Mackerel Snappers

How to explain even
the toughest teachings
about God and his Catholic Church.

Spencer Allen

Nihil obstat   Rev. Dylan Schrader
Censor librorum

Imprimatur   + Most Reverend John R. Gaydos,
Bishop of the Diocese of Jefferson City
May 9, 2013

The Imprimatur is a declaration that a book is free of doctrinal or moral error. No implication is contained in this declaration that the individual granting it agrees with the contents, opinions or statements in this work.

Cover Art   Author photo courtesy of Debbie Sackman.
Image of the Ignatius *Catholic RSV Study Bible* used with permission from Ignatius Press.

ISBN:1482637596

ISBN-13:9781482637595

DEDICATION

For P. B. and J.

And Taters

CONTENTS

PART 2 AUTHORITY 58

PART 3 SALVATION 151

ACKNOWLEDGMENTS

So many people have been instrumental in helping me learn the faith as I have. Beyond that, Mgsr. Robert Kurwicki and His Excellency, bishop John R. Gaydos have provided me the opportunity to teach in the wonderful Jefferson City Diocese at the great Cathedral of St. Joseph. Fr. Dylan Schrader has given much time to reading those essays, correcting my imprecise language and making sure that my attempts to explain things in a simple way do not threaten the integrity of the clear truth expressed by our Church. Randy England has been a consistently wise guide in the process of publication, and Josh Korte, Joyce Tarbet and Tyler McClay have been invaluable in reading early drafts and giving much needed criticism. My wife Christy has been so patient over the years as I've given time to writing and speaking on the faith. And finally, my children, to whom the book is dedicated, have given me the inspiration to study our faith. I learn it so I can explain it as well as possible to them, so our family can spend eternity together in God's glory.

INTRODUCTION

"Wherever the bishop appears let the congregation be present; just as wherever Jesus Christ is, there is the Catholic Church."
-*Ignatius of Antioch, "Letter to the Smyrneans" VIII, (circa AD 110).*

In the spring of 2012, I debated a Church of Christ preacher. After a couple of casual meetings, we arranged for the public event to take place at a neutral location. I didn't advertise this too much within the Catholic community. For one, this was my first public debate, and it was against an experienced and intelligent preacher. So, in the event that I should fall flat on my face, I'm not proud to say there was a bit of damage control in my decision. Second, I wasn't particularly interested in a cheering section even if I should do well. I saw the debate less as a sparring match, and more as an opportunity to communicate the Catholic viewpoint to individuals who might not have been exposed to it otherwise.

Despite my opponent advertising .the event in the local newspapers, the turn-out was decidedly dominated by attendees from the Church of Christ, including one teenage fan who had gone so far as to print a t-shirt displaying my opponent's face.

I believe I won that debate. I say that without much personal pride at all, as my opponent was certainly the more talented public speaker (and had *much* cooler transitions for his PowerPoint slides). His practiced cadence and well-time inflections came from a few years behind a pulpit. I'm certain I did very well, though, because there were just too many questions and objections that my opponent could not answer. This had nothing to do with my own personal cleverness, but everything to do with the fact that the Catholic Church is built upon such a solid and unshakeable foundation. Because history and Scripture overwhelmingly point to the truth of the Catholic Church, the arguments more or less write themselves.

An *apologist* is an individual who offers an explanation or defense for something. There are plenty of books or resources on apologetics available, but my reason for publishing this book is to provide a resource for individuals who probably have no background in apologetics or theology, and may not have really developed an interest in learning more deeply about Catholicism in the first place. Most of the chapters build upon stories with which most readers will relate. Through these personal anecdotes, I attempt to ease more deeply into specific teachings. My book is written with the hope of reaching the man who might secretly be doubting the existence of God, or the woman who is struggling with understanding her son's same-sex attraction. I wrote it for the family lacking motivation to go to Mass or the Protestant father-in-law who doesn't understand why his grandchildren pray to Mary.

Just recently, I loaned a member of my family some reading material. Though not all of these books were religious, I knew she was experiencing anxiety over whether or not God existed, so I included a book examining the evidence for the existence and divinity of Christ. She apparently started on this book first and called me within a week amazed by what she was reading.

We spoke for about an hour, with me doing my best to answer questions about the Trinity, Jesus, and faith. "I never learned any of this in Catholic school," she said, going on to conclude that her Catholic education had not been very good.

I told her that it wasn't necessarily true that her Catholic schools have done a poor job of teaching the faith, though that was possible. Rather, even the best schools can only teach as well as the students are prepared to receive, which is limited to their age.

"You only went to Catholic school until 8th grade," I told her. "Imagine if a doctor tried to perform surgery using only what he learned up until the 8th grade. Or if an architect tried to design houses using the math and science he learned only through high school." Many adults Catholics are living or even rejecting their faith based on an 8th grade or high school understanding of it.

Jesus delivered a very rich and very deep set of teachings. But somehow many Catholics are convinced that what they learned up through 8th grade religion class with Sr. Esther (if they even went to Catholic school) was the sum total of the very best the Church has to offer.

No wonder adult Catholics leave for other religions, vote in such large numbers against core Christian principles or reject key teachings of their own Church.

Most people want to do the right thing and want to believe what is true, but have never had anyone explain it to them well. The title of this book, "Mackerel Snappers," comes from a derogatory term once directed at Catholics. When the requirement to abstain from meat was binding on all Fridays, Catholics were stereotyped as fish eaters. The teaching on Friday penance, like most of the teachings in this book, are often rejected *because* they are misunderstood. More than that, Catholics fail to realize that the teachings of their Church are not opinions. They are not just one interpretation among many. The dogmas of Catholicism are facts, and God intended for all Christians, not just Catholics, to believe in the Immaculate Conception, the true presence in the Eucharist, and Purgatory, to name just three of the many essential teachings.

In addition to helping readers understand their faith on an adult level, this book is intended to help parents explain their faith to their own children. In the New Testament, the apostles did not spend their time setting up Catholic schools or leading Sunday school classes. Rather, they taught fathers and mothers, the heads of households, who then raised their own children in the faith. It was so foreign to the apostles to evangelize to children that when the little children attempted to approach Jesus, the apostles attempted to hold them back (Matt 19:14). Jesus corrected them and welcomed the children, of course, but the primary ministry of Christ and his followers was to adults. Today's parents need to reclaim their special role as the first heralds of Christ in the lives of their sons and daughters.

As addressed in a later chapter, Catholics do not look to the Bible alone as our authority. Though not inspired, the writings of the early Christians are extremely important in understanding how people practiced Christianity in the earliest years. Many of these authors wrote while the apostles were still alive. Also important are the writings of Church councils, such as modeled by the Council of Jerusalem in Acts, when doctrine was settled by deliberation among the apostles. But most of this book relies on Scripture and logic alone since this is the background of most non-Catholic Christians one might encounter. Unless otherwise noted, all Scripture quotations will be from the *Revised Standard Version*, Catholic edition. This beautiful translation is well-respected among Catholic and Protestants. However, any reputable translation of the Bible would work for deeper study of quoted verses.

While the chapters are intended to be comprehensive, they focus on some groups more than others. The reader is much more likely to answer the door on a Saturday morning to find a Mormon missionary, rather than a Muslim, standing there, which is why I have an entire chapter devoted to the Latter Day Saint Church and not Islam. In addition, some challenges or questions are more appropriately addressed than others. Most Catholics will probably go their entire lives without being challenged by a member of the Church of Christ on why our churches have organs. But almost every Catholic has been asked questions about Mary or Purgatory. Some topics are covered within broader chapters, such as a treatment of the Assumption in the chapter on the Immaculate Conception, so the index in the back is designed to guide the reader in finding answers to particular challenges.

While there are not enough pages to address every possible question or challenge that may arise, my intent is to provide the intellectual tools to find those answers and the confidence to know that, no matter how challenging the objection, Christ and his Catholic Church have delivered a truth that is sharper than any two-edged sword.

1
Roadblocks

1

YOU'RE IN GOD'S ARMY NOW

Saint Michael the Archangel,
defend us in battle.
Be our protection against the wickedness and snares of the devil.
May God rebuke him, we humbly pray;
and do Thou, O Prince of the Heavenly Host -
by the Divine Power of God -
cast into hell, Satan and all the evil spirits,
who roam throughout the world seeking the ruin of souls.
    -St. Michael the Archangel Prayer

In the Fall of 2010, I stood on stage to introduce the keynote speaker of the first annual "Apologetics Boot Camp." At that time, I was president of a non-profit organization that had raised money to bring well-known Catholic speakers to the area. The idea of a boot camp came from the exhortation in *Ephesians*, which is worth quoting in its entirety:

Finally, be strong in the Lord and in the strength of his might. Put on the whole armor of God, that you may be able to stand against the wiles of the devil. For we are not contending against flesh and blood, but against the principalities, against the powers, against the world rulers of this present darkness, against the spiritual hosts of wickedness in the heavenly places. Therefore take the whole armor of God, that you may be able to withstand in the evil day, and having done all, to stand. Stand therefore, having girded your loins with truth, and having put on the breastplate of righteousness, and having shod your feet with the equipment of the gospel of peace; besides all these, taking the shield of faith, with which you can quench all the flaming darts of the evil one. And take the helmet of salvation, and the sword of the Spirit, which is the word of God. Pray at all times in the Spirit, with all prayer and supplication. To that end keep alert with all perseverance, making supplication for all the saints, and also for me, that utterance may be given me in opening my mouth boldly to proclaim the mystery of the gospel, for which I am an ambassador in chains; that I may declare it boldly, as I ought to speak (6:10-20).

Our speaker for the conference, Tim Staples, served our country as a Marine, so he was the ideal guest for our first "Boot Camp," which drew a few hundred attendees from throughout the state. I took the stage first, attempting to set the tone for the day.

"I want to ask you a few questions, and I want to hear a loud and clear *hoorah!* in response," I instructed. "Are you ready to learn to defend your faith?"

Hoorah!

"Are you ready to get excited about being Catholic?"

Hoorah!

"Are you ready to welcome Mr. Tim Staples to the stage?"

Hoorah!

As I stepped down and Tim took over, I felt pretty satisfied with how the conference had opened. That was when a man in the front row grabbed my arm on my way from the stage. He very clearly informed me that a Marine would never say *Hoorah!*

Then, over my shoulder, I heard Tim Staples pause from his routine for a moment. "The first thing we're gonna have to do," he said, "is get away with all of this 'Hoorah' stuff. Can I hear an *'Oorah?'*"

Sigh … Well, at least the rest of the conference went well.

We are in spiritual battle

The title "Church Militant" isn't heard as often as it once was. The very idea of battle is one that seems completely contrary to the Christian message of love and compassion. But the Holy Spirit was intentional when he inspired Paul to exhort us to arm ourselves.

This is not a battle against other men, but with evil spirits, the "rulers of this present darkness." A battle is waged around us, even as we relax on the couch in the evening, tuned into reality television. Scripture gives us several glimpses of this in stories of individuals overtaken by possession, such as the man in Mark 5, whom Christ and the apostles encountered in the graveyard of the Gerasenes. This man, strong enough to break the chains by which he was bound, cried out day and night and cut himself with stones. He was possessed by many demons (5:1-20).

Throughout history, great and holy men have fought daily with the demonic forces who sought to scare them from their life administering the sacraments, and even today possession remains a threat to those who abandon the sacramental life and give themselves, instead, to unholy pursuits.

Our part in the fight against evil calls for prayer, fasting and participation in the sacraments. To this end, we have an army of angels on our side, as seen in 2 Kings 6:17. After Elisha's prayers, his servant's eyes were open and he saw a hillside covered with flaming chariots and horses.

This battle, though, calls not just for a life in pursuit of holiness, but of truth. As the passage from Ephesians instructs, our loins are to be girded with truth, our shield is to be faith, and our sword is the Word of God. Without a knowledge of the truth and a willingness to share it with others, we are soldiers walking onto the battlefield without armor.

It is a contradiction in terms to call oneself a dedicated Christian and not undertake the duty to spread truth to others. It has become a common thing for individuals to claim that their faith is a "private matter," and certainly we should not be boastful. But Scripture exhorts us to "always be prepared to make a defense to anyone who calls you to account for the hope that is in you, yet do it with gentleness and reverence" (1 Pet 3:15). Jude's epistle appeals to us to "contend for the faith" (1:3).

Scripture never tells us to keep our faith private, but rather to take our lamp from beneath the bushel (Matthew 5:15), warning that God will spew the lukewarm from his mouth (Rev 3:16).

Is sharing the faith judgmental?

Of course, telling others about the faith sometimes means having conversations that are uncomfortable. It means confronting behaviors in others that are destructive to their souls.

It is at this point in a Christian's relationship with others that he is scolded for being judgmental. *Who are you to tell me whom I should and shouldn't have sex with? Read the Bible – it says not to judge.*

This jab – that Christians are being *unchristian* by telling others how to live their lives – is one that causes many among us to shy away from having conversations about morality.

Scripture certainly does tell us to avoid judging. Jesus speaks against judging others by their appearances (John 7:24), and in Matthew, he warns against hypocrisy, saying that we should not criticize another's behavior when we are engaged in a worse behavior ourselves (7:3). There is a difference, though, between a man who sins and then repents and a man who persists in sin. So even though we are all sinners, it isn't hypocrisy to speak to others about their behaviors if we have truly repented of our own.

And certainly we are not to judge another person's eternal destination. That I might see a man sinning tells me nothing about his knowledge of that sin, his mental or emotional condition, or the state of his life that might have led to that action. It definitely does not tell me whether he will later repent.

But we can judge actions as sinful.

Is it judgmental to tell a man that it is wrong to beat his children? Or to tell our teenage nephew that it is wrong to kill himself with methamphetamines? These behaviors are harmful to our bodies or to others, so why would it then be judgmental to warn others against behaviors that are harmful to their souls? Isn't the possibility of eternity in Hell worse than any damage to the body that comes from illegal drugs?

Far from telling us not to judge sinful behavior, Scripture commands it. Christ commands us to approach anyone who sins against us (Matt 18:15-17). Paul tells the Corinthian church to drive out the wicked from among them (1 Cor 5:12-13).

Some shy from approaching family or friends with words of correction, afraid of conflicts and hard feelings. But Christ warns that he did not come to bring peace on earth, and that his hard teachings would be a sword that would divide even members of a family (Matt 10:34).

When we judge the behavior of others, it is an act of love, as long as it is done with the gentleness and reverence Peter mentions in his first epistle (3:15). Atheist Penn Jillette has a YouTube video where he recounts the story of a Christian who attempts to proselytize him. Far from being offended, Jillette is touched that this man cared enough to attempt to convert him.[1]

If a Christian believes that following Christ is *the* way to Heaven, Jillette asks, how much would that man have to hate a non-believing friend not to tell him about it?

Sin is toxic to our souls. To bite our tongue out of fear of offending another is an act of cowardice, not love. This is expressed perfectly in the book of Leviticus:

> You shall do no injustice in judgment; you shall not be partial to the poor or defer to the great, but in righteousness shall you judge your neighbor" (Lev 19:15).

Summary:
- Never say "Hoorah" to a Marine;
- We are engaged in a great spiritual battle which depends on a strong sacramental life and personal witness of the Good News;
- Scripture calls us to have enthusiasm for defending the faith;
- We cannot judge anyone's eternal destiny, but we can judge behavior as sinful and harmful in order to warn and guide others.

---

[1] *Penn Says*, http://www.youtube.com/watch?v=ZhG-tkQ_Q2w

2

YOU *CAN* HANDLE THE TRUTH!

"It is the truth that possesses us, it is something alive! It is not we who possess it; rather we are grasped by it."
- *Benedict XVI*

D uring a recent vacation, I ran out of gas for the first time in my life. The light had come on to warn me as we were driving on the interstate, but I was confident that I could make it a few more miles to our exit ramp.

In fact, we did make it that far – exactly *just* until our planned exit ramp. Ten minutes later I was jogging along the road, trying to find the gas station that our GPS told me was a few blocks ahead.

Some things are objectively true

People understand how truth works in most of their daily lives. *Prettier. Tastier. Desirable.* These are opinion words. *True* and *false* are not.

The low fuel light meant the tank was nearly empty, whether I wanted it to be or not. It wasn't simply the car's *opinion* that we were nearly out of gas. The dashboard and I could not have just agreed to disagree.

In most instances, people understand that there are objective truths and don't mind sharing these truths with others. Being correct doesn't make one person better than another. For example, suppose I get into an argument with my brother over whether or not my truck is powered by a team of gerbils on exercise wheels. Once we open the hood, it will be obvious that one of us is incorrect. The other man knows more about cars.

So why should religion be different? Discussing differences with civility and open-mindedness is a lost art. Politics has helped do this to us. While a great amount of political doctrines *are* opinion, media treat them like facts.

People are often wary of any sort of abstract fact at all. Otherwise important conversations end too quickly in a truce. *I have my opinion*, says the man who was just proven wrong, *and you have yours.* Coexist bumper stickers echo the modern myth that all religions are created by God and equally true.

But religious doctrines are factual assertions, not opinion.

Either God exists or he does not. It is impossible that he exists for me and doesn't exist for you. If God exists, then atheists need to know about him. If not, then worship is a waste of time.

If Christ exists and is God, then Muslims and Jews are in error. This doesn't make them bad people. Just incorrect.

Catholics believe that Christ started the Catholic Church. This is not an opinion. Catholics are wrong or they are right.

Purgatory exists or it doesn't. Christ is truly present in the Eucharist or he isn't. Mary was either a sinner or she wasn't.

The idea that all religions are from God and are equally true is impossible since different groups believe things that are completely in opposition to the beliefs of groups. Jesus claimed that nobody came to the Father except through him, which means that either Christianity is a sham for being based on such an exclusive claim or that any religion other than Christianity is a false path to the Father.

If proof exists for the truth of our religious beliefs, then it is important to discuss that proof and to convince others of it. Christ prayed, in John 17, that his followers would be united. Paul echoed this by appealing to the idea that there should be no divisions among us (1 Cor 1:10).

Today, many choose their church based on the group's reputation for great fellowship, inspiring preaching or engaging young adult programs. But these truly are matters of opinion. Truth isn't measured by casserole dishes and youth group t-shirts.

Opinions have their place. They are perfect for a debate over the most talented contestant on *American Idol*. But the Good News that God has revealed is more than a matter of personal taste.

Summary:

- Religious beliefs are often treated as opinions, but statements that are either true or false are not opinions, but assertions of fact;
- Specific religions hold teachings that directly contradict other religions' teachings;
- Because contradicting beliefs cannot both be true, some religions are more true than others.

3

HOW "FAITH" CAUSES ATHEISM

"If anyone says that the one, true God, our creator and lord, cannot be known with certainty from the things that have been made, by the natural light of human reason: let him be anathema."
-*Vatican I*, Dei Filius, *Canons (1870)*

When I was a senior in high school, I took a philosophy class. Dr. Roberts was gone one particular day, and our substitute, a "born-again Christian," took offense to something we were reading that day. She then committed the cardinal sin for teachers in a public school and began telling us that we needed to stop reading the nonsense our teacher had assigned and instead accept Jesus Christ as our personal Lord and Savior.

By that point in my life, I had decided I was no longer a Christian, and wavered between atheism and indifference. However, one of my classmates, Ion, was not wavering at all and was an outspoken atheist.

What happened next confirmed for me that I did not want to be a believer.

17

Ion challenged the substitute, telling her that he believed that her God was fiction. He asked the sub how *she* could believe in some magical man in the sky?

"I believe because I have *faith*," she said with confidence.

Ion smiled and glanced around at the rest of us, who were stunned into silence by the exchange. "Well I have faith, too," he said. "I have faith that God is a big, pink cow."

The substitute's face grew red and her voice heightened. She told Ion how offended she was by his mockery. Not about to back down, Ion told her that he was just as offended by her rejection of his rose-colored bovine deity.

Thankfully the class was nearly over at this point because the two of them continued the verbal shoving match, putting her faith against his until the bell signaled the time to change classes.

We had a different substitute the next day.

"Faith" is not a warm feeling

I don't remember what philosopher we were reading, but I do remember the real lesson I learned that day: if this woman represented the best Christianity could do against atheism, I didn't want to waste my time with prayers and parables.

Unfortunately, this is the experience that so many teenagers and adults are experiencing today because Christianity has been stained by a horribly incorrect definition of "faith." It is worth repeating this again: the definition of "faith" that most of our society uses is *wrong*. More than that, it is *dangerous* and destructive.

Faith is not a warm feeling in our hearts. It is not a belief without evidence. It is not an emotional assurance or, as the Mormons call it, a "burning in the bosom."

Christians have come to think it is a good and virtuous thing that one should believe in God without proof for his existence. Atheists see such blind faith as a source of ridicule.

But this kind of faith – this naïve kind of hope in God – is not the way that Scripture defines it. The biblical definition is given by the author of Hebrews, who writes that "faith is the assurance of things hoped for, the conviction of things not seen" (11:1). To flesh this out a bit, faith is a virtue given to us freely by God, and it is the means by which we believe all that God has revealed.

Note that faith is not belief *that God exists*. Knowing he exists is a prerequisite to faith.

Proof of God's existence precedes faith

God does not ask us to believe in him without any proof. Instead, Paul tells us that God placed proof of his existence all around us: "Ever since the creation of the world his invisible nature, namely, his eternal power and deity has been clearly perceived in the things that have been made" (Rom 1:20).

God gave us evidence that he exists and he also gave us the intellectual tools to connect the dots. *This* is what I didn't understand as a teenager – the existence of God can be argued from scientific, historical, and philosophical evidence.

Some Christians feel that doctrines are not matters for logic or discussion, but Scripture disagrees. The epistles, especially those of Paul, are filled with logical arguments for the existence of God and of what he has revealed. For instance, Paul reasoned with the Athenians that their pagan deities were false and that the "unknown God," to whom they had dedicated an altar, was the one, true God worshiped by the Jews (Acts 17:23).

Earlier, in Acts 8, Philip reasons with the Ethiopian Eunuch, converting him through the proof of the Old Testament prophesies, which Christ had fulfilled.

The writings of the first century Christians, such as Justin Martyr and John Chrysostom, show their efforts to convert others through arguments and evidence, and in Ephesians 4:11, Paul writes that some of us are called to be teachers and evangelists, instructing others in the faith.

Those who think we are called to believe without any proof often look to the story of Thomas who demanded to see and touch the wounds of Christ before he believed in his resurrection. Christ said to him, "Have you believed because you have seen me? Blessed are those who have not seen and yet believe" (John 20:29). But for those who think Thomas was criticized because he wanted evidence, this isn't the case. He already had *plenty* of evidence. Thomas was aware of the prophesies Christ had fulfilled, and he had witnessed many healings and miracles first hand. He had heard from the other apostles, who testified to the risen Lord. All of this should have been enough for him to take Christ at his word that he would rise again, but still he doubted.

Evidence of God

For me, once I began to explore the evidence for God, I was overwhelmed by how convincing the case of his existence could be made. One piece of evidence might be explained away. Two pieces of evidence, and an atheist has to start doing logical gymnastics. But when all of the evidence is taken as a composite whole, it is a *certain* conclusion that God exists and has revealed himself to the world.

There are several great books and resources that outline and describe the various arguments for God, such as *The Handbook of Catholic Apologetics*, by Peter Kreeft and Ronald Tacelli, or for younger readers, *Prove It: God*, by Amy Welborn. This book is not a place for a thorough examination of such arguments, but some are worth mentioning as especially powerful in my own adult conversion.

Existence of a spiritual plane - Each of us has self-awareness. We are not merely rational creatures, but we are individuals who are witnessing the universe from a perspective that nobody else will ever know. The odds against my own existence are beyond computation. What if two *different* cells, out of millions, had combined into an embryo inside my mother? What if my parents had never met? What if the same were argued about their parents, grandparents, and every necessary biological event through the history of mankind. Yet here I am, as if my soul were created specifically and intentionally.

Need for a beginning - The physical universe appears to have come into being. Things which come into being, based on evidence before us, appear to need a cause. Yet we cannot have one cause after another, into infinity. This would be like having a chain held up by one link after another, without finally discovering a link that is anchored to something solid and fixed. If everything that comes into being needs a cause, then there must be something *uncaused* which exists by its very nature. Atheists often try to refute this proof, called the *Kalam* argument, by reasoning that if everything needs a cause, then something must have caused God. Note, though, that the argument didn't say "everything needs a cause," but that "everything that comes into being" needs a cause. Therefore, there must be something that exists that never came into being and which demands existence by its very nature.

Some attempts to get around the beginning include the ideas that our universe is just one of many "universes" that came into existence within a *multi*verse, from which new universes are infinitely created. Additional theories have also been proposed.

Aside from the fact that there is no actual scientific proof for these theories (they are just as much speculation as atheists claim faith to be), modern physics and cosmology make these theories highly improbable, if not impossible.

The 2003 publication of the "Borde, Guth, and Vilenkin Theorem" argued the error of modern theories which attempt to avoid the necessity of a beginning to space and time. The B-G-V theorem demonstrates that universes which have been expanding through history must have had a space-time finite past and a cosmological beginning.

On the occasion of Stephen Hawking's 70th birthday, Alexander Vilenkin, co-author of that theorem, appeared at a meeting of scientists at Cambridge University. *New Scientist* called his talk the "worst birthday present" ever, as Hawkings is not a proponent of a cosmic beginning. Vilenkin argued that the universe is not infinitely old, presenting scientists with the problem of explaining its beginning without the existence of a force outside of space and time.[2]

Need for a designer - Our common sense tells us that when we encounter things that appear to be complicated, organized, and suited for a purpose, there must have been a designer. If an alien landed on our planet and discovered a camera and a rock, he would surely recognize the camera, not the rock, as resembling very basic engineering, concluding that an intelligent being created it. When we observe the delicate and complex organization of everything from cells to the natural universe, such a conclusion is reasonable. After all, if the laws of physics were tweaked even in the slightest, the universe as we know it could not exist or sustain life. Here are just a few of the many examples of this apparent fine tuning:

---

[2] Lisa Grossman, "Why Physicists Can't Avoid a Creation Event," *New Scientist,* January 11, 2012.

- gravitational force constant (adjusted slightly would make stars too hot or too cool for life);

- ratio of number of protons to number of electrons (adjusted would prevent formation of planets and stars due to taxation of gravity);

- velocity of light – adjusting would affect the luminosity of stars, making them too great or too insufficient for life.[3]

The evidence for a designer is so convincing that a very outspoken atheist, Antony Flew, eventually made a public pronouncement of his conversion to belief with the publication of his book *There is a God: How the World's Most Notorious Atheist Changed His Mind.*[4]

Another consideration with design is that nothing can be greater than its source without outside influence. Water, for instance, doesn't rise above the level of its source. Yet, somehow irrational matter and energy has arranged itself into beings which move, and think, and write sappy love notes as teenagers.

Miracles. - There are so many miracles that are beyond naturalistic explanation, but which point specifically to Christianity. Some claims of miracles are hoaxes, and atheists seize on these to claim that all miracles are false. However, others are powerful in their testimony.

In Lanciano, Italy (700 AD), a priest who was doubting his faith was saying Mass before several congregants when the host and wine turned into actual flesh and blood. This miracle was investigated by the World Health Organization in 1973. Even more amazing, the five globules of blood always balance a scale when weighed, even when several are placed on one side of the scale and

---

[3] Dr. Hugh Ross, *Big Bang Refined by Fire*, 1998. Reasons To Believe, Pasadena, CA (1998).
[4] Harper One Publisher (2008).

only one on the other. It is as if God is attempting to show that Christ is fully present in each drop of consecrated wine.

In 1947, a girl named Gemma de Giorgi, who had been born without pupils, was brought by her grandmother to Padre Pio. Though her abnormality left Gemma blind, her grandmother asked for Padre Pio to heal her. After the priestly blessing, Gemma was soon able to see, while she still did not have pupils.

The *incorruptibles* are saints who, upon their death, were buried with no expectation that their bodies would do anything but decompose. In some cases the bodies were interred in saturated ground, or they were covered with lime to encourage decomposition. Years later, perhaps when these saints were exhumed to obtain relics, the bodies were discovered to be soft and as unblemished as the day they died, even while bodies buried in the same area had decomposed. No natural explanation exists for this phenomenon, especially as it is specifically Catholic saints who are preserved. Some notable saints, such as St. Bernadette of Lourdes and St. John Vianney, remain on display today. Their bodies, preserved from decay, stand as a reminder of how their holiness is an antidote to the sin that returns our bodies to dust in the first place

Now, another story about faith, this one from the movie *Indiana Jones and the Last Crusade*. Having discovered the location of the Holy Grail, Jones is passing through a series of traps and comes to a ravine that is apparently too deep and wide to cross. It appears that one step would lead to certain death. As his dying father cries out for him to hurry, Jones takes a deep breath and steps out over the ravine in a *leap of faith*. His foot lands securely upon a stone bridge that had previously been camouflaged by the pattern of stones.

Jones did not simply *hope* there was a bridge. He didn't have a warm feeling that it existed.

Rather, he had passed through the other tests because his father's diary, which had been reliable so far, assured him that his step into apparent emptiness would not lead to his death.

So this is the *true* definition of faith. God has given us evidence of his existence and, through faith, the ability to comprehend it with our intellect. Once we have accepted him as an authority in our lives, we can trust that those things he reveals to us are true. Paul stresses this in 2 Corinthians 5:7, where he discusses the promise of eternal life and writes that we "walk by faith and not by sight." Faith excludes both vision and doubt. The existence of Heaven, of angels, of grace, and of the nature of the Trinity – these things are matters of faith because God, whom we know to exist, does not lie and has revealed these truths to us. We do not need to see them to believe.

Summary:
- Faith does not mean belief without evidence;
- Historical, scientific and logical evidence demonstrates with certainty that God exists;
- Since we know a God exists who created everything, we can trust what he has revealed to us;
- This revelation is given through prophets, Christ and the apostles, and through Scripture;
- Faith is the gift by which we can understand and trust in that revelation.

4

ANSWERING ATHEIST OBJECTIONS

"Since God is the highest good, He would not allow any evil to exist in His works, unless His omnipotence and goodness were such as to bring good even out of evil."
-Augustine (Enchiridion xi)

Several years ago some friends and I went on a fishing trip in the lakes between Minnesota and Canada. In order to keep bears out of camp, we tied our food into a bag hoisted into the trees. Unfortunately, one morning we left the bag on the ground while we ate breakfast.

The first guy to notice our guest happened to be taking a bathroom break against a tree barely fifteen feet away from the bear. After he leaped over the nearest pup tent to join us, we chased the bear off with rocks. It returned twice more, each time getting more aggressive. Knowing we needed to relocate our camp, three of the guys later left to fish for supper while the rest of us remained behind to pack up the gear. The bear had consistently come in along the same path each visit, so after our work in the camp, we gathered rocks and positioned ourselves several feet above that trail, ready to ambush him from above if he returned.

Some time passed before I felt the presence of something behind us. I turned slowly. The bear was on our ledge, watching us watch for him.

Conversations about the faith can be this way. Despite our best preparations, we find our objector has devised some question or objection that enters through a path we had not anticipated.

Following up on the chapters about belief in God, this chapter tries to anticipate some of the more common questions and challenges from atheists. By no means is every question answered, but the ones chosen set the basic premise upon which a number of other answers can be found. Some objections, such as the assertion that God would need a creator, too, are answered in other sections of the book.

Christians are one god away from atheism

Here is another attempt at cleverness from the atheist community. Christians, some claim, do not believe in the gods of the Egyptians, the Greeks or the Norse.

"You refuse to believe in all of these Gods," an atheist suggests, "and you think this is reasonable. I simply believe in one fewer god than you."

But there is a big difference between one and nothing.

Christians refuse to believe in the gods of ancient pagan cultures, as well as any other god whose existence is not backed by any proof.

Rather than play little games of subtraction, atheists and Christians should move to the real question of what evidence exists for the Judeo-Christian God.

Truth requires scientific evidence

This argument holds that only those things which can be shown through the senses and scientific inquiry are worthy of belief (a.k.a. *naturalism*). Atheists who use this approach often demand falsifiable experiments demonstrating that God exists.

The problem is that our minds are not the measure of reality and, in addition, many things can be known to be true which are not able to be proven through test tubes or double-blind experiments. For instance, it cannot be shown through replicable experiments that a dog evolved from a simpler type of creature, but atheists generally believe this. Naturalists would simply claim that there appear to be sufficient signs pointing to evolution. Theists would say the same thing about God; plenty of evidence points to his existence, even if he does not fit under a microscope.

There is something silly about the very idea that we should only believe in things which can be proven scientifically. If this statement is true, then we should be able to demonstrate it scientifically. However, it is impossible to demonstrate scientifically that truth can only be known scientifically.

Can God create a stone too heavy for himself to lift?

Christians believe God is omnipotent, which means "all-powerful." The classic argument against this is the claim that, if God is all-powerful, he should be able to create a stone so heavy he cannot lift it. If he fails to do so, he has revealed a limit in his power. If he succeeds, then he similarly has created a limit in his power. Either way, atheists claim that this shows that the argument for an omnipotent God is illogical.

However, omnipotence means having every power that actually exists, and divine self contradiction is not one of them.

God is also omnipresent, meaning he is in all places at once. However, the land of Lilliput is imaginary, so God is not there. Does this mean he isn't really omnipresent since we've found a place where he doesn't exist? God cannot exist in places that are pretend, and he cannot possess powers that are pretend, either.

The Old-Testament God seems like a thug

This is a tough one, for sure. And the main reason is because our 21st century sensibilities are so different from the culture we experience in the Old Testament. It's hard enough trying to understand the childhood of our own parents, not to mention the lives of people who lived thousands of years ago.

The culture described in the Old Testament is a brutal one. Communities such as the Canaanites engaged in behaviors like child sacrifice and ritual prostitution.

Our God is a merciful one, Old Testament or New. He takes no pleasure in the death of the wicked, but hopes for their repentance (Ez 33:11). For instance, rather than rashly wiping out Nineveh because of the sins of its people, God sent a prophet to try to reach their hearts (Jonah 4:11). He was willing to spare Sodom and Gomorrah for the sake of a handful of righteous (Gen 18:25).

He even tolerated the Canaanites for four years (Gen 15:13-16) but eventually he was moved to respond to the persecution of the Israelites and the threat of influence from this pagan culture.

Life is a gift from him that he can revoke for any reason that he deems sufficient. Immorality is, by definition, offending God by going against his will. Since God cannot violate his own will, his acts cannot be, by definition, immoral.

Why would God order the extermination of the entire Canaanite culture? For one, he knew that if even a remnant of that people remained, they would assimilate with the Israelites (Deut 20:18), who were intended to be a people set apart. As the great physician, God saw it necessary to remove the influence of the entire culture, just as the entirety of a diseased limb might require amputation. Even the children were to be subject to this judgment, which seems to most offend our modern sensibilities. However, with God's omniscience there is a greater plan at work. Allowing the children to live without their parents and culture might very well be a less merciful act than allowing their immediate entrance into Heaven. God also has knowledge of what spiritual fate these children might have matured into if they grew up with the Canaanite influences still imprinted in their formation.

This event, as well as other difficult passages in the Old Testament, must also be understood in light of the language of the inspired authors. Even though the text is inspired and inerrant, it is written through human pen. So God is often given human attributes (called *anthropomorphical* language) or events are described as they appear (*phenomenological* language) because the human mind is incapable of fully grasping the divine. For instance, though God is sometimes described as angry, vengeful, or jealous, he does not really experience emotions as humans do, because that would mean that our unchangeable God is actually changeable. It would also mean that emotional pain exists in Heaven and that God is dependent upon us for fulfillment. Rather, our God is perfectly just and "jealous" in the sense that an act against his will (which means directing our loves to something other than God), results in the consequences of divine justice. He certainly doesn't mope around all day, looking at photographs of us and wondering what we ever saw in that idol.

The long and short is that Scripture contains passages that are hard to fully digest. Even so, this is far from an argument to *disprove* God. At best, it shows us that we believe in a God that is just more difficult to figure out than our limited imaginations will allow. Would anyone want to believe in an almighty power who was so simple as to be perfectly predictable?

An all-good God would not create tragedy

As the story of *Genesis* tells us, man was originally made to live in a paradise. Presumably, that paradise would not have included things such as earthquakes, tsunamis or forest fires.

God created our universe from nothing. But in the process of doing so, he also took chaos and brought it into order. When first created, the earth was "formless," and God gave it form (Gen 1:1). He separated the light from the dark, bringing order to our days (1:3). In short, God is order.

In the original sin, Adam and Eve rejected God and moved themselves and subsequently their offspring (including us) away from God. Since it is God who holds all things in order, to move from him puts us into a state of disorder, which affects our own physical and emotional health, as well as the stability of our world.

So it is true that God is all good and that natural disasters are a result of humanity's movement, through sin, away from that source of good. God does not actually cause these disasters. There is a difference between God's *positive* will and his *permissive* will. He positively, or actively, wills some things to happen. His permissive will is when he does not cause things to happen, but allows them because he foresees ways to bring good out of them.

Scripture contains examples of God not just allowing, but actually causing events that would appear tragic to us, such as the great flood and the plagues of Egypt. While God cannot cause moral evil, such as the heinous act of a criminal, he is perfect justice and can act in such a way to correct an unjust situation. Even if deaths resulted, this would not be a sinful act, as addressed in the earlier section on the Canaanite genocide.

Until his great plan is revealed to us in Heaven, we cannot always recognize how God brings good out of tragedy. As a result of some tragedy, some who otherwise have no spiritual life might turn to prayer for the first time. Our response to catastrophes builds up the body of Christ as individuals of good will put their energy and resources into the welfare of others. It could also be that God foresees and allows disasters in some cases because he is saving some individuals from a greater evil in the future, such as the death of a child who would otherwise have lost his adult faith.

Did an all-good God create sin?

Darkness is not a thing. It is the absence of light.

Cold is not a thing. It is the absence of heat.

Darkness and cold are both synonyms for emptiness, or *privation*. Sin is another example of the privation of something that ought to be present. God does not create sin. He is all good, but as explored in the last answer, movement away from God is movement away from good.

Sin is not a thing. It is the absence, or privation, of good.

Much evil is done in the name of religion

This excuse is a bit of a strange one, but still a common reason that individuals give for rejecting religion. That an individual might kill another and claim religion as his motivation really says nothing about whether or not God exists. At best, it shows that the individual belongs to a religion that is misguided in its doctrines.

Most likely, however, evil done in the name of religion is the result of evil intent that is looking for a way to justify its actions in the name of God.

John Hinckley Jr. attempted to assassinate Ronald Reagan, supposedly in an attempt to impress Jodie Foster, for whom he had an obsession. This doesn't say anything about Jodie Foster, and it certainly doesn't prove her nonexistence.

Why Doesn't God heal amputees?

The hidden assertion in this question is that spiritual healings, whether they happen in Scripture or at Lourdes, are all fakes and easily staged. *But growing a new leg* – that would be a miracle!

While this question is a favorite among contemporary atheists, it is really a red herring (see chapter on fallacies). For one, it shouldn't surprise us that we don't see healed amputees, as God often seems to restrain his miracles to just a few degrees shy of knock-you-upside-the-head obvious. He wants our love for him to come with a bit of work and struggle so that our faith might be toughened like iron tested in fire. Or perhaps, just as Christ desires us to participate in our own salvation, his healing touch prefers to empower the body's cooperation through its own healing process, which does not include regeneration of limbs. The one exception would be replacing of the soldier's ear (John 18:10), but even then the action was an attempt to correct Peter's misguided act.

Most importantly, though, Scripture shows that Christ had something in mind that was superior to just being a divine ER doctor. He came, primarily, not to heal our bodies, but to heal our souls, and the types of afflictions he healed seemed to be picked specifically to communicate a spiritual reality to his followers. He explained, when healing a blind man, that God allowed his blindness "that the works of God might be made manifest in him" (John 9:3).

33

Christ healed the blind, preaching that one's eyes should be opened to the truth.

He healed the lame, preaching that one should walk in faith.

He healed lepers, preaching that he would cleaned away sin.

He resurrected the dead, preaching all of us shall one day rise.

In other words, Christ did some amazing miracles, but the core focus of his ministry was to get people to Heaven. His healings often served as metaphors – as physical signs of the spiritual reality of his ministry. They are hints of the sacraments, through which physical signs actually cause a spiritual reality.

What about unanswered prayers?

In Twain's *The Adventures of Tom Sawyer*, Huck Finn gives prayer a chance, asking for some fishing gear. He dismisses the idea of God as nonsense when his prayers are not answered.

God answers our prayers, but not always in the way we expect. Isaiah reminds us that the goal of prayer is to align ourselves with God's will: "For my thoughts are not your thoughts, neither are your ways my ways, says the Lord" (55:8-9).

God always answers *yes* to our prayers when we ask for those things that align with his will, such as wisdom, forgiveness and salvation (Jas 1:5; 1 John 1:9, and Rom 10:13).

Would God create a place like Hell?

Many Christians today reject the idea of Hell, and others maintain that it could not possibly be an eternal state. Atheists perceive the natural discomfort with the idea of a giant oven, where devils enslave the damned.

Hell does exist, as a later chapter explores. It is not populated with red-horned creatures with pitchforks. Rather, it is a state of pain and misery that comes from an individual's rejection of God.

So how could a loving God cast someone into Hell and leave him there for eternity?

Imagine a saddened husband, whose wife left him for another man. To ask how God would cast a sinner out of Heaven is like asking this man why he kicked his wife out of the house. Why won't he let her come back? Rather, that estranged husband has begged and pleaded for his wife to return, but she has so completely emptied herself of any love for him that she ignores his phone calls and throws away his letters.

Hell is a place of our choosing. Those who go there have died in a state of resolute rejection of God and his love. They can never leave Hell to go to Heaven because they have so emptied themselves of love that there is not a spark to ignite the fire of repentance. Like the abandoned husband, God has sent these sinners graces through their lives to call them back home, but they have rejected these offers for reconciliation. After their death, their eternal state reflects their final moments.

God is not the one who throws away the keys to Hell. As C.S. Lewis wrote, "the doors of Hell are locked from the inside."[5]

Summary:
- **Atheists must answer the evidence for God, not dismiss him through word games;**
- **Scientific inquiry is not the only way to know something as true;**
- **God cannot contradict himself;**

---

[5] *The Problem of Pain.*

- Evil is the absence of good, resulting when man moves away from God, the source of good;
- God's healing work serves a purpose greater than just our medicinal needs;
- Christians must strive to align their prayers to God's will, not the other way around;
- Hell exists and those who go there do so of their own choosing.

5

A FEW *BAD* MEN?
RESPONDING TO SCANDAL

Turning and turning in the widening gyre
The falcon cannot hear the falconer;
Things fall apart; the centre cannot hold;
Mere anarchy is loosed upon the world,
The blood-dimmed tide is loosed, and everywhere
The ceremony of innocence is drowned;
The best lack all conviction, while the worst
Are full of passionate intensity
-William B. Yeats, from "Second Coming"

I was riding with some friends a few years back, and when the subject of the Catholic Church came up, one remarked, "You know, the Catholic Church has quite a colorful history." As the conversation proceeded, it became clear that her perception of Catholicism was based on occurrences of scandal.

Does the Church claim to be immune from evil?

Does the existence of scandal within our past and present

nullify our claim to be the Church that Christ established? Put another way, when scandal occurs (it has before and will continue to), is that reason to leave Catholicism and find a less "colorful" church home?

When people refer to Church scandal, they are usually referring to one of these events:

- The Inquisitions
- The Crusades
- The treatment of Galileo
- Something Pope So-And-So did once upon a time
- Indulgences
- The "fact" that the Catholic Church "chained up the Bible, forbid it to be read, and burned people at the stake for translating it, yada, yada, yada"
- The priest abuse crisis

The first thing that any Catholic should realize when addressing scandal is that, no matter what clever rationalizations might exist, the truth is that real evil has been done by real individuals, causing real pain in real lives. The most important thing that one can do in conversations like these is to listen and attempt to empathize. It shouldn't surprise anyone that someone might leave the faith because of the behavior of others. As Mahatma Gandhi is alleged to have said, "I like your Christ, I do not like your Christians. Your Christians are so unlike your Christ."

Putting it in perspective

However, the pendulum swings both ways, and in the process of expressing indignation at real incidents of scandal, some have distorted facts or made unfair assumptions.

The Inquisitions - Spanish Inquisitions are sometimes

portrayed as a period when the Catholic Church sought out and killed Jews and Protestants. Some exaggerated anti-Catholic claims put that number at nearly 100 million killed, when the real number is closer to a few thousand. The Inquisitions were not at all a blanket persecution of non-Catholics. Rather, in the 15th century, a number of non-Christians were pretending to convert in order to gain political office, while secretly practicing their original faith. The Inquisitions began as investigations into this, with offenders turned over to the state for punishment. At that time, heresy was punishable by death, just as it was in Protestant communities.

Galileo - Anti-Catholics occasionally use Galileo as an example to show that the Church is anti-science, torturing the poor scientist for promoting a heliocentric model of the universe. Rather, the Church had already welcomed speculation as to the mechanics of the universe, especially from Copernicus. Galileo got in trouble for taking his science a step to far, pushing bad theology. Regardless, there is no evidence that he was tortured as a result.

"Hitler's pope" - Pope Pius XII has been painted as an anti Semite in recent years for ignoring the plight of the Jews. This claim did not really exist before a 1963 play called *The Deputy*. In truth, Pius and other Church officials attempted to keep a low profile to avoid drawing attention to the fact that they were working to hide thousands of Jews and to issue documents to allow these individuals to pretend to be Christians. Despite the modern smear campaign, the Jewish community of the time recognized the Church's contribution, so much so that, in addition to issuing a public statement of gratitude, the Chief Rabbi of Rome converted to Catholicism after the war and chose the Pope's name for his own at baptism.[6]

There are much more thorough books for giving detailed analyses of many of these items. Patrick Madrid's *Pope Fiction* and

---

[6] Jimmy Akin, "How Pius XII Protected Jews," www.catholic.com.

H.W. Crocker III's *Triumph* are excellent sources for getting a more balanced understanding of the Inquisitions, the Crusades, Galileo, and scandalous stories of various popes.

But the main point with any of these is that even the most "damning" evidence proves nothing but that sinners exist in the Church, just as Christ claimed they would.

The abuse scandal

Just after the turn of the 21st century, the church had a very dark season. It seemed one story after another hit the front pages of our papers, though a close examination shows that the vast majority of these cases happened many years ago, and that the Church seems to have seriously cleaned up her seminaries and parishes long before being "forced to" by pressure from the media.[7] So many cases came out at once because many were not revealed to the public at the time. There are some practical reasons for this, but there were also some inexcusable reasons, such as the relocation of accused priests to new parishes. However, one of the harms caused by this is that people are now under the impression that there is something inherently disordered about the Catholic priesthood, which caused this scandal.

The number of abuse cases within the Catholic Church is no greater, and in some cases less, than in other Christian groups. One study by three major insurance companies showed that the reported incidents of clergy abuse in Protestant communities is greater than the total number of reports about Catholic clergy.[8] Is this a reason to throw stones at our non-Catholic brothers and

---

[7] *The Nature and Scope of the Problem of Sexual Abuse of Minors by Catholic Priests and Deacons in the United States,* John Jay College of Criminal Justice. February 27, 2004.

[8] Rose French, "Report: Protestant Church Insurers Handle 260 Sex Abuse Cases a Year," *Insurance Journal.* June 18, 2007.

sisters? Of course not, but the next time someone makes a priest joke, it might be helpful to steer him to these resources.

Beyond religious institutions, the incidents of abuse and cover up in secular institutions, such as public schools, is even more alarming.[9] The National Center for Missing and Exploited Children maintains that incidents in Catholic Church are no higher than in other institutions.[10]

What does this show us? That sex abuse, like all sin, is a symptom of a damaged society, a people still scarred by our fallen nature. Scandal will happen, but we must now examine whether or not this challenges the integrity of our Catholic Church.

Consider the scandal with which the Old Testament church was plagued. Temple priests abused the offerings, David committed adultery and murder, and many leaders fell into idolatry. Yet, it would have been a time for God's wrath had any of the Israelites decided to break away because they wanted to start a new church, free from such scandal. In fact, Jesus confirms the authority of the Scribes and Pharisees, despite their faults, because they sit on the chair of Moses (Matt 23:2).

A Church of sinners, as Christ intended

Many claim that the New Testament church is different and that Christ would never have built a church that was headed by sinners. Yet, we need look no further than his own twelve apostles to see that this claim is erroneous. These men bickered among themselves over who was greatest in Heaven, they neglected prayer, all but one abandoned him at the crucifixion. Thomas doubted and Peter denied. And one can't forget Judas, who sold our Savior to

---

[9] *Educator Sexual Misconduct: A Synthesis of Existing Literature*. U.S. Department of Education (2004).

[10] Ernie Allen, president of National Center for Missing and Exploited Children, as reported in *Newsweek*, April 7, 2010.

his death for few silver coins. Our bishops are the successors of these apostles, so why would we hold them to a higher standard than the men that Christ, himself picked.

Scripture tells us that the true church, will have sinners, even among the leadership. Acts 20:28-30 warns of grievous wolves among the flock. Matthew 13 contains the parables of the net that collects good and bad, and the weeds among the wheat.

Rather than being free from scandal, the true Church will instead be *marked* by scandal. Consider Luke 22 and John 13, where we discover that Satan had entered Judas to help tempt him to great sin. While Judas is completely responsible for his decision, Satan knew that if he could lead one of the leaders of the new church to sin, it would cause scandal and lead many astray. Is it any surprise that he is still at work today? He knows that for every person who leaves because of a *colorful* history, he has won another small battle in the great war. So one of the identifying marks of the true church (not the most important) will be the evidence of Satan's most vicious attacks.

Truth and holiness come from God, not man

God does not promise that his church will be free from sinners, but he does make clear that *despite* sinful leaders, his church will always be the pillar and bulwark of the truth (1 Tim 3:15). In Matthew 16, Christ insists that the gates of Hell will not prevail against his church, and John writes that the Holy Spirit will guide the church to all truth (16:13).

Even acknowledging sinners, the Church is full of many saints, whose lives are full of holiness. Even so, the Church's holiness does not find its source in men and women, but in God. He is also the source of the truth, through Scripture, Tradition, and his infallible guidance from error. A Christian should never leave the truth of Jesus because of the scandal of Judas.

The Church is also holy because of its sacraments, which also receive their power from God. St. Francis was once asked what he would do if he learned that the priest administering mass had three concubines on the side. His answer: "When it came time for Holy Communion, I would go to receive the Sacred Body of my Lord from the priest's anointed hands."

Lastly, we must remember that scandal is our cross to bear. When sin sends pain through the body of Christ, it hurts us all, but we must remember that God makes all things work together for good (Rom 8:28), and he will always be there to lead us through the darker moments and make the mystical body more vibrant and healthy than ever before.

Summary:

- Through 2,000 years of Church history, incidents have occurred when Christians, even in positions of authority, have committed great sin;
- Catholics must develop empathy and pray for victims of any scandal;
- The sex abuse "crisis" in the Catholic Church has been exaggerated by media and is no worse than in other institutions;
- As he did with Judas, Satan targets Church leaders with great temptation, hoping to draw Christians away from Christ through scandal;
- The Church's holiness comes from God, not man.

6

BIG AND RICH ... AND HOLY?
THE "WEALTHY" CHURCH

"Love for widows and orphans, prisoners, and the sick and needy of every kind, [are] as essential to [the Church] as the ministry of the sacraments and preaching of the Gospel. The Church cannot neglect the service of charity any more than she can neglect the Sacraments and the Word."
-Pope Benedict XVI, God Is Love *(Deus Caritas Est), 2006, paragraph 22*

"If the Church is so interested in helping the poor," many will reason, "why doesn't she sell off all her possessions and grandiose churches and use the money to buy food for the needy?"

This objection never seems to come from someone who has, himself, sold off all of his own possessions to feed the poor. Even so, the concern is valid. After all, our social teaching has its roots in the Scripture insistence that we are to feed and clothe the least among us, and this must be taken to heart by any truly devout Catholic. Yet, when people make this attack on the Catholic

Church, there is a bit of a distraction at work.

How wealthy is the Church?

My wife and I took a tour of Vatican City a few years back, and I was overwhelmed by the beauty of the art and architecture that filled those great walls. What many do not realize about much of this art, however, is that most of it actually doesn't belong to the Church. Rather, out of love for Christ, many great artists and institutions have loaned these invaluable pieces to the care of the Vatican and for the edification of its many visitors.

Some other pieces of art and architecture, on the other hand, do belong to the Church only because they were not loaned, but given – a free gift of time and talent offered up by an artist out of love for his Lord and Savior. Selling these works undermines the original intention of those whose brushes and chisels crafted them.

So, what of the possessions that remain? Those buildings and works that were purchased with money that might just as easily have gone to the poor? Liquidating the possessions of the Church would probably not even feed all of the world's poor for an entire year. The United Nations reported in 2004 that aide to the poor totaled almost $8 billion a year, whereas the Vatican real estate is valued at around $900 million.[11] But having the grandeur of such art on display provides for the inspiration of millions of souls through countless generations. How many souls would be uplifted if these treasures were tucked away in private collections?

In addition, past decisions cannot be evaluated based upon the present context. For instance, while it might be argued that the Church's finances today do not justify the construction of magnificent churches and the purchase of elaborate works of art,

---

[11] David Waters. "Sell the Vatican, Feed the World?" *The Washington Post,* October 16, 2009.

one must remember that at the time much of this was purchased, the concern did not exist. Much of the art work that we consider "priceless" today was little more than a commissioned assignment at the time. The materials used in such art were much more readily available. And it was the construction of these great cathedrals that put years of food on the table of the many artisans needed.

Should more be done for the poor?

Is it so wrong that the Church should hold some wealth? For many non-Catholics it would seem so, but their "local" churches do the same thing, putting aside money for later projects, missionary excursions and emergency funds.

Imagine if you took the collective wealth of every Baptist church within our country – it would surely rival what the American Catholic Church can boast. However, because the Church is a collective institution, with a centralized structure, her finances appear to be more massive than they really are.

Today the Catholic Church ranks as *the largest* charitable organization in the world.[12] In addition, less than 10% of the spending of the American Catholic Church goes to parishes and dioceses – the rest goes to charity, education and (the vast majority) to health care.[13] Almost no other institution is doing more to bring food and basic necessities to the poor and disadvantaged. From organizations such as the St. Vincent de Paul Society to missionary work in third world countries, anyone who would make the statement that the Church doesn't attend to the needs of the "least among us" simply doesn't pay much attention to the great good our church has done for those in need.

In *Schindler's List* the title character eyes the ring on his finger,

---

[12] "Earthly Concerns" *The Economist.* August 8, 2012.
[13] Ibid.

agonizing over how many more Jews he could have saved had he only tried harder and sold more of his possessions. Similarly, some will continue to demand that the Church is not truly holy until she has sold all of her possessions to buy bread for the poor. These words have a familiar echo. It was, after all, Judas Iscariot who first made these charges as a woman anointed Christ's feet with expensive oil. "Why was this ointment not sold for three hundred denarii and given to the poor?" he asked. But Jesus said, "Let her alone, let her keep it for the day of my burial. The poor you always have with you, but you do not always have me" (John 12:5-6).

As the Catholic Church has shown, we can feed the poor *and* preserve great beauty in art and architecture. The poor need beautiful Cathedrals, too. The Church's primary mission is to bring salvation to the world, and to do so, the church must remain a visible, or sacramental, sign of the glory of Christ. While Christ was a humble man, we recognize that he is our God, and that the visible glory of the magnificent churches and artwork send a message to the world. The Church is a beacon of light which proclaims that *here* is salvation. As the feet of our Savior had been anointed with oil, *here* you will find the assembled bride of the living God, adorned in all her glory.

Summary:
- Many of the Church's vast collection of treasures are actually either on loan or gifts;
- Selling the Church's wealth would not actually feed the poor for very long;
- The decentralized nature of non-Catholic communities makes their wealth less obvious;
- The Church is the largest charitable organization in the world;
- The preservation of great art and architecture serves the purpose of uplifting souls to the glory of God.

7

THREE-CARD MONTE:
LOGICAL FALLACIES

"I've seen a good many little girls in my time, but never one *with such a neck as that! No, no! You're a serpent; and there's no use denying it. I suppose you'll be telling me next that you never tasted an egg!"*

"I have tasted eggs, certainly," said Alice, who was a very truthful child; "but little girls eat eggs quite as much as serpents do, you know."

"I don't believe it," said the Pigeon; "but if they do, why then they're a kind of serpent: that's all I can say."
-*Lewis Carroll,* Alice's Adventures in Wonderland.

When my grandfather was dying, I got acquainted with the hospice minister. Ralph introduced himself as a Christian apologist and invited me to visit his website. When I later did so, I discovered a "Bible study" for Catholics. Intrigued, I worked through the study and found myself growing increasingly frustrated. One question after the next was carefully worded to trick Catholics into thinking their faith is unbiblical. For instance, one question asked how many works it takes to "earn" one's way into Heaven. The question was followed by a series of biblical citations demonstrating that no amount of good works can earn salvation. However, the Catholic Church does not teach that one can earn God's grace. This question, like so many in Ralph's study, was "begging the question" in hopes that a less informed Catholic would begin questioning his faith.

Only a sucker takes the bet in a game of three-card monte, the conman's game that appears and disappears on a street corner as suddenly as a candy wrapper in the wind. You spot the queen, follow her under and over, to the left, right, and middle and ... which card? This card? Sorry, brother, that's an eight of spades.

Ralph's study was an example of Christian three-card monte. It's common to encounter arguments that take a similar approach in steering people from their faith. Sometimes this is done intentionally, and sometimes the fallacy comes from someone who simply doesn't realize the logical leap he is taking in his argument.

Fallacies are those verbal tricks, those logical sleights-of-hand, that shift the focus during otherwise rational discussions. One moment the Catholic apologist is proving the Immaculate Conception of Mary and suddenly – sorry, wrong card – the topic has turned to the Inquisitions. Catholics who desire to defend the faith effectively need to be familiar with how to identify and respond to at least the most basic of these arguments, keeping a conversation on the right track.

Some fallacies distract the conversation

Begging the question - When begging the question, one starts with an assumption that has not been proven and asks a question or makes a challenge based on that assumption.

Fallacy: Do you really want to be associated with a religion whose leader, the pope, is the anti-Christ?

The question works on the assumption that the pope is the antichrist, forcing another to consent to this whether he gives a "yes" or "no" answer.

Shotgun approach – In the movie *The Matrix*, superhuman skills give the main characters the ability to dodge fired bullets. Sometimes, when encountering a Catholic who knows how to defend his faith, a frustrated objector will fire, not a single bullet, but an entire shotgun load of arguments, hoping that at least some of them will stick.

Catholic: As you can see, John 20 clearly shows that Christ gave the authority to forgive sins to the leaders of His Church.

Objector: You know, it really doesn't matter. I could never have any confidence in a Church that started the inquisitions, teaches that people should pray to Mary, and sacrifices Christ over and over again every Sunday …

Avoiding the question – As with those who attempt a shotgun approach, objectors to the faith often change the subject when presented with an answer or question that proves too challenging.

Catholic: Don't the passages in Romans 11 and Hebrews 10 indicate pretty clearly that a man can lose his salvation?

Objector: I'm not interested in reading some passages you've taken out of context. I want you to explain how a loving God would allow someone to turn away from him.

Straw man– Just as a man made of straw can easily be blown over, so can the very flimsiest support for the very strongest of doctrines. Often one will encounter someone who presents and demolishes an obviously weak argument for a Church teaching. This individual hopes he will give the impression of dismantling the entire teaching.

A straw man argument against homosexual relationships might propose that the Church's objection is based solely on the idea that homosexual couples cannot have children, one of the primary ends of marriage. If so, this logic would conclude, homosexual couples have just as much justification to marry as infertile or elderly individuals.

However, the Church's teachings on homosexuality are deep, complex and solid, and it would be disingenuous to dismiss the teachings based on the superficial defeat of a straw man argument.

Name Calling (*ad hominem*) – While one would hope that name calling only popped up on the playground, it is still common when adults disagree. Catholics will often find their best efforts to explain the faith dismissed as the words of a "papist" or "idolater." Name calling can also take the form of condemning another group morally. I remember one conversation a few years back when, in the middle of a conversation about Pope Pius XII, the other individual brought up the abuse crisis and attempted to dismiss all that I had said on that note.

Shifting burden of proof – Similar to an argument from silence, we must always remember that the burden of proof rests on he who wants to challenge the accepted view.

Fallacy: Show me where the Bible says that it's okay to follow your "Sacred Tradition"?

The Israelites accepted Scripture and Tradition, as did the Christian church until the reformation. Since the idea of Scripture-alone is a break from what was understood to be the norm, the burden of proof is on the other party (though Tradition can certainly be proven through Scripture). For more on this, see the chapters on Scripture and Tradition.

Red herring – A red herring is a fake, or misleading proof that often distracts or confuses the issue at hand. A red herring may be a perfectly legitimate concern thrown into an argument to which it has no relevance. "Well, Senator Smith may have increased jobs, as you say, but I can't vote for anyone who doesn't support our schools."

Fallacy: Who cares if you can prove the early Christians were Catholic; I don't remember anything about the early Christians chaining up Bibles.

The speaker, who obviously realizes his opponent has proven a point, quickly throws in a desperate odd-ball challenge that has little to do with the discussion at hand.

Formal fallacies use faulty reasoning

Syllogistic errors – In a syllogism, three "terms" are set up to form a logical train-of thought that looks like this: "All dogs have four legs. Rex is a dog. Therefore Rex has four legs." One common syllogistic error occurs when two premises make an invalid claim based on similarities: "Rex is a dog. All poodles are dogs. Therefore Rex is a poodle."

Fallacy: When you look at Catholicism, you see so many of the trappings of Pagan belief: worshiping on the day of the "Sun" god, god-eating, a venerated mother and child. Catholicism is just Paganism warmed over.

The fact that there are apparent similarities between Catholicism (even Christianity) and Pagan beliefs is far from proof that Catholicism is simply glorified paganism, as some groups would like to claim. This argument fails on many levels.

In truth, similarities between two groups can be explained a few other ways, including pure coincidence. Another consideration is that there is not really much proof that Christian beliefs came *after* the pagan beliefs they supposedly resemble. Very possibly the pagan groups lifted practices from the Christians.

More probable is the consideration that God has planted the truth in every man's soul. Though sin distorts our ability to be in tune with it, fragments of that truth still come through even in those who completely reject Christianity. One shouldn't be surprised to see glimpses of Christianity – glimpses of the truth – color the otherwise made up beliefs of non-Christian religions.

One of the most important points to make here is that some fringe Protestant groups will make the claim that Catholicism came from paganism because they see similarities, such as examples of a virgin birth or a resurrected God in some pagan belief systems. What they fail to realize is that atheists make that same claim about *all* of Christianity. So if the similarity to Paganism charge discredits Catholicism, it discredits all of Christianity. If Protestants have a defense for why there is no connection, then Catholicism has the same defense.

Circular reasoning – If a man attempts to reach down and pick himself up off the ground, he'll be doing the same thing that Bible-only Christians attempt by demonstrating that the Bible claims inspiration for itself. *Anything* can claim inspiration for itself (e.g. Everything in this book is inspired!), but only that which can be verified by an outside authority stands on firm ground.

Catholic: How do we know that the Bible is inspired?

Fallacy: 2 Timothy 3:16 tells us it is.

Catholic: How do we know we can trust 2 Timothy?

Fallacy: Because it is in the Bible, which is inspired.

Rather than using circular reasoning, a Catholic would answer that history records that Christ, who did and said things that proved his divinity, gave the Catholic Church the authority to bind and loose on behalf of God, and that this Church declared a set of writings, the Old and New Testament, to be inspired. This argument (when explained fully) starts from solid base and ends with a solid conclusion.

Band wagon – This fallacy argues that if most people buy into a belief, it must be true.

Fallacy: Oh, most Catholics don't agree with the Church on birth control. The pope is so out of touch.

Just because everyone else is doing it doesn't make it a good idea: "For the gate is narrow and the way is hard, that leads to life, and those who find it are few" (Matt 7:14).

Argument from silence (proving a negative) – An argument from silence maintains that because nobody ever spoke against a certain belief, that belief must have been accepted. An example: "I've seen no historical writings disproving the idea that Abe Lincoln was a vampire killer, so I'm free to believe it." It would be impossible for one to prove that Abe Lincoln didn't kill vampires since the topic probably never came up in his journals or other documents. The burden of proof is on he who makes the outlandish claim.

Fallacy: The Bible never says Christ didn't have children or get married, so I can believe it if I want to.

The Bible also doesn't tell us that the apostle Paul wasn't an alien visitor from the Planet Z-907. However, because Scripture doesn't condemn every wild idea afloat in the imaginations of men doesn't give us permission to validate these ideas.

Slippery slope - A might lead to B, so A is bad. Often this approach gives an improbable worst-case scenario to a proposition: "If we legalize a sin-tax on alcohol and tobacco, the next thing you know they'll be putting higher taxes on gum to prevent cavities."

Fallacy: If we allow the government to outlaw abortions, then what's to stop them from outlawing contraception? Eventually, they'll be outlawing premarital sex and arresting consenting adults who are simply enjoying each other's company.

The challenge assumes that a ban on abortion is an attempt to "legislate morality," when it is really an effort to defend life. While Catholics reject contraception and premarital sex, it is silly to say that these behaviors are threatened legally by an abortion ruling.

False Dichotomy - There are two types of people in the world, those who read and enjoy this book and those who don't love Jesus.

How's that for a lead?

The idea that people are either fans of this book or are infidels is just another example. Of course, not all either-or propositions are fallacious, but the types thrown at Catholics often are, and the term for this is a *false dichotomy*, or a false choice: *Either you can follow some pope or you can follow God*. While the papacy is a subject for another chapter, the Catholic apologist can identify and defend a third option, which is that following the pope is following God, just as much as to obey a deputy is to obey the sheriff, himself.

Argument from Ignorance – An attempt to humble another through the use of esoteric knowledge is a common tactic in discussions of faith. Arguments from ignorance happen, for instance, when an individual is told that "if you only understood the original Greek," a biblical teaching would make much more sense. While learning biblical Greek is certainly a way to grow closer to Scripture, as Catholics we understand that Christ did not design a faith that would be accessible only by those who are skilled in linguistics. He gave us the Spirit-guided Church as the final arbiter in all matters of doctrine.

Faulty cause and effect – B follows A, so A causes B. This happens often, not just in religious discussions, but political debates, where an event or policy is thought to cause a later event, even though no correlation has been established. For instance: "Cancer rates rose substantially the year after more fluoride was added to the water. We must eliminate the dangerous poison."

Fallacy: The sex-abuse scandal would never have happened had the Catholic Church not insisted on celibacy among its priests.

Just because the discipline of celibacy existed before the abuse crisis does not indicate that it caused – or even contributed – to it. On the contrary, studies show that abuse is just as prevalent among clergy from non-Catholic denominations. In fact, most abuse happens at the hands of married men, often family members of the victim. The fact that the Catholic Church has the unique discipline of celibacy, however, has made it an easy target (and celibacy an easy explanation) for the crisis. This is explored more fully, with documentation, in the chapter on scandal.

Hasty Generalization – A Protestant minister once told me of all the Catholics he met who didn't know Scripture or have a good relationship with Christ. However, to assume that the individuals he refers to represent the whole of Catholicism is to commit the fallacy of "hasty generalization." This fallacy is carried to an even more dangerous extreme by assuming that the sinful or apathetic behavior of certain members of the group is a means by which the integrity of that group as a whole can be judged.

These fallacies and their rebuttals all deserve deeper exploration, and there are many more that could be added to the list. One must, of course, be careful that he does not become focused on winning debates when the real goal is to win souls. That said, exercising how to hold a logically consistent and cohesive conversation is a skill that can only strengthen our ability to answer the invitation of the Lord in Isaiah 1:18:

Come now, and let us reason together...

Summary:

- Logical fallacies are verbal sleight-of-hand tricks that people use (sometimes without realizing it) to win arguments;
- Some fallacies, such as red herring and the shotgun approach, are designed to distract the conversation from the topic at hand;
- Other fallacies, such as bad analogy and circular reasoning, include reasoning errors;
- When discussing the faith, Catholics should be aware of these fallacies, both to avoid using them and to avoid falling for them.

Authority

8

THE TRINITY: FUZZY MATH?

"It is the attribute of God, of the most high and almighty of the living God, not only to be everywhere, but also to see and hear all; for he can in no way be contained in a place ... The three days before his luminaries were created are types of the Trinity: God, his Word, and his Wisdom."
-Theophilus of Antioch, To Autolycus 2:15 (AD 181)

Right now God is watching your great-grandchild die. He is, right now, watching your great-grandmother being born. Right now God is watching Napoleon invade Italy and is watching, sometime in the future, the discovery of a cure for a terrible disease.

God is eternal, and sometimes people think this means that he never ages and never dies. And while these things are true, *eternal* means much more than this, including the reality that time and space are his creations, and he exists outside of them. All things that have happened and will happen are happening *right now* for God.

It should be mind-boggling to think about God. As much as

he has been humanized by Hollywood, he is not George Burns or Morgan Freeman. He is an infinite, immutable, omnipresent, omnipotent, omniscient being.

It is a form of prayer to contemplate these things, attempting to grow closer to our creator, but knowing we will never understand the sum total of him.

He is beyond comprehension, yet he is simple. Sovereign, but granter of mankind's free will. All powerful, but victim upon the cross. He very well could have authored the Whitman line: *Do I contradict myself? Very well, then I contradict myself, I am large, I contain multitudes.*

And nothing about God seems a greater contradiction than the Trinity. Three, but one. And it is this that makes for the greatest mystery of Christianity.

What Scripture tells us about God

There is only one God: this is a very prominent point in the Old Testament, with the polytheistic pagan cults competing for attention (Deut 6:4; Isa 43:10; John 17:3);

Three different *persons* are identified as God: the Father (John 17:3), Jesus Christ (Col 2:9; Tit 2:13; Heb 1:8, 10), and the Holy Spirit (Acts 5:3; Heb 3:7-10; 10:15-17) are each identified as God;

These three persons are distinct from one another: This is shown by their cooperation and interaction with each other (John 17; 14:12-17; 16:10; Acts 2:32–33);

The three persons are often invoked and shown operating with equality to one another: (Matthew 28:19; 2 Cor 13:13, Heb 9:14). The three persons appear to be operating with the same will and intent.

Three in one. The math doesn't seem to add up. The reason? Because it isn't about math at all. The above Scripture makes clear there are three *persons* in one *nature*. "Person" is who someone is. "Nature" is what someone is. For instances, humans all have human nature in common. God the Father, the Son and the Holy Spirit all have divine nature in common.

The difference is that an individual's human nature is tied directly to his individual identity. Of my three sons, though each has human nature, Bryce is gentle and imaginative, Jack is mischievous and independent, and ten-month-old Tate just likes to follow his mommy around the house all day. Each has his own will and intellect shaping his nature, making them separate humans.

However, the three persons of the Trinity do not just *have* divinity, as my boys each have human nature. God *is* divinity, and because divinity cannot be separated like human nature can, the Father, Son, and Spirit are perfectly united in will, intellect and substance, which means they are *one* God, not three parts to God.

This is why, in the creed at Mass, we say that Christ is *consubstantial* with the Father. "Con" means "together" or "same." They exist with the *same* substance.

Why, then, are there three distinct persons?

God is perfect knowledge

Picture a pear.

When a person imagines a pear, no matter how perfectly, all he has is an idea of a pear in his head. Man can form a similar image of anything that he knows (at least as well as he knows it).

When God forms an image in his head, it becomes reality. God envisioned light, and as soon as he said "Let there be light," it appeared. Psalm 148 says of God, "He commanded and they were created" (verse 5).

I might be able to form an image of someone I know. If God did that, however, he could create an image that actually formed into that person.

And before there were people, puppies, dandelions, angels, or .... even a universe, God still had perfect knowledge. And his knowledge was of the most perfect thing in existence, himself. Just as an individual might form a mental picture of herself, God formed an image of himself. Because his knowledge is perfect, everything about who God is went into this image.

And, as with the pear, God's perfect image of himself isn't just a thought, but is actually manifested as a second person. This is what is meant by saying Jesus is begotten of the Father (John 3:16), not created, as with the pear. Christ is a person formed of God's self-knowledge. Just as all of us express our knowledge through our words, Christ is called the divine "Word" (John 1:1). Christ is the "reflection" of God's glory, the "very stamp of his nature" (Heb 1:1-3). He is, in Paul's words, the "image of the invisible God" (Col 1:15).

Because Christ is the "image" of the Father, everything that is true of the Father's nature is also true of the Son's nature. The Father is eternal, and so is Christ. The Father is divine, and so is Christ. The Father's will and Christ's will are the same. They share the same intellect. The two persons are *one* God.

God is perfect love

Because we are made in God's image and he is knowledge, we have knowledge. We also have love because God is love.

When someone loves another, he pours everything into that love. A husband who holds back from his wife and family is giving love imperfectly.

Through all of eternity, the Father and the Son have existed. The Father has poured himself completely into his love for the Son. The Son has done the same in his love for the Father. Their very divinity is poured into that love, as well as their shared intellect, will and eternal nature. The love manifests as a third divine, but distinct, person: the Holy Spirit. The word that theologians use for this is that the Father and the Son "spirate" (breathed out) the Holy Spirit.

Is the Holy Spirit a person?

Some groups deny the third person of the Trinity. The Jehovah's Witnesses believe that the Holy Spirit is not a person, but a force (like electricity) that emanates from the Father. This idea falls apart quickly, though, when one considers that the Holy Spirit does conscious things, such as teach (John 14:26) and witness (Heb 10:15-16). When was the last time that electricity ever did those things? In addition, the Spirit's divinity is affirmed in 2 Cor 3:16-18, when he is called Lord.

So when Christians speak of the three-in-one Trinity, we are speaking of one Divine nature that, through perfect knowledge and perfect love, exists as a family of Father, Son and Holy Spirit.

What is a mystery?

The Trinity is a mystery. This doesn't mean that we cannot know anything about it, which is what some people assume the word means. Rather, a mystery is that which can only be known through what God has told us.

Natural reason alone can't lead us to know about God's triune nature without divine revelation. We also cannot hope to understand a mystery fully with our limited intellects. Author Frank Sheed, in *Theology and Sanity*, describes a mystery as a great hall of priceless art. The deeper into the hall we travel, the more astonishing each new print is than the last. One can never reach the end, but only travel further and experience even greater art.

Likewise, the Trinity is a concept that grows more amazing and awe-inspiring as we further understand and contemplate it, though we will never fully understand the nature of God, despite our best efforts. We only travel deeper into the mystery.

After all, who would want to worship a God who was so simple that humans could figure him out? We haven't even figured out the tax code, and God is definitely greater than that, but we can know some things – some basic elements about the Trinity. To contemplate the relationship between the three divine persons is one of the highest forms of prayer for Christians, and the more we know about the three-person God, in whose image we were created, the more we understand about ourselves.

Summary:
- Scripture tells us that there is only one God, but three divine persons sharing that divine nature;
- These divine persons act in harmony with one another;
- Christ, the Word, is the reflection of God manifested as a second eternal person;
- The third person of the Trinity is the *spiration* of the love between the Father and the Son;
- The Holy Spirit is an actual person within the Trinity, not merely a force;
- A mystery cannot be fully grasped, but can be understood more deeply as we grow in knowledge of our creator;
- Understanding the Trinity helps us to understand ourselves.

9

THE GOSPEL TRUTH:
IS SCRIPTURE RELIABLE?

"Those divinely revealed realities which are contained and presented in Sacred Scripture have been committed to writing under the inspiration of the Holy Spirit. For holy mother Church, relying on the belief of the Apostles, holds that the books of both the Old and New Testaments in their entirety, with all their parts, are sacred and canonical because written under the inspiration of the Holy Spirit, they have God as their author and have been handed on as such to the Church herself."

-Dei Verbum (Dogmatic Constitution on Divine Revelation), *Promulgated by His Holiness Pope Paul VI on November 18, 1965.*

As Catholics we believe the Bible is inspired, or authored by the Holy Spirit through the pens and minds of men. But let's pretend that we do not believe this.

Whether or not the Gospels are inspired really doesn't provide the *only* answer to whether or not they are reliable. After all, an American would have to be insane to doubt whether Abraham Lincoln existed and was president. None of us have ever seen or met him; however, journals, letters and personal accounts of his life exist today, many of them written by people who knew Lincoln firsthand. None of these works are "inspired," but they are still reliable texts, and they provide research material to discover more about the Great Emancipator.

Likewise, there are four Gospels accounting for the birth, life and death of Jesus Christ. Two of these were written by apostles, Matthew and John. The other two were written by disciples of the apostles. Mark was a follower of Peter and most likely learned the complete story of Jesus from this close companion of our Lord. Luke was a disciple of Paul, who also did not know Jesus during his earthly ministry. However, at the start of his Gospel Luke explains that the contents of it are based on careful research:

"Inasmuch as many have undertaken to compile a narrative of the things which have been accomplished among us, just as they were delivered to us by those who from the beginning were eyewitnesses and ministers of the word, it seemed good to me also, having followed all things closely for some time past, to write an orderly account for you, most excellent Theophilus, that you may know the truth concerning the things of which you have been informed" (Luke 1.1-4).

So of the four Gospels, we have three eye witness accounts (one relayed through Mark from Peter) and one carefully researched narrative. Aside from inspiration, the gospels have established credibility.

But weren't the Gospel writers biased?

If the early Christians were trying to start a new religion, some argue, they have a strong bias toward fabricating information to create the "myth" of Jesus. This criticism falls apart very quickly, however, when several things are considered:

The apostles had nothing to gain by spreading fiction – Many early Christians died for their beliefs, including eleven of the twelve apostles. With no riches or power, but only martyrdom to gain by threatening the powers that be, one can assume that the early disciples at the very least believed what they were writing.

Non-Christians wrote about Christ, too - Though atheists claim that Christians "invented" Christ, Jesus is also written about by early pagan and Jewish authors, who had no motivation to spread myths that threatened their own beliefs. Jewish historian Josephus wrote about many Gospel figures, including Jesus, John the Baptist, and Pontius Pilate.

Consistency and variations in the Gospels – The four Gospels tell a story of Jesus that is very consistent, especially Matthew, Mark and Luke, which are noted for being harmonious in their content. That these four sources would tell such a similar story points to a set of actual historical events that guided these authors. In fact, the Gospels are similar enough that some try to claim that the four authors just copied off one another. However, there are notable variations in how events are recalled and explained by the different authors, which is less likely to have occurred if the authors had just used the same source.

No dissenting histories – At the time of Jesus, when most people did not know how to read or write, oral tradition was extremely important. From children to adults, people learned to memorize large portions of information and to transmit it reliably. The Gospels contain the claims of some major events, and large numbers of individuals converted because of them. Had the events in the Gospels not happened, there would have been a number of early Jewish and Pagan authors who would have attempted to set the record straight, but these are all but non-existent.

Historical track-record of the New Testament – The Gospels have shown to be reliable when compared to other historical accounts. Even parts of the Gospels that were, at first, thought to contradict history were later shown to be accurate. An example is the Pool of Bethesda from the fifth chapter of John. At first, historians did not think this pool existed until evidence was found for it in the 19th century.

Do the Gospels contain contradictions or errors?

The Gospel accounts contain details that, when compared with one another, appear to create contradictions or errors. However, these apparent contradictions are often a result of several factors:

The authors were writing to different audiences, so different facts or details were emphasized. Mark, for instance, was most likely writing to a Roman audience while Luke was probably writing to a Greek audience, so they each had a different name for the location of the crucifixion based on the name their audience would have used (either Calvary or Golgotha).

The authors used figurative language, such as poetry, hyperbole and idioms, and were not always intending that their words be understood at face value.

Our understanding of biblical geography/culture is lacking. The book of Acts records that Christ ascended from Mt. Olivet (1:9,12), but Luke had him ascending from Bethany (24:50,51). However, Bethany is actually on the slope of Mt. Olivet. Since Luke also authored Acts, it is unlikely he was contradicting himself.

The authors in biblical times wrote with a different structure than many authors do today. Mark often leaves out details or occurrences he considered less significant and wrote about events in a sequence that feels as though they happened one right after the other. And sometimes the authors ordered events as they thought of them, rather than the order in which they occurred. Though the

Holy Spirit inspired the Gospels, he didn't dictate them word for word, but worked through the minds of the authors.

The reliable transmission of the Gospels

That the Scriptures might be written accurately is one matter. Their accurate transmission to modern readers is another.

The original texts of Scripture no longer exist. They were composed on papyrus, which is not able to withstand decomposition over extended lengths of time. This shouldn't be surprising. After all, no originals exist even of Shakespeare's plays. However, the Bible retains a remarkable amount of historical integrity – much more than many other ancient writings whose preservation is not questioned.

The dating of the writing of most New Testament documents is around 50 – 90 AD, and many 1st century fragments remain today. Beyond those, the oldest existing copy of any New Testament manuscript is from 200 AD, about 150 years later. The ancient manuscript that comes closest is Homer's *Iliad*, with 500 years of difference from composition to the oldest copy. For Aristotle's work, it is 1200 years, the same as with Sophocles.

We have around 24,000 fragments or entire copies of early New Testaments, with just under 6,000 of them in Greek. For the *Iliad*, it is just over 1,700; 100 or so for the works of Aristotle; and about 10 for the works of Sophocles.

Finally, even if a single New Testament document or fragment did not exist today, almost all of it could be pieced together just from quotations within the writings of the early Church fathers.

One would expect, with all of the early copies of the New Testament, that if the Holy Spirit were not at work the integrity of the content would have suffered. However, out of all of the copies, an amazing consistency exists, with very few lines in dispute among early texts. Even so, it is important to note here that, while the original text was inspired, translations and copies of it were not. The *King James* Bible, for instance, is an uninspired translation of ancient Greek texts. As will be explored in the chapter on Scripture and Tradition, even the concerns over translator and copier error are non-existent in the Church that Christ built.

The reliability of the Gospels is a subject that can and does fill books that go into much deeper detail. However, once the Gospels are established as a reliable source of information, one can take the next step of examining what proof they have to offer as to the existence of a man named Jesus Christ, and whether or not that evidence is compatible with good historical scholarship.

Summary:

- The Gospels are based on first-hand accounts, careful research and reliable oral transmission;
- No credible case can be made that bias corrupts the integrity of the Gospels, especially as they are supported by non-Christian sources;
- Perceived contradictions or errors are the result of the reader's ignorance of audience, literary style and cultural factors;
- The Gospels were recorded with a level of integrity that surpasses many other ancient documents;
- The Scriptures were preserved with integrity by the Holy Spirit for readers 2,000 years after their composition.

10

A CHIP OFF THE ETERNAL BLOCK: THE DIVINITY OF CHRIST

"We are not playing the fool, you Greeks, nor do we talk nonsense, when we report that God was born in the form of a man."
-Tatian the Syrian (Address to the Greeks 21 (AD 170)

J esus was either a liar or a lunatic.

C.S. Lewis, author of *The Chronicles of Narnia* and other famous titles, used his book *Mere Christianity* to articulate this argument against the claim from atheists that Christ was not God, but just a good and wise man, much like Gandhi. That there was nothing divine about Jesus is a popular claim in today's culture.

But Jesus did not act like a man who was just wise and good. He acted like a man who believed he was God. He made statements putting himself on the same level as God, and claimed the ability to heal, forgive sins and to rise from the dead.

He was either a liar or he was delusional. Or he was God.

And given that he didn't just make amazing promises, but also fulfilled them, one can conclude that he is exactly who he and the Gospel writers claimed him to be: the only begotten Son of Yahweh, true God from true God, consubstantial with the Father.

Another group who challenges the divine nature of Christ is the Jehovah's Witnesses, whom most have encountered on their front doorstep, perhaps on a Saturday morning when the doorbell rings. The Witnesses started in the late 19th century after a preacher named Charles Taze Russell began studying with the Seventh Day Adventists, known for their anti-Catholicism. He eventually developed his own religion. Christians should be skeptical of any religion that was developed by a man in the 1700's, rather than by Christ himself, but many are easily swayed by the *apparently* convincing arguments of these missionaries.

Does Christ claim to be God?

One of the most straightforward claims of the Jehovah's Witnesses is that Christ never makes the statement, "I am God." While these exact words may not appear in the New Testament, Jesus make certain claims that only God would be qualified to make. Examples include John 8:58-59, where Christ assumes the title of "I am," which God uses for himself in Ex 3:14; In Heb 1:6-8, Rev 1:8, and Rev 22:13, divine titles and attributes are assigned to Christ. In addition, Christ is known as the incarnate Word, and John 1:1 makes clear that "The Word was God." Isaiah 9:5-6 refers to him as "mighty God." In order to refute some of these verses, such as the opening passage from John's gospel, the Jehovah's Witnesses have altered many verses in the translation of their *New World* translation of the Bible.

Paul expresses it clearly in Colossians 2:9, when he writes that, in Christ, "the whole *fullness of deity* dwells bodily."

In order to get around the verses that testify to Christ's divinity the Jehovah's Witnesses claim that Jesus is actually the

Archangel Michael. They cite as an authority for this 1 Thessalonians 4:16, which reads that Christ will descend from Heaven with an "archangel's voice." The Witnesses are assuming that the angel's voice belongs to Jesus, but instead it is an archangel announcing his triumphant return. Hebrews 1:5-6 emphasizes that Christ is superior to angels:

> "For to what angel did God ever say, 'Thou art my Son, today I have begotten thee'? Or again, 'I will be to him a father, and he shall be to me a son'? And again, when he brings the first-born into the world, he says, 'Let all God's angels worship him.'

Only God is worthy of worship, and while Christ has the authority to rebuke Satan (Matt 4:10), angels do not (Jude 9).

Is Christ inferior to God?

The Witnesses will point out that Christ does, in many instances, appear to be inferior to God the Father. However, their misreading of this comes from a poor understanding of the two natures of Christ, who is fully human and fully divine. Christ has been equal to the Father through all eternity. He is God's knowledge of himself manifested as a second eternal being, equal and united in divinity, will and intellect with the Father. However, the sins of man separated us from God in a way that an appropriate sacrifice needed to be offered to atone for them. The debt was too large for mankind to pay.

God desires for us to be with him in Heaven, so Christ took on human nature in order to die on our behalf. As Paul wrote in Philippians, he "emptied himself, taking the form of a slave, coming in human likeness" (Phil 2:7).

Having two natures, Christ also has two wills (a human and divine will). When the Jehovah's Witnesses or other groups point out verses where Christ appears to be inferior to the Father, they are failing to realize that these are examples of where Jesus is speaking from the perspective of his human nature.

Christ fulfills Old Testament prophesies

The prophets whose words are recorded in the Old Testament spoke on behalf of God to guide the people of Israel. In doing so, however, the prophets often offered hope, especially in times of persecution and exile. A messiah would be sent to redeem God's people. Some very specific prophesies were made about this promised individual:

> Isaiah 32:3-4; 35:5-6- His ministry will include miracles curing the blind, deaf, lame and dumb;
> Isaiah 53:3 - He will be rejected by His people;
> Daniel 9:24-27 gives a precise prediction of Jesus' arrival;
> Psalm 22:16; Zech 12:10 - His hands and feet will be pierced;
> Psalm 22:18 - they will divide His garments among them.

Not only did these prophesies accurately foreshadow the life and death of Jesus, but there are over 300 Old Testament references and prophesies that were fulfilled by him. The prophets wrote decades or centuries before Christ, but were able to predict very specific details, including his miraculous acts. This indicates his divine influence over their proclamations.

Historical claims

In the Easter story alone, very specific historical claims point to the divinity of Christ and his unique authority over all false prophets in establishing the one, true faith:

- The knowledge of the location of his burial, as he was placed in a tomb owned by Joseph of Arimathea, who was a member of the Jewish Sanhedrin (Mark 15:46);
- Jesus' tomb was found empty by a group of women

(Mark 16:1-4; Acts 2:29; 13:36; 1 Cor 15:4);

- The risen Christ appeared to many witnesses, including 500 at one time (1 Cor 1-11);
- The martyrdom of the disciples, who had witnessed the miracles of Christ firsthand.

The first two of these claims are believable because they are so *unbelievable*. If the story of Christ were made up, how likely is it that the author of this "fiction" would have been a member of the Sanhedrin, the group that condemned Jesus. Would he have offered a burial spot reserved for a member of his family? Likewise, in the Jewish culture of the first century, a patriarchal structure existed and women's testimony was not highly respected. If the account of the empty tomb were fictional, the author most likely would have arranged for the male apostles to discover it.

Making these accounts even more convincing is the reality that no contradictory evidence exists. People were converting to Christianity in enormous numbers, upsetting the Jewish and Roman culture. These conversions were based upon historical claims that Christ had died, that an identified man had given his tomb to Christ, that the tomb had turned up empty, and that hundreds had seen Christ alive again.

If this were all fiction, there surely would have been detractors recorded in ancient writings:

"No Jesus of Nazareth was crucified on that day."

"There was no empty tomb! The body of Christ lies there still!"

The most convincing evidence for the historical fact of Jesus' death and resurrection is the martyrdom of most of the apostles.

Many religions, such as Islam, have their devout martyrs. The difference is that the martyrs of other religions often go to their deaths to affirm something they *believe*, but have not witnessed firsthand. For instance, Joseph Smith, the founder of Mormonism, claims to have had several encounters with divine beings that happened while he was alone, and he reports that he "returned" the golden tablets from which he supposedly translated the Book of Mormon, making them unavailable for archeological scrutiny.

The Jews did not believe in a messiah that would rise from the dead, so the twelve were not inclined to expect that (Luke 24:11; John 20:25). Even Thomas was so doubtful that he refused to believe the words of his fellow apostles. Yet, when threatened with their lives, the apostles had no choice but to continue to proclaim the death and resurrection of Christ because they had witnessed it firsthand. If the events of Jesus' death and resurrection had not happened, the apostles would have known it was all a lie. Would they really have gone willingly to their painful deaths?

Many people claim that the various religions are all equal paths to the peak of the same mountain. However, only one religion is based upon verifiable historical occurrences, such as the fulfillment of prophecy and the events at the end of Jesus' life. And this is why Jesus is able to make the bold claim that he, and he alone, is the way, the truth, and the life, and that nobody gets to the Father except *through him* (John 14:6).

Summary:

- Christ cannot simply be a "good" man, and unless he is the God he claims to be, he is either delusional or a liar;
- Christ claims to be God and does many things that only a divine person could accomplish;
- Christ cannot be the Archangel Michael, as Scripture shows he is superior to angels;
- Christ only appears inferior to God when he speaks from the perspective of his human nature;
- Historical facts speak to Christ's divinity.

11

LIES OF BIBLICAL PROPORTIONS: CATHOLICS AND THE BIBLE

"I would not believe the Gospel if the authority of the Catholic Church did not move me to do so."
-*Augustine,* Against the Fundamental Epistle of Manichaeus, *chapter 5*

Sometimes I forget that not everyone picks up on my dry sense of humor. Once I had an aide who wanted a teaching job and asked to do a lesson that I could observe. She told me one of the stories from Genesis that she'd like to cover.

"That's fine," I said. "But I'd prefer a lesson on 1 Samuel 6."

Not everyone is immediately familiar with this story, which is the one where the Philistines steal the Ark of Covenant. As punishment, they are inflicted with a bad case of mice infestation and hemorrhoids. Even after they return the Ark, the only way they can rid themselves of the curse is to melt down their valuable gold and make it into five golden mice and five hemorrhoids. So, long story short, this young lady didn't realize I was joking, and she proceeded to prepare a lesson on this story.

For kindergarteners.

As one might predict, after working into the early morning to complete the lesson (including making a cardboard Ark of Covenant), she wasn't amused when I discovered what she had done and informed her that I had just been kidding.

It is a safe generalization to say that most people aren't familiar with the story of the Philistines and their golden hemorrhoids. For some reason there don't seem to be a lot of sermons about it.

I felt bad about the misunderstanding. After all, what she was only attempting the very important job of helping these students to know the Scriptures.

Catholics have a reputation for not being familiar with the Bible, and in many cases I would say that is true. We could all spend more time with God's written word, but the same could be said about many Protestants I have met. Beyond our need to be more familiar with the Bible, however, there are a number of myths about Catholics and Scripture that are worth debunking.

In an earlier chapter, I mentioned Ralph, the hospice minister who wrote the anti-Catholic Bible study. He was very fond of perpetuating these silly whoppers. Ralph and others like him continue to spread these myths, so Catholics should be aware of how to respond when encountering them.

Catholics added books to the Bible

Catholic Bibles are a bit larger. There are seven additional books in the Old Testament of Catholic Bibles: Tobias, Wisdom of

Solomon, Judith, Sirach, Baruch, and 1st and 2nd Maccabees. Daniel and Esther are also longer in Catholic Bibles.

These books are called the *deuterocanonical* books, from the Greek word for "second canon," which does not mean they are "second" to the other books, but that they were selected later. Protestants will sometimes refer to them as the *Apocrypha* to imply that they are not part of the real Scriptures. The rejection of these books is usually based on the premise that they are not inspired because they weren't included in the Hebrew Old Testament, also called the Palestinian canon..

But where did God specify that only the books in the Hebrew Old Testament are inspired?

By the time of Christ, there were actually a few versions of the Old Testament, and nobody had definitively settled which was the official version. There was the Palestinian canon and there was the version that Catholics use today, called the Septuagint. Some Jews went only by the first five books of the Bible, called the *Pentateuch*. There were other versions floating around, as well.

Christ and the apostles preached using the same Old Testament as Catholics do (or at least a version very similar to it). We know this because as many as two-thirds of the Old Testament quotes in the New Testament are from the Septuagint Greek.

Modern speculation from some historians is that a Jewish council was held in Jamnia in the late first century. At this supposed council, the seven books in question were officially rejected. There is no historical proof that this council took place, but even if it had, why would any Christian follow the guidance of a council of Jews *after* the time of Christ. Wouldn't they have had a motive to reject any books that supported a competing religion?

Sometimes Protestants will object to the seven extra books, claiming that they are never quoted in the New Testament. In the debate mentioned in the introduction, my opponent attempted to make this argument. Actually, these books are not quoted word-for-word, but each of them is paraphrased in the New Testament. Interestingly, several Old Testament books that Protestants *do* accept are not quoted in the New Testament either: Ezra, Nehemiah, Esther, Song of Songs, Ecclesiastes, Lamentations, Obadiah, Zephaniah, Judges, 1 Chronicles, and Nahum. So, by the logic of these objectors, these books also need to be removed.

Catholics added the Deuterocanonical Books in AD 1546 at the ecumenical council of Trent

Councils will sometimes "proclaim" something officially that has actually been believed by Christians for some time. However, at some point the belief starts to be questioned, so the Church needs to come out officially to reaffirm this belief.

The Catholic Old Testament that we have today had been in use for a considerable length of time. Proof of this is that even early Reformation Bibles contained these books, though they were often moved to an appendix. However, when Protestant reformers eventually attempted to remove these books, the Council of Trent officially solidified the Old Testament canon.

The Catholic Church burned people at the stake for attempting to translate the Bible into the common language

The official language of the Catholic Church is Latin. For this reason, documents and Scripture had been written in Latin for centuries during the history of the Church. Most of the laity before the printing press were illiterate anyway and relied on the educated Church clergy to preach the Word of God. As Paul wrote, "faith comes from what is heard" (Rom 10:17). But of those who could read in the Middle Ages, the language they read *was* Latin.

Some anti-Catholics claim the Reformers attempted to translate the Bible into the common language and that the Catholic Church burned men such as John Wycliffe at the stake for this act.

Actually, there were already Bibles translated into the common language by the time Wycliffe produced his Bible. Actually, there were several of them, authorized and commissioned by the Catholic Church. What Wycliffe was condemned for was creating a translation of the Bible that was unauthorized and filled with theological problems, much as Protestants and Catholics alike today criticize the Jehovah's Witness' *New World Translation*.

That Wycliffe or others were executed as heretics is a stain upon Church history. However, at that time, execution was the state-administered punishment for heresy. Catholics were also executed by Protestant governments, such as in Calvin's Geneva.

Catholics were forbidden to read the Bible

The last section looked at Wycliffe's error-filled translation of the Bible. His was not the only one to produce such a work, and the Church was concerned about what would happen when the lay faithful began reading translations that contained flawed theology.

Imagine a Christian parent who discovered that his child was doubting the divinity of Christ. Searching his child's room, he discovered that his son was reading a Jehovah's Witness translation of the Bible, along with propaganda from this group. That parent would be justified in wanting to separate his son from this dangerous influence. It isn't the Bible reading that the parent objects to, but the translation.

There is also danger in the reading of Scripture that is independent from what is called "Sacred Tradition" and the "magisterium," a word that refers to the authoritative teaching office of the pope and bishops. Sometimes, fearing that individual reading would lead to erroneous doctrine, individual priests may have discouraged personal Bible study. This is unfortunate, but it is important to understand the motive of wanting to make sure that the Bible is taken in the context of the *entire* word of God, which was not recorded only in written form.

The Catholic Church chained up the Bible during the Middle Ages.

Yes, this happened, and for the same reason your bank might chain up a pen or telephone booths had chained phone books – so they would not be carried off and would remain for all to use.

As will be explored in the next couple chapters, Bibles were copied by hand before the invention of the printing press. The resulting rarity of these books made them very expensive, so much so that usually one or two copies existed in each church, rather than one per household or person.

Catholics changed their list of Ten Commandments from the list in the Bible

Anti-Catholic sources will sometimes refer to the Vatican website, where it appears that the second commandment, "Thou shalt not make graven images," has been removed.

The two lists of the commandments appear in Exodus 20:1-17 and Deuteronomy 5:6-21, and neither of them numbers the commandments. In fact, when one reads carefully, there are more than ten commandments, so in order to get that number, some educated guesswork has to go into deciding which of the commandments are consolidated.

Catholics understand the making of graven images for worship as being the same as having a false god before us, so we combine these two. However, the Church understands "coveting" a neighbor's wife as different than coveting his goods. One is more linked to lust, and the other envy.

Protestants, however, typically separate the graven image commandment but combine the last two.

Interestingly, the traditional Jewish numbering is different still. Jews referred to the Ten Commandments as the *Decalogue*, which means "ten words." The first "word" was "I am the Lord, thy God." They then combined into one, as Catholics do, the two commandments about false gods, and also combined, as Protestants do, the two commandments about coveting.

Long story short, Christians are to take to heart each of the commandments, regardless of the numbering.

All Christians can do a better job of spending time with God's written word. As the next couple chapters will examine, the Bible is not just a book for Catholics, it is a Catholic book, and our spiritual lives should feed upon it. As St. Jerome once wrote, "Ignorance of Scripture is ignorance of Christ."

Summary:

- Catholics preserve the Old Testament from which Christ and the apostles preached;
- Wycliffe and others like him were condemned for producing error-filled translations and without authorization;
- The Church has tried to protect the lay faithful from falling into the error of reading bad translations or by reading Scripture out of the context of Sacred Tradition and the Magisterium;
- Catholics did not remove the commandment concerning idols, which is really part of the commandment forbidding worship of false gods;
- Catholic worship is saturated with Scripture.

12

VERY BAD BASEBALL:
IS THE BIBLE *ALONE* OUR AUTHORITY?

"But beyond these [Scriptural] sayings, let us look at the very tradition, teaching and faith of the Catholic Church from the beginning, which the Lord gave, the Apostles preached, and the Fathers kept."
-Athanasius, *Four Letters to Serapion of Thmuis*, 1:28 (AD 360)

Anyone who has coached little league sports before knows there are effective strategies and not so effective strategies.

See if you can figure out which this is:

A new coach, determined not to pollute the game of T-ball with opinions on how the game should be played, gives each of his five-year-olds a copy of the book of rules and says to be ready for the big game in a couple weeks.

A good team needs a good coach. While the book of rules may explain that one hits the ball with the bat, a good coach demonstrates how to choke up, follow through, and slide into second without a mouthful of dirt. With each child left to make sense of the book on his own, the team would be a mess by the first game.

With that in mind, should Christians follow the Bible alone?

This question is *the* question that Catholics should ask when dialoguing with other Christians. This was the central topic in the debate mentioned in the introduction to this book. The Church of Christ preacher I debated, held the affirmative that Scripture is the all-sufficient authority for Christians. Sometimes this viewpoint is called *sola Scriptura*, Latin for Scripture alone.

The next two chapters will look systematically at the case I built for a foundation of Scripture along with Sacred Tradition.

Catholics should have a strong regard for Scripture. It is the inspired Word of God transmitted to us in written form. As it is inspired, it is also inerrant and serves as an authority for Christians.

The Church of Christ, echoing the sentiments of various Protestant groups, believe that Scripture alone is our authority. Their unofficial motto is to "speak where Scripture speaks and be silent where Scripture is silent."

The next chapter will examine a number of practical, logical and historical reasons why a Scripture alone foundation is impossible. In this chapter, though, Scripture itself will be the main witness, testifying on behalf of Tradition as equal to the Bible in the formation of Christian doctrine.

The end conclusion will show that to "speak where Scripture speaks and be silent where Scripture is silent" is, itself, self-contradictory and unbiblical. It is a tradition of men.

What is Sacred Tradition?

Sometimes Catholics distinguish between "small t" tradition

and "capital-T" Tradition. Sacred Tradition does not refer to things that have always *just been done that way* or to customs, such as the putting up of a Christmas tree. Sacred Tradition is also *not* a set of teachings that are new or different from what is in Scripture.

Rather, Catholics believe that Christ and the apostles delivered a set of teachings and that those teachings were preserved and passed on in two forms, written and oral (or, on occasion, demonstratively). For instance, Scripture tells us that we must be baptized and Tradition demonstrates the proper way this is done.

To return to the sports analogy, the book of baseball rules and procedures must be put together with a coaching tradition. The book of baseball rules shows that one must hit the ball with a bat. The coach shows how that looks. He teaches the kids to judge a pop fly and how to steal a base.

Or to use another analogy, God gave us two eyes so that we can look at the same thing from two different perspectives, giving us depth perception. Scripture taken by itself (or Tradition alone) is the same as trying to catch a ball with one eye closed. Christianity without depth perception results in doctrinal misjudgments.

What does Scripture say about itself?

Scripture testifies that it is difficult to interpret: Peter writes that Paul's letters are "hard to understand" and that "untaught and unstable *people* twist [them] to their own destruction, as *they do* also the rest of the Scriptures" (1 Pet 3:16).

Think of the logic here. Many *sola-Scriptura* Protestants claim that an untaught man can pick up the Bible and learn the teachings of Christianity, but according to Peter, the *untaught* end up twisting the Scriptures to a destructive end.

Scripture testifies that it is limited in development: One would think that, had he believed Christians were to follow the Bible alone, the apostle John would have made sure to commit everything he knew to Scripture. Rather, at the conclusion of his last two epistles, John writes that he has many more things to communicate, but "I would rather not use paper and ink, but I hope to come to see you and talk with you face to face, so that our joy may be complete" (2 John 12; 3 John 13).

In his Gospel, John shows a similar acknowledgement that paper and ink is insufficient to fully communicate the fullness of Christ: And there are also many other things that Jesus did, which if they were written one by one, I suppose that even the world itself could not contain the books that would be written. Amen" (21:25).

Protestants often make the mistake of assuming that any reference to the "Word of God" means a reference to Scripture. But Christ is the Word made flesh (John 1:1). Scripture is merely a reflection of the ultimate Word, and anyone who has ever tried to write an obituary for a beloved grandfather or parent knows that it is impossible to truly capture a person's essence on paper. How could one suppose that pen and ink is sufficient to sum up the revelation of God made flesh. Christ became man to demonstrate and proclaim the Good News, so he wants a Church that demonstrates it and proclaims it, too.

Scripture testifies that we are to also follow oral Tradition: Paul writes in 2 Thessalonians that we are to "stand firm and hold to the traditions which you were taught by us, *either by word of mouth or by letter*" (2:15). If Christians are to follow the Bible alone, why did Paul put oral teachings on par with epistles? In the next chapter he commands the Thessalonians to "keep away from" those not acting according to Tradition (3:6). In 1 Corinthians, he echoes this sentiment by asking his audience to "maintain the traditions" he delivered to them (11:2).

Sola-Scriptura Christians will sometimes point to verses which appear to condemn traditions, but these are referring to the Jewish traditions that were no longer binding upon Christians, such as circumcision. As seen by the verses above, Christ-centered traditions are just as authoritative as Scripture.

Scripture testifies that Traditions are also the Word of God: My debate partner asserted that Scripture never calls Traditions inspired. This was an outright falsehood. "Inspired" means given by the inspiration of the Holy Spirit, which is absolutely true of Tradition. Peter wrote that the things they preached were given by the Holy Spirit (1 Pet 1:12).

Paul wrote to the Thessalonians that in hearing him preach, they "received the Word of God" (1 Thes 2:13).

Scripture testifies that Tradition is preserved by the Spirit: Sometimes non-Catholics try to discredit Tradition by claiming it is like the telephone game, wherein the message gets corrupted as it passes from one person to the next. That would absolutely be the case if Tradition were not the Word of God and preserved by the Holy Spirit, who is promised to guide us to all truth (John 16:13). In the chapter on the reliability of the Gospels, it was demonstrated how well the Scriptures were preserved compared to other ancient manuscripts. The same Spirit responsible for this also preserved Sacred Tradition.

Not only does Paul write that the Holy Spirit will protect the "sound words which you have heard from me" (2 Tim 1:13-14), but Isaiah prophesies that the word of God, through the Spirit of God, will be placed in the mouth of the believer and never depart from his mouth or that of his descendants (59:21).

That prophecy in Isaiah is echoed in the New Testament when Paul writes to the Romans that the "'word is near you, in your mouth and in your heart' (that is, the word of faith which we preach)" (10:8).

Scripture testifies that the Sacred Tradition is meant to be transmitted orally: Speaking of the words that Timothy "heard" from him, Paul does not command his disciple to write them down, but rather to "commit these to faithful men who will be able to teach others also" (2 Tim 2:2).

Finally, Scripture never – ever – tells us to follow the Bible alone: The conclusion of this chapter will look at several passages that Scripture-only Protestants typically use to support this approach, followed by an analysis of these verses in context.

2 Timothy 3:16 - All scripture is inspired by God and profitable for teaching, for reproof, for correction, and for training in righteousness, that the man of God may be complete, equipped for every good work.

This verse is the classic defense of Scripture alone. As Catholics, we acknowledge that Scripture is inspired. But this verse does not claim that Scripture is "sufficient." Rather, Paul describes it as "profitable." Other translations use the word "purposeful" or "useful." Saying Scripture is *useful* is far from proving it to be all that a Christian needs for truth.

At this point in my debate with the Church of Christ preacher, he pointed out that even if the word "purposeful" was used, the verse goes on to show that Scripture makes a man of God "complete, thoroughly equipped for every good work."

Except *that isn't what the verse says*. Rather, Paul writes that doctrine, reproof, correction and instruction perfect a Christian. Notice what Paul writes to the Ephesians:

And his gifts were that some should be apostles, some prophets, some evangelists, some pastors and teachers, to equip the saints for the work of ministry, for building up the body of Christ, until we all attain to the unity of the faith and of the knowledge of the Son of God, to mature manhood, to the measure of the stature of the fullness of Christ; (4:11:13).

Here he does not even mention Scripture, but shows that it is the work of apostles, prophets, evangelists, pastors and teachers that perfect the saints and brings us into the fullness of Christ. And how do these individuals do this? Through doctrine, reproof, correction and instruction. It is *these* things that make the man of God complete and thoroughly equipped for every good work, and Scripture is useful to that end.

To illustrate, let's take the same passage from 2 Tim 3:16 and change some of the words to demonstrate the grammatical structure:

All fuel is given by God, and is profitable for cars, for airplanes, for buses, for motorcycle travel, that the man of God may be complete, thoroughly equipped for every good trip.

In this case, using the very same structure, one can see that fuel isn't sufficient for "every good trip." Rather, the vehicles that get us there are, and fuel is useful (or purposeful) to make them run, just as Scripture must be combined with Sacred Tradition.

Proverbs 30:5-6 - Every word of God proves true; he is a shield to those who take refuge in him. Do not add to his words, lest he rebuke you, and you be found a liar.

Catholics would agree wholeheartedly with this verse – that one should not add to the Word of God. However, as shown earlier in this Chapter, the "Word of God" is not just Scripture, but also Tradition.

2 Thessalonians 1:8 – [When the Lord Jesus is] … inflicting vengeance upon those who do not know God

and upon those who do not obey the gospel of our Lord Jesus.

As with the previous verse, this one does not even refer to Scripture, but rather the gospel of our Lord. "Gospel" simply means "good news," and Tradition contains the good news just as much as Scripture. Many other verses that also refer to the "word" or "gospel" are often used to try to support the Bible as our only authority (Psa 18:28-30; 1 Pet 1:22-23; John 17:17).

Revelation 22:18-19 - I warn everyone who hears the words of the prophecy of this book: if any one adds to them, God will add to him the plagues described in this book, and if any one takes away from the words of the book of this prophecy, God will take away his share in the tree of life and in the holy city, which are described in this book.

This passage from Revelation is one that Catholics can agree wholeheartedly with. Nobody should add to or take away from God's prophecy. In fact, it was non-Catholics who removed seven books from the collection of Scriptures during the Reformation.

That said, this verse presents even bigger problems as a Bible-alone verse. The warning in Revelation applies to "this book," which is Revelation, itself. God was speaking specifically about the vision he gave to John, not to Scripture as a whole.

1 Corinthians 4:6 - I have applied all this to myself and Apol'los for your benefit, brethren, that you may learn by us not to go beyond what is written, that none of you may be puffed up in favor of one against another.

Because this verse refers to "what is written," *sola-Scriptura* Christians assume it must be talking about the Bible, warning against going beyond the written word. However, the passage nowhere mentions the Bible. Perhaps Paul was referring to the

Talmud, The Mosaic law or the Old Testament scriptures. Actually, there is reason to believe he was referring to something completely different. A couple verses earlier, he writes:

> This is how one should regard us, as servants of Christ and stewards of the mysteries of God. Moreover it is required of stewards that they be found trustworthy. But with me it is a very small thing that I should be judged by you or by any human court. I do not even judge myself. I am not aware of anything against myself, but I am not thereby acquitted. It is the Lord who judges me. Therefore do not pronounce judgment before the time, before the Lord comes, who will bring to light the things now hidden in darkness and will disclose the purposes of the heart. Then every man will receive his commendation from God. (4:1-5).

Paul is writing about salvation. We are not to judge him and "go beyond what is written." Very probably he is referring to the Book of Life mentioned in Revelation 22. Because we do not know whose name God has written in this book, we are not to "go beyond" it by trying to judge one another's salvation.

John 10:35 - If He called them gods, to whom the word of God came (and the Scripture cannot be broken) ...

Once again, Catholics can give a big "Amen!." Scripture should not "be broken," and Sacred Tradition does no such thing.

Rev. 1:11 – "Write what you see in a book and send it to the seven churches."

This verse is often used to support Scripture alone because John is commanded to write, not pass orally, the revelation. However, in upholding Sacred Tradition, Catholics do not claim that Scripture isn't important. Of course there are things which are appropriate to be written. But in this instance, John is in exile and cannot preach the word. The best way for him to record his vision is in written form, but this does not mean that he would not have preached it if not in exile.

John 20:31 - but these are written that you may believe that Jesus is the Christ, the Son of God, and that believing you may have life in His name.

This verse will make another appearance in the chapter on eternal security. Here, John is simply giving a reason as to why he wrote the contents of his Gospel, that we may believe in Christ. This is a far cry from claiming that Scripture, alone, is sufficient to know all that was revealed for a Christian life. Scripture, in this case, is "purposeful," just as Paul told Timothy it would be.

The Bible, itself, tells us that Scripture is insufficient for a complete understanding of Christianity. As one would predict, if the inspired Word tells us that Scripture alone is bad Christianity, we would also see practical and historical problems with trying to apply that approach over the 2,000 year history of the Church. The next chapter will demonstrate that this is exactly what one finds.

Summary:
- Scripture testifies that it is difficult to understand and not sufficient for understanding revelation;
- Scripture testifies that Sacred Tradition is given by the Holy Spirit and is meant to go hand-in-hand with Scripture;
- Christ is the Word of God, and both Scripture and Traditions are reflections of his revelation;
- Scripture never tells us to follow the Bible alone.

13

BUT WAIT, THERE'S MORE!
MORE PROBLEMS OF *SOLA SCRIPTURA*

*"We are obliged to yield many things to the Papists--that with them is the
Word of God, which we received from them; otherwise we should have
known nothing at all about it."*
-Martin Luther, *Sermons on John 16 [LW 24]*

One of the odd joys of parenthood is reminiscing about
the days before the technology that our children know.
"We didn't have our own televisions in the backseat,"
my wife told my daughter. "We had to count blue cars or read
books during ten hour trips to a vacation." I joined in with my
own stories of two-dimensional video-games and pay phones.

As Christians, we are also spoiled by our modern access to
Scripture. Our Smartphones and tablets give us instant access to
any translation, and even before this, free Bibles were as available
as your nearest Campus Crusader or hotel nightstand. It is an easy
day and age to claim that Christians should follow the Bible alone.

The last chapter explored what Scripture, itself, had to say
about its own role in the life of a Christian: that it is meant to be

read in tandem with Sacred Tradition. This chapter is going to travel back in time to the days of Christ and the apostles and show why, through the past 2,000 years, a *sola Scriptura* approach to Christianity has been impossible and dangerous.

33 AD[14]

There exists one, true Church.

At this point the teaching ministry of Christ has reached its climax with his death upon the cross and the start of the Church on Pentecost. Jews and Christians of this period certainly had their Scriptures, but they were in the form of the Old Testament that they had known since childhood (2 Tim 3:15).

Today we have nothing that Jesus, himself wrote. Nor did he ever command his apostles to write down everything.

All Christians today would agree that one cannot come to a knowledge of Christ through the Old Testament alone, so at this point in history, one would have to follow the oral teachings of Christ, his apostles and others who had been entrusted to preach these sounds words.

Going by the Bible alone was impossible at this point.

50 AD

At this point, Christ ascended nearly two decades earlier, and the apostles continue to preach the Good News. So far there is still not a completed New Testament, but this is a likely date for Paul's first epistles, which are the earliest writings in the New Testament.

---

[14] The calendar we use today most likely does not accurately pinpoint the date of Jesus' birth, but for the sake of this timeline, we'll assume he was born in 1 AD.

Even so, these were written to specific audiences. The letters to the Corinthians, for instance, went specifically to Corinth. While this community would eventually share the letter with other Christians, this would take time.

For the next few decades, certain groups would be exposed to certain writings, but no one group had a complete New Testament, so going by the Bible alone is again impossible.

100 AD

By now each book in the New Testament has most likely been written. We are still faced with the problem that certain books were written to specific communities, who probably passed copies of them around. It is arguable that certain communities might have collected a number of the twenty-seven books we have today.

However, because God never gave an inspired table-of-contents, nobody knows which books are for sure inspired. There seems to be agreement that the writings of the apostles are given by God. Peter, for instance, attests to Paul's works as Scripture (2 Pet 3:16). But Christians at this time disagree over which books belong in the "canon" (collection of books).

Some will argue that 2 and 3 John, 2 Peter, Revelation, Hebrews, and James do not belong in Scripture.

Others defended the Scriptural status of writings that many today have never heard of: *The Shepherd*, Clement's letter to the Corinthians, the *Didache*, the epistles of Barnabas and the letters of Ignatius.

Today, when Protestants are asked how to determine which books should have gone in the New Testament, they argue for inclusion of the writings of the apostles and their disciples. However, Mark and Luke were not apostles. They were disciples of apostles, but so were Barnabas (cousin to Mark and actually called an apostle in Acts 14:14) and Ignatius (disciple to John).

At this point, there is no consensus as to which books go in the New Testament, so going by the Bible alone is still impossible.

200 AD

Still no consensus. Still no Bible-alone Christians.

300 AD

Not at this point, either.

367 AD

At this point scholars *finally* identify the first list of New Testament books that is identical to ours, today. It appears in the 39th Festal Letter of Athanasius.

There still isn't unanimous consensus, but at least it appears we are closer to that. By now the apostles have been dead for a couple hundred years, at least. This means that the Church, made up of the body of believers, is left to sort out the New Testament without the guidance of Jesus and his chosen twelve.

Upon what are they basing this?

For one, books are included which have been identified, from the beginning, as inspired. Other books are included which are recognized as being used frequently in worship. Finally, others are used which conform with the accepted doctrines of the time.

This is huge.

The doctrines of the first few centuries were not derived from Scripture alone. Rather, Scripture was sorted by how it conformed with the accepted doctrines. And how were those doctrines passed on until then? Through oral teachings.

This means that one can go back and read the writings of early Christians, non-inspired though they are, and see firsthand what those men and women believed who learned directly from the apostles and their disciples. These writings are available to anyone on the internet, as well as collected in books like *The Faith of the Early Fathers* (in three volumes) by William A Jurgens.

Many well-known Protestant pastors, anxious to model their communities after the first Christian churches, have gone to the writings of these Christians. What they discovered, in the first couple centuries, were Christians who believe in the necessity of baptism, the real presence of Christ in the Eucharist and the importance of bishops, among other Catholic teachings. And if it quacks like a duck, walks like a duck, and confesses to a priest like a duck … it must be a Catholic duck!

This also tells us that the first centuries did not give us a Bible-based Church, but a Church-based Bible.

However, at this point the canon of Athanasius was not authoritative, and others disagreed with him, so we still do not see the certainty or reliance on Scripture that allowed for Christians to obey the Bible alone.

393, 397 AD

At this point, late in the fourth century, the twenty-seven books of the New Testament are settled definitively. This happens at the Church Councils of Hippo and Carthage. These are Catholic councils, presided over by Catholic hierarchy, who sent their decisions to the pope in Rome for ratification.

Protestants often reject the idea that the Catholic Church put together the New Testament (despite the chronicle of history), claiming that the Holy Spirit is responsible for identifying Scripture. This is true. The question, though, is by what tool the Holy Spirit did this work. It turns out that the Spirit guided a human institution, long after the apostles, to act infallibly. Nobody should be surprised by this. After all, the Council of Jerusalem in Acts also shows the Church leaders gathering to decide an issue that wasn't clear to them before.

The Councils of Hippo and Carthage are just segments in a long line of the Catholic Church following the biblical example of using councils to help develop doctrine.

At this point, it can be argued that Christians finally have a complete New Testament. The only problem that remains now is that almost no Christian, except for the learned and powerful, can read it. Most were illiterate and not at all wealthy.

Bible-only Christians could not have existed at this point.

1440 AD

By this point, over 1,000 years have passed without the ability to mass produce the Bible. The printing press will be invented this year by the inventor Johannes Gutenberg. God's written word has been preserved through all of this time by the Catholic Church. The Bible is copied, one carefully stroked letter at a time, by monks who have devoted their lives to God. Some of them went blind during the careful, exacting work.

It is estimated that, if one were to adjust for inflation and different currency, owning a Bible during this time period would cost the equivalent of a nice house today. Most of us wouldn't have owned one, and most Christians were illiterate anyway. Without a printing press previously, there was no cultural motivation to teach individuals to read.

Bible-only Christians would not have existed at this point.

1517 AD

Martin Luther posts his Ninety-Five Theses on the door of the Wittenberg Church. He and the other reformers preached a doctrine called *sola-Scriptura*, holding that any Christian should be able to read and interpret Scripture for himself. With the exception of the Orthodox Christians[15], there is one Christian community.

Over the next few years, that *one* Church will splinter as different individuals come to different interpretations of Scripture.

1980 AD

Bible-only Christianity has existed now for over 400 years. By this point, there are 20,800 different groups claiming to be Christian but in disagreement over doctrine and practice.[16] This number increases at a rate of about 270 new "churches" a year.

1985 AD

22,150 different denominations.[17]

TODAY

The fragmenting of Christianity continues, and the start of it can be traced to the idea that Christians should follow their own personal interpretation of Scripture, guided by the Holy Spirit. However, Christians disagree on key doctrine. The number of distinct Christian groups listed together in the Yellow pages is scandalous.

---

[15] Orthodox Christians will be discussed in the chapter on authority.

[16] *Dictionary of Christianity in America* [Protestant] Downers Grove, IL: Intervarsity Press, 1990.

[17] In this case "denomination" is used to refer to a specific group. Some use it to refer to a group that belongs to a hierarchical structure, so some clarification is necessary.

If the Holy Spirit is guiding each of these groups to its interpretation, then the Spirit must be schizophrenic.

When I debated the Church of Christ preacher, I put a still shot up of a video which shows six basketball players playing a passing game.[18] This clip asks the viewer to count how many times one of the teams passed the ball. As the action continues, an individual dressed as a gorilla walks onto the screen and begins moving about, beating his chest for the camera. When the video ends, the viewer is asked how many times the ball was passed. Then he is asked if he saw the gorilla.

Most people do not.

Our minds work in such a way that the power of suggestion influences one's perception. Christianity works the same way. Many read Scripture and think the doctrines of their denomination are perfectly obvious, but this is because the power of suggestion, not the Holy Spirit, is guiding their reading.

Any modern Christian, relying on his own critical reading skills, will fail to infallibly interpret a 2,000 year old text.

The trouble with different translations

Very few individuals today can read the original Greek (or Hebrew or Aramaic) text, and must rely on translations. However, translations are colored by biases. As will be seen in the chapter on the Jehovah's Witnesses, a biased translation can be quite dangerous. Some try to read from various translations to get around this, but how does an ordinary Christian sort the translations out without a knowledge of the original language.

---

[18] *The Invisible Gorilla*. Christopher Simons and Daniel Simmons. www.theinvisiblegorilla.com, © 1999.

Notice the following passages, from different translations:

Acts 20:28 – "Therefore take heed to yourselves and to all the flock, among which the Holy Spirit has made you overseers, to shepherd the church of God which He purchased with His own blood" (*New King James Version*).

Acts 20:28 – Pay attention to yourselves and to all the flock, among which the holy spirit has appointed you overseers, to shepherd the congregation of God, *which he purchased with the blood of his own [Son]*" (*New World Translation*).

The second translation, taken from the Bible of the Jehovah's Witnesses is a valid translation of the Greek, but the wording makes it easier to deny the divinity of Christ.

Difficulties in reading Greek

In order to be a Scripture scholar, one must first have the time to devote to this pursuit. Most people have busy lives, filled with the business of raising kids and earning a living. In addition, one needs very developed critical reading skills and an understanding of biblical culture to digest certain references or idioms.

Learning a biblical language like Greek is quite an obstacle for many Christians. Here is an example text: "πορευθέντες οὖν μαθητεύσατε πάντα τὰ ἔθνη, βαπτίζοντες αὐτοὺς εἰς τὸ ὄνομα τοῦ πατρὸς καὶ τοῦ υἱοῦ καὶ τοῦ ἁγίου πνεύματος."

Greek grammar also works differently than English, and the endings of words change to indicate case, gender, mood, etc. There can be dozens of forms of the same word, depending on how it is used in a sentence, and each of those forms affects meaning and spelling.

If that was difficult, it gets worse. *Koine* Greek did not use punctuation or spacing, so the earlier passage would read:

"πορευθέντεςοὖνμαθητεύσατεπάντατὰἔθνηβαπτίζοντεςαὐτοὺςεἰς τὸὄνοματοῦπατρὸςκαὶτοῦυἱοῦκαὶτοῦἁγίουπνεύματος."[19]

This passage is from Matthew 28:19 for those who haven't figured it out.

Here are a couple of passages demonstrating the difficulties that Greek poses for translators:

Luke 23:43 - And Jesus said to him, "Assuredly, I say to you, today you will be with me in Paradise" (*New King James Translation*).

Luke 23:43 – "And he said to him: 'Truly I tell you today, you will be with me in Paradise'" (*New World Translation*).

In these passages, is Christ saying that he will be with the thief in Paradise *today*? Or is he saying that *today* he tells the thief that they will end up in Paradise together (which fits the speaking style of Christ and makes sense, since Christ didn't ascend to Heaven until a later day). Both are valid translations since there were no commas in the original text. The comma placement is guesswork.

Textual variants in early manuscripts

Even if one gets past the problem of reading Greek, he must still contend with the reality that we do not have the original inspired biblical texts to help sort out variations in the early copies that do exist. These variations can influence translation:

Luke 2:14 "Glory to God in the highest, And on earth peace, goodwill toward men" (*New King James Translation*).

---

[19] The Greek used at the time actually would have used all capital letters.

Luke 2:14: "Glory to God in the highest, And on earth peace among men with whom He is pleased" (*New International Version*).

The *New King James* passage relies on a textual variant that has since been discovered to be different from earlier translations. The difference is substantial. Rather than portraying God as sending peace and goodwill to all men, as the popular Christmas greeting holds, the earlier translations show that he is actually sending peace to men who are of good will, or favored by him.

Finally, the Bible-alone Christian is faced with the problem of authority. If two preachers both read Scripture diligently and pray for guidance from the Spirit, but both reach a different conclusion, to what source do they turn to settle the disagreement?

The answer to this comes in the following chapter.

Summary:

- **The New Testament did not get completely written until decades after Christ's ministry;**
- **Several centuries passed before Christians agreed on which books went into the Bible;**
- **The final "table of contents" for Scripture was settled by the Catholic Church at the Councils of Hippo and Carthage;**
- **Not until after the printing press could individual Christians have their own copies of the Bible, and most people were illiterate until after that point, anyway;**
- **The Reformation splintered Christianity into tens of thousands of disagreeing groups;**
- **Reading Scripture for oneself presents many very substantial challenges.**

14

THE STRONG ARM OF THE DIVINE LAW: THE INFALLIBLE POPE

"I think it my duty to consult the chair of Peter, and to turn to a church whose faith has been praised by Paul ... My words are spoken to the successor of the fisherman, to the disciple of the cross."
-*Jerome, To Pope Damasus, Epistle 15 (AD 377)*

What is your pillar and foundation of truth? This question is a good one to consider for a chapter on authority. We'll revisit the answer at the end.

Early one summer, I was driving home with two of my sons. On this particular night, I was overly occupied with some thought or the other, so it wasn't until I heard, "Daddy, look, a police officer," that I realized I had been speeding.

"Actually, that's a sheriff," I told him, "Daddy was probably going too fast and he wants to talk with me about it."

Several minutes later, with a ticket in the passenger seat, I pulled away. I explained to the boys that it wasn't actually the sheriff, but one of his deputies, and that we're glad they do such a good job making sure everyone follows the rules of the road.

The leaders of the Church are deputized with Christ's authority

The idea of a deputy is an important one for Christians to understand. We live in a culture that has experienced a great deal of disappointments from leaders in all areas of society. One of the consequences is that, in faith, people tend to move toward a mentality that Christians should listen to Jesus alone, and that no human authority really carries any weight. What could some man in Rome have to tell me about how to live my life and what to believe? What are his man-made rules to me?

However, God also believes in the idea of a "deputy" acting on the behalf of authority figures. In the Old Testament, David established a kingdom whereby the king's authority was entrusted to a prime minister. In Isaiah 22:22, God promises that he "will place on his shoulder the key of the house of David; he shall open, and none shall shut; and he shall shut, and none shall open."

The events in the Old Testament exist, in part, to help us understand the New Testament. Christ sat upon the "throne of his father David" as our new king (Luke 1:32). Knowing how the Davidic king operated his kingdom indicates how Jesus operates.

Jesus knew that one day he would return to Heaven and that his followers would need a "prime minister," or deputy, to guide them in his absence. He also knew that his followers would be familiar with the above quote from Isaiah. So, when he chose Peter to head his Church, he said, "I will give you the keys to the kingdom of heaven, and whatever you bind on earth shall be bound in heaven; and whatever you loose on earth shall be loosed in heaven" (Matt 16:19). The promise of binding and loosing was later extended to all of the apostles (Matt 18:18), but the keys were given specifically to Peter.

Four important things are communicated here:

- Christ echoed the words of Isaiah, telling us that Peter would have the authority that was given to the prime minister in that passage;
- Peter would be able to make authoritative decisions on earth ("bind and loose"), knowing they would be in conformity with God's plan;
- The prime minister position in the Old Testament was one of succession, and those who heard Christ's words understood he intended for Peter to have successors too;
- In Matthew 18:18, Christ extended the ability to bind and loose to all of the apostles, but gave the keys exclusively to Peter, putting him as the head.

The deputy, I explained to my oldest son, had a badge on his chest that the sheriff himself put there. And even though the sheriff is the one in charge, he told the deputy that whoever listened to him, listened to the sheriff, too. And whoever rejected the deputy rejected the man who gave him the badge. If I hadn't listened to that deputy, I would have ended up in the sheriff's jail.

Christ used almost identical words to tell the leaders of his Church that, when they spoke, it was really Christ speaking: "He who hears you hears me, and he who rejects you rejects me, and he who rejects me rejects him who sent me" (Luke 10:16).

Peter's place of primacy among the apostles

Of the twelve apostles, Peter had a special place of authority. Not only did he receive the keys to the kingdom, but he stands out in the narratives of the New Testament:

- Peter heads any list of the apostles (Matt 10:1-4; Mark 3:16-19), and sometimes he is the only one mentioned by name (Luke 9:32);

- Peter spoke for the apostles (Matt 18:21; Mark 8:29), including preaching on their behalf at Pentecost (Acts 2:14-40);

- Peter led the council held at Jerusalem (Acts 15).

Peter is also the apostle who is singled out to strengthen the faith of the others (Luke 22:32). Christ decided that this simple fisherman would have a place of primacy among the others.

Who is the Rock? Who is the good Shepherd?

In an attempt to discredit the Catholic claims about Peter, non-Catholics will point out that God is the rock of our salvation (2 Sam 22:3) and Christ is the good shepherd (John 10:11-21).

This is true, but as a sheriff shares his authority with a deputy, Christ himself applied these titles to Peter. In John, he asks Peter three times to feed his sheep (John 21:15-17).

In the passage from Matthew 16, Christ gives Peter the title of "rock." Peter's previous name was Simon. Often in Scripture, individuals are given a new name by God to signify a change in their identity. When Peter correctly answered Christ's question, our Lord blessed him and then said, "You are Peter, and upon this rock I shall build my Church."

When I mentioned this in my debate with the Church of Christ preacher, he argued that *Petros*, the Greek word for Peter, actually means small stone and that *Petra* means rock. According to him, Christ was saying that Peter was a small stone compared to the large rock of Christ. Others argue that the "large rock" is not Peter, but his statement of faith.

However, as I pointed out, this argument is a red herring. *Petros* is simply the masculine form of the feminine *petra*, and Christ couldn't give Peter a feminine name. What my debate opponent pointed out about *petra* and *petros* also was no longer true in the Greek of the New Testament (*Koine* Greek), which had relaxed the grammar of the older *Attic* Greek.

Finally, several early Christian writings indicate that the Gospel of Matthew was actually not written originally in Greek, but Aramaic, the language of the Hebrew people.

In summary, Christ's words to Peter were, "You are *rock*, and upon this *rock* I build my church."

What infallibility is, and isn't

Some very striking promises were given to Peter and the apostles. Jesus promised that whatever they bound or loosed on earth would be honored the same in Heaven. This does not mean, of course, that God waited around in Heaven to see the decisions of the apostles. Rather, as promised in John 16:13, the Holy Spirit would lead the Church to all truth.

Before going further to explain what infallibility *is*, it is worthwhile to explain what it is not.

First, infallibility is not impeccability. Some assume Catholics to believe that the pope cannot make mistakes or commit sin. Obviously, nothing could be further from the truth. The pope, like all men, is capable of sin and personal error. As discussed in the essay on scandal, the Bible never promises that the leaders of the church will be free from sin.

Second, infallibility is not divine revelation. Mormons believe that their modern-day prophets receive new public revelation from God, but Catholics do not believe this of the pope. We agree with

Protestants that public revelation ended with the close of the apostolic period. The pope is not on God's e-mail list. To make a pronouncement, he must consult Scripture and Tradition, praying for guidance.

Yet men are, in and of themselves, fallible. So how could Christ know that these human leaders would not spread error?

He knew this because the integrity of the Church is not built on the power of men, but on the promise of God, who would never create a Church that could be corrupted by sinners.

Infallibility means this – and only this – that when the Pope (or the bishops in communion with him) teaches official matters of faith and morality, intending it to be binding on all Christians, God *will not let him teach in error.* When the pope makes an infallible statement, he is said to make it *ex cathedra,* which means "from the chair" of Peter. However, this is not the only way that teachings can be infallibly known. Infallibility also refers to the "ordinary and universal" magisterium, which includes those teachings that have been taught by the Church through the history of Christianity. For instance, while a pope has never made an *ex cathedra* statement on homosexuality, but marriage as a union between a man and woman is infallibly defined nonetheless.

Infallibility is simply the guard rail that keeps a pope from driving the entire church off the curb. Far from being some superhuman power, it is a divine restriction put upon any man who receives the seat of Peter from the unbroken line of succession.

And this is why Christians can trust the official proclamations of the pope, as well as those received from doctrinal councils, such as the council of Jerusalem in Acts 15, where the issue of circumcision was still unclear, and deliberation among the Church leaders settled the matter.

Didn't Paul rebuke Peter?

Sometimes, to counter Catholic claims about infallibility, non-Catholics will point to Galatians 2:11-21, where Paul rebukes Peter for drawing back and not eating with the Gentiles. Actually, this is a perfect illustration of how some misunderstand infallibility. Obviously Peter can teach infallibly since he penned two inerrant epistles in the New Testament. However, infallibility does not protect a pope from bad actions, and in this case, Peter is not being chastised because he *taught* in error, but because he *acted* in error.

Hierarchy and succession

If it made sense that Peter and the apostles were important to spread the Good News in the first century, how much more do we need this gift today, with civilization cluttered by modern distractions. Christ deputized the apostles because he understood that our sinful nature separated us from hearing the divine guidance of the Holy Spirit as clearly as we otherwise would After his ascension, we would need a visible guide.

Our Lord prayed for unity in John 17:21, and Paul makes clear that this is a doctrinal unity (1 Cor 1:10). To see the danger of moving away from the unity offered by Peter or his successor, one can look at the Orthodox Churches, which broke from Rome in the eleventh century. Since then, the various Orthodox groups have broken into ethnic communities and have been unsuccessful in uniting for a doctrinal council. And, as seen in the chapters on Scripture, the rejection of the Church by the Reformers has created tens of thousands of independent groups with differing doctrine.

Those who reject the idea of an authoritative Church often claim that they only follow Christ. However, as Scripture attests, the Church is the fullness of Christ (Eph 1:22-23), so to reject the Church is to reject Christ.

The deputation of a prime minister in the Old Testament was meant to be an office with succession, as was intended by Christ in deputizing Peter.

The early Church also had a hierarchical structure, with elders (a.k.a. "presbyteroi" or priests) and bishops ("episkopoi") leading the Church (Acts 20:17,28). Unlike in many Christian communities today, where pastors and elders are selected by democratic vote, in the New Testament elders are appointed to a Church (Acts 14:23; Tit 1:5). There is no example of decision by congregational vote in the inspired text.

The authority of a Church leader came either from direct commission by Christ (such as in with Paul) or by a laying on of hands from a Church leader (1 Tim 5:22). If that laying on of hands confers authority, then the true Church today must be one with an unbroken line of authority stretching back to an apostle or a direct commission by Jesus.

The testimony of the early church

While the introduction of this book explained that the chapters would rely almost exclusively upon Scriptural quotations, looking back at the writings of the early Christians is key here. Did they understand that the apostles would have successors, as Catholics do, or that they would not, as most Protestants believe? Keep in mind that these quotes are from men who wrote during Christianity in its purest form. These writings came from the very culture that selected which books went into the New Testament, so we can be assured they would be acting in accord with the Scriptural model. In the first two cases, the dates are early enough that some of the apostles were most likely still alive:

"And thus preaching through countries and cities, they appointed the first-fruits [of their labors], having first proved them by the Spirit, to be bishops and deacons of those who should afterwards believe. Nor was this any new thing, since indeed many ages before it was written concerning bishops and deacons. For thus saith the Scripture a certain place, 'I will appoint their bishops in righteousness, and their deacons in faith.'... Our apostles also knew, through our Lord Jesus Christ, and there would be strife on account of the office of the episcopate. For this reason, therefore, inasmuch as they had obtained a perfect fore-knowledge of this, they appointed those [ministers] already mentioned, **and afterwards gave instructions, that when these should fall asleep, other approved men should succeed them in their ministry** ... For our sin will not be small, if we eject from the episcopate those who have blamelessly and holily fulfilled its duties."

-*Clement, Epistle to Corinthians, 42, 44 (AD 98).*

"For what is the bishop but one who beyond all others possesses all power and authority, so far as it is possible for a man to possess it, who according to his ability has been made an imitator of the Christ of God? And what is the presbytery but a sacred assembly, the counselors and assessors of the bishop? And what are the deacons but imitators of the angelic powers, fulfilling a pure and blameless ministry unto him, as...Anacletus and Clement to Peter?"

-*Ignatius, To the Trallians, 7 (AD 110).*

"But if there be any (heresies) which are bold enough to plant themselves in the midst Of the apostolic age, that they may thereby seem to have been handed down by the apostles, because they existed in the time of the apostles, we can say: Let them produce the original records of their churches; **let them unfold the roll of their bishops, running down in due succession from the beginning in such a manner that [that first bishop of theirs] bishop shall be able to show for his ordainer and predecessor some one of the apostles or of apostolic men,**--a man, moreover, who continued steadfast with the apostles. ...To this test, therefore will they be submitted for proof by those churches, who, although they derive not their founder from apostles or apostolic men (as being of much later date, for they are in fact being founded daily), yet, since they agree in the same faith, they are accounted as not less apostolic because they are akin in doctrine...Then let all the heresies, when challenged to these two tests by our apostolic church, offer their proof of how they deem themselves to be apostolic. But in truth they neither are so, nor are they able to prove themselves to be what they are not. Nor are they admitted to peaceful relations and communion by such churches as are in any way connected with apostles, inasmuch as they are in no sense themselves apostolic because of their diversity as to the mysteries of the faith."

-Tertullian, Prescription against the Heretics, 33 (AD200)

Pillar and Foundation?

Protestants and even Catholics try to question the infallible authority of the Pope, but few think through the implications of this. The following thought experiment shows how, if infallibility does not exist within Catholicism, all of Christianity is in trouble.

The immaculate conception of Mary has been infallibly defined.

Let's suppose the Catholic Church is wrong on this teaching on Mary, then this means that the Church is not infallible.

If the Catholic Church is not infallible, then any teaching that comes from her is questionable.

Until the fourth century, there was much disagreement on what the exact nature of Christ was, with some questioning his divinity or humanity. The Catholic Church, at the Council of Nicaea, defined the divinity of Christ and the formulation of the Trinity.

If the Church is not infallible, we cannot be sure we have

properly defined the Trinity.

As seen in the chapters on Scripture, the Catholic Church also defined which books belong in the New Testament. If the Church is not infallible, we have to question whether the right books were included.

However, Christ did not create a Church of confusion. He did not design that Christianity would splinter into thousands of shards. He put in place a means by which those who sought unity could find it, and he did not do this by Scripture alone.

Returning to the opening question of this chapter, Scripture tells us very clearly what the pillar and foundation of truth is for a Christian (1 Tim 3:15).

It is the *Church* of the living God.

Summary:

- Christ deputized the apostles to act in his name and with his authority after he ascended;
- Peter had a special place of prominence among the apostles;
- To ensure the unity that Christ promised, the successors of Peter are protected from error;
- The New Testament Church was one of hierarchy and succession;
- If the Catholic Church is not infallible, Christians must question the very New Testament upon which so much of their faith is based.

15

DO ONLY CATHOLICS GO TO HEAVEN?

"Basing itself on Scripture and Tradition, the Council teaches that the Church, a pilgrim now on earth, is necessary for salvation: the one Christ is the mediator and the way of salvation; he is present to us in his body which is the Church. He himself explicitly asserted the necessity of faith and Baptism, and thereby affirmed at the same time the necessity of the Church which men enter through Baptism as through a door. Hence they could not be saved who, knowing that the Catholic Church was founded as necessary by God through Christ, would refuse either to enter it or to remain in it."
-Lumen Gentium 14.

During lunch with a preacher named Chris, with whom I had been dialoguing for a while, he mentioned that his uncle had passed away a couple months back, and that he had been asked to do the funeral.

"My uncle never came to Church," Chris explained. "He didn't have a place for Christ in his life and didn't demonstrate the fruits of conversion. So when I gave the sermon at his funeral ..."

He paused here, and I attempted to finish the thought for him. "You expressed hope that he had a deathbed conversion?"

"No," he said, obviously taken back slightly that I had been so off mark. "No, this was a man who had lived a life of the flesh. He had never been a part of a Christian Church, and had never been baptized. I had to explain to his family that even though he would not be admitted into Heaven, he would want them to repent, believe, and be baptized so that they would not suffer the same fate as he is now facing."

Chris's particular religious group does not even allow musical instruments in their worship services because they do not believe that the New Testament authorizes them. As do Catholics, they believe that baptism is necessary for salvation, but do not recognize the baptism of infants as valid. Chris was always clear that, even though we met occasionally for lunch and dialogued in a friendly way, he did not consider me a Christian. He could not call me a "brother" in Christ, and did not believe that I would inherit eternal glory if I did not repent and get baptized as an adult.

Our modern sensibilities tell us that we should take offense at such a conclusion. *What do you mean I'm not going to Heaven?* But it didn't really bother me that Chris had identified me as a future log in Satan's fireplace. It was not an attempt to insult me, as a person, but rather the logical conclusion he had reached considering the facts that a) he believed the Bible teaches that one must be baptized as an adult to go to Heaven and b) I had not been.

Catholics have sometimes been accused of having the same attitude toward other Christians. I still occasionally hear others claim that "when I was in school, we were taught that anybody who isn't Catholic goes to Hell."

So does the Church teach this? Did it ever?

The short answer, of course, is no. But it does teach that

outside the Catholic Church there is no salvation. Isn't this the same thing? Not quite, but for Catholics who don't understand this teaching, significant mistakes can be made in understanding how salvation works in the lives of others.

Do non-Christians go to Heaven?

Let's start with Jesus, who stated very clearly that he was the way, the truth, and the life, and that nobody comes to the Father except through him (John 14:6).

Period. End of discussion, right?

According to Jesus, who is God, Buddha is not a path to Heaven. Nor is Taoism or the various Hindu deities.

If this quote from Jesus were taken in isolation, this would mean that everyone who is not a Christian is destined to Hell.

But just a chapter later, Jesus clarifies that people are only guilty of sinning against him *if* he had preached to them first, but that after he preached to them, they had no excuse for not believing in him (John 15:22; cf. 9:41).

The Church calls it invincible ignorance when someone doesn't know about Jesus or hasn't accepted him through no fault of their own.

This answers the question of what happens to a man on a remote island who never meets a missionary. If God reads a desire in that person's heart to know him, but the native never learned about Christianity, he can gain Heaven based on his desire.

Other reasons a person might be invincibly ignorant might include someone with a psychological roadblock, such as a man who was emotionally abused by his Christian father and has rejected the faith of his childhood. Or a woman who had been raised by atheist parents and had not yet been exposed to a compelling reason to look into Christianity. In the latter case, she might be considered "without sin," as Christ said, because she had not yet been preached to.

However, if someone consciously rejects Christ or the opportunity to learn about him, that person is making a conscious decision to reject any promise that Christ makes to his followers.

The Church as the fullness of Christ

Taking this a step further, Christ did not come just to free us from our sins, but to start a Church that would guide Christians as a "pillar and bulwark of truth." Paul, in Ephesians, tells us that the Church is not separate from Christ, but is actually the "fullness" of our Lord and savior (1:23). The Church is actually the mystical "body of Christ" (1 Cor 12:12 13).

The Church is not some separate thing from Christ. It is united to him and is the way he continues his work. It is the means by which he distributes his grace and preserves his truth.

Christ identified this Church as more than just a community of believers. He defined it as a visible structure, led by Peter and his successors and committed to the certain beliefs that Christ and the apostles delivered, such as the true presence of Christ in the Eucharist and the need for baptism.

So, it turns out that Chris was right when he claimed that baptism was necessary for salvation, as scripture makes clear (John 3:5; 1 Pet 3:19-21). But as with those who never had the opportunity to learn about Christ, some individuals have not been baptized because the sacrament was never made available to them. If God sees that, given the chance, they would have accepted him through baptism, these individuals can be baptized "by desire."[20]

This applies to the Catholic Church as a whole. If non-Catholics learn that the Catholic Church is true, but reject it anyway, they are rejecting Christ (Luke 10:16). Even more than that, if someone rejects the Catholic Church because they intentionally avoided learning about what Christ had revealed, that person is responsible for neglecting his own salvation.

We are responsible for what we know.

There is hope for the woman who grew up in a Southern Baptist community and never met a Catholic. Or for the man who leaves Catholicism because he was scandalized by the abuse crisis. Or the teenager who has been so emotionally invested in her Pentecostal upbringing that she never questioned it.

There is even hope for Chris's uncle, who might have psychological or intellectual roadblocks that Chris was not aware of when declaring his uncle eternally damned.

The Catholic Church, with its sacraments and the gift of infallibility, is the instrument of Christ's continued work on earth. Because of this, salvation does not come from any other source.

This doesn't mean that there are not elements of grace and truth in the various Protestant communities. Even though baptism, marriage and Scripture itself find their source in the graces of the Catholic Church, their use in non-Catholic worship does not eliminate the graces they confer.

And as for truth, only the Catholic Church fully preserves what Christ and the apostles delivered, but fragments of this truth have influenced the teachings of Protestant and even non-Christian

---

[20] *Catechism of the Catholic Church,* No. 1257-1261

religions, such as Mormonism and the Jehovah's Witnesses. Even Paul recognized the seeds of truth among the Athenians, who worshipped many Gods. While those people were far from Christian, they had an altar standing in tribute to the "unknown God" (Acts 11:23), showing that they recognized the deficiencies in their recognized deities. Paul seized upon this opportunity to preach to them about the one true God in Jesus Christ.

In the same way, Catholics are called to recognize the desire of non-Catholics to know the truth that God has revealed and to respect these separated communities for their attempts to be instruments of grace and truth. But, as Paul did with the Athenians, we must not let our journey stop there, but we must preach the Good News of Jesus Christ and the Church he established, through which he has guided his flock for two-thousand years.

Summary:

- Christ is the way, the truth and the life. He is the only path that leads to the Father;
- The Church is the fullness of Christ on earth and whoever rejects the Church rejects Christ;
- Some people, however, are not aware of the teachings about Christ and his Church and are not responsible for their own ignorance;
- Any truth that exists and any grace available to non-Catholics still comes from the source of grace, which is Christ acting through the Church he established.

16

IN HELL ON A MEAT RAP?
CAN TEACHINGS CHANGE?

"I've been gone a long time now. It's not even a sin anymore to eat meat on Friday but I'll betcha there are still some guys in Hell doing time on the meat rap, right?"
-George Carlin, Special Dispensation, 1972.

Once upon a time, Catholics had the derogatory nickname "mackerel snappers" because it was church discipline that we would abstain from meat every Friday of the year (not just during Lent, as we are accustomed to doing now). It was considered grave sin (and mortal sin if full consent and knowledge are involved) to violate this Church law. In the sixties, that discipline was relaxed in the United States.

However, the fact that it is no longer a grave sin to eat meat on Fridays outside of Lent has been a frequent means of attack against the Church's teaching authority. Comedian George Carlin, a fallen-away Catholic, once asked what would happen to the guys in Hell on a meat rap.

The short answer is this: There isn't one person (nor has there ever been a person) who is in Hell on a "meat rap."

Carlin was looking for a punch line, but, there are those (including our Protestant friends) who are genuinely misinformed about the teachings of the Church. I've had a number of conversations with Protestants who point at the change regarding meat on Fridays as a flaw in the Church's authority.

The difference between discipline and dogma

First off, one needs to understand the difference between a dogma and a discipline. Teachings of the Church that are based on the public revelation, given once-for-all during the apostolic period cannot be abolished or changed (though they may be developed over time, such as has happened with the Christian definition of the Trinity). A male-only priesthood, the perpetual virginity of Mary, and the divinity of Christ, for instance, are dogma. We do not have the option to disbelieve these teachings, and the Church will never *change its mind* on them.

On the other hand, the Church was established by Christ to shepherd over His flock and to act in a parental role (hence calling priests "Father"), and any parent knows that sometimes children need temporary rules to address certain situations. For instance, we don't have a rule limiting video game time in our house. If, however, I started to perceive that the kids were spending too much time with the Wii, I would create a rule limiting their use of it. These situational rules are called disciplines. Unlike dogma, disciplines can change. They can disappear and be revised at the Church's will, depending on her perception of the need for that discipline. Disciplines include the celibate priesthood and abstaining from meat on Fridays.

But as is the case with dogmas, we do *not* have the option to disregard disciplines. I can't count how many times I've heard people dismiss some rule of the Church with the cavalier, "Oh, that's just a *man-made rule.*" Even "Bible-only" Protestants shouldn't have a problem with disciplines. There are examples of them in Scripture, after all. One in particular is when Paul stresses in the eleventh chapter of the first epistle to the Corinthians that women must wear head coverings. Yet, today almost no Christian Church, Protestant or Catholic, requires this, dismissing Paul's instructions as a cultural rule, applying to that specific community during that specific time. Other biblical disciplines include restrictions against women speaking in church or having authority over men (1 Cor 14:33-35; 1 Tim 2:8,11-12). Paul also prohibits a woman from wearing braided hair, gold or pearls (1 Tim 2:9). If the Bible can put forth changeable disciplines, then the Church that Christ established can do the same.

The disciplinary rules of the Church can no more be dismissed than could Paul's exhortation to Corinth. After all, in Luke 10:16, Jesus tells the leaders of the Church that whoever rejects them rejects God. In Matthew 16 and then again in Matthew 18, he tells them that whatever they bind or loose on earth is bound or loosed in Heaven. In John 21 Jesus tells Peter three times to feed his sheep, putting him as the visible shepherd on duty after the Ascension.

In these and other places in Scripture, Christ is deputizing the leaders of his Church, especially the leader of the apostles, Peter (and we know what happens when we disobey a deputy).

And when we disobey a "man-made" rule, if that rule was made by the authority of Christ, which was vested in the leaders of the Church, we are essentially telling Christ that our judgment is better than his. That he made a mistake by putting these men in charge of us. That the Church he establish was a flawed institution.

Christians who ignore disciplines are committing the same sin as Adam and Eve, who ignored God's warning not to eat from the tree and decided (under the temptation of Satan) that they knew better than he did. There is nothing inherently evil about a piece of fruit, after all, but there is something inherently evil about asserting that we are superior in intellect to God.

Likewise, there is nothing inherently evil about meat or consuming it on Fridays, but there is something gravely sinful in telling the Holy Spirit-guided Church and the Pope which heads it that we know better. The Church has the parental authority to set up disciplines that might steer us from our earthly attachments and help us focus more on Christ.

Adam and Eve were not banished from the Garden on a "fruit rap."

Nor is anyone in Hell on a "meat rap."

But there *might be* plenty of people in Hell on an *I-will-make-up-my-own-rules-and-to-Hell-with-the-Church-and-its-God-vested-authority* rap.

And, to answer George Carlin's question, they would still be there today.

Why did the teaching change?

Fridays have traditionally been a day of penance in the Church as a weekly reminder of Christ's death upon the cross on Good Friday. The idea of going meatless of Friday was a discipline created to ensure a universal sense of sacrifice among the faithful.

However, in 1966 the US bishops released American Catholics from the requirement to give up meat on Fridays outside of Lent. Instead, abstinence from meat is encouraged, but is no longer the *only* prescribed means of penance.[21]

---

[21] *On Penance and Abstinence*, November 18, 1966.

Many mistakenly think the bishops simply did away with meatless Fridays. Rather, their intent was to encourage abstaining from meat on Fridays, but allow the faithful to pick an individual form of penance that might be more meaningful.

Didn't Paul warn about apostate groups who would forbid marriage and the consumption of certain foods?

A common attack on Catholicism is built upon Paul's warning in 1 Tim 4:3 to beware of certain groups because they advocate avoiding certain foods and forbid marriage.

Paul was speaking specifically about heretical groups that had risen up at that time, especially certain gnostic sects, who taught that the flesh is evil. If, as anti-Catholics sometimes claim, he was warning about any group that forbids the eating of certain foods, then the apostles themselves would be at fault for writing that one should abstain from the meat of strangled animals (Acts 15:20).

Unlike the gnostic sects, who forbid certain foods absolutely, the Church recognizes the goodness of food, but sets certain days on which the faithful can join together, as one body of Christ, in its penitential act. Marriage, too, is seen as a good and holy thing in the Church, unlike in the groups that Paul wrote about, and no man or woman is forbidden to marry. However, men called to the priesthood (at least in the Latin rite) are selected from among those who have chosen to devote themselves to a life of celibacy for the sake of the kingdom.

Too many rules?

When Protestants complain that the Catholic Church has invented too many rules, the implication is that a simple "love Jesus" Christianity is superior.

Has the Church "invented" too many rules?

Or have we just "invented" too many sins?

As all Christians agree, our primary "rules" are to love God and to love our neighbors. If we did this perfectly, we wouldn't need any other rules, but our nature as creatures of the flesh mean that we keep straying and each rule of the Catholic Church is simply a way of addressing a new sin (or distraction from Christ) that we've invented.

Consider a marriage (which is appropriate considering who our bridegroom is). The one rule in a marriage is love your spouse. However, should the husband start failing in that duty, it might, over time, appear that the wife is too legalistic.

He starts sleeping in and missing work - she comes up with a rule that, if he loves her, he'll start getting up on time so the paycheck keeps coming home.

He is a workaholic, so she comes up with the "rule" that all electronics are shut off in the evening.

After a while, that husband might complain that his "legalistic" wife has too many rules, but in reality, he has invited too many imperfections into his love for her.

Likewise, the rules of the church are there to address the myriad ways Christians devise to show less love for Christ. We don't respect the Eucharist, so the Church asks for a pre-Eucharistic fast. We start sleeping in on Sundays, so the rule is that Mass is an obligation.

If we just loved Christ so perfectly that our every act was an expression of our love for him, all rules would go away. If we desire for the Church to stop *inventing* rules, perhaps we just need to stop *inventing* sin.

Necessity, after all, is the mother of invention.

Summary:

- Disciplines, unlike dogmas, are meant to be rules to guide the faithful in particular situations and cultures; they are subject to change;

- The rules regarding abstaining from meat on Fridays and the celibate priesthood are disciplines;

- Fridays still remain a day of penance within the Church, and Christians are encouraged to abstain from meat or to engage in a penitential act of their choosing;

- The rules of the Church are in response to behaviors that are threatening to the spirituality of Christians or the honor due to our Lord.

17

HEY, WHOSE GLASS OF MARTYR BLOOD IS THIS? IS THE CATHOLIC CHURCH THE WHORE OF BABYLON?

"The figure of the great harlot, and the influence she wields, is also interpreted as referring to impurity."
-Josemaría Escrivá Ascent of Mount Carmel, 3, 22

In general, it's a mistake to try to engage in apologetics in hostile forums on the Internet, especially for someone as bull-headed as I am. Posting in an atheist forum, for example, is bound to get a person a dozen replies to every one post. For anyone with a full-time job or a family, it is impossible to keep up with the responses, and I've concluded that some of the individuals who seem to post every five minutes must be the heirs of some great railroad tycoon's money, with nothing to do but sit around and make sure to win every single argument on the web.

On a forum devoted to ex-Catholics, I met a woman named Cassie. She, another Catholic, and I appeared to be the only ones who had discovered this website, but it didn't matter. Cassie had the energy of several posters. I stuck with the debate for a while, intent to help her see the light, but I eventually realized that it didn't matter how articulately I argued the Catholic faith, Cassie wasn't willing to reason. She had seen a few videos which supposedly made the case that the Catholic Church is the Whore of Babylon prophesied in Revelation. Convinced of that, she knew that every one of the Church's teachings must be in error.

I added this chapter after seeing several signs and flyers pop up around town for a "Prophecy Seminar," which promised to expose the anti-Christ and the Whore of Babylon. After discovering the program was sponsored by the 7th Day Adventists, I could pretty well guess how that presentation would go.

A number of descriptions from the book of Revelation and elsewhere in Scripture depict the anti-Christ, the Whore and the Beast; and some fringe groups preach that the Catholic Church fits the bill. A surprising number of people buy into this theory, which has been rejected by most reputable Protestant scholars.

Signs of the "Whore of Babylon"

The number of the beast, 666 (Rev 13:18): The number 666 has been the source of a lot of fascination, especially in horror movies. Ancient languages used letters that also acted as numbers. Some groups, such as the Seventh Day Adventists, attempt to find the sum of 666 in titles for the pope. This has been so unsuccessful that Ellen Gould White, the founder of the Adventists, had to invent a title for the pope: *Vicarius Filii Dei*, or Vicar of the Son of God. The pope is not known by this title and never has, but rather by "Vicar of Christ." The letters in this title do not add up to 666 in any ancient language. The irony is that Ellen Gould White's own name actually *does* add up to 666 in Roman numerals. But she is not the anti-Christ, either. Most biblical scholars believe that 666 refers to Nero Caesar, who persecuted the Christians.

Golden Chalice (17:4): The mention of a golden chalice seems to fit perfectly with the Catholic Church's celebration of the Eucharist. That is, of course, unless one ignores that the chalice mentioned in Revelation is not a cup of Christ's blood, but of God's wrath (Rev 14:19). Gold has always been a part of true worship (Ex. 25:38–40, 37:23–24) because it gives greater glory to God. As can be seen in the Gospel of Mark, God desires that he be given honor with the finer items in life (14:3-9).

Possessing great wealth (Rev 17:4): As discussed in the chapter on the Catholic Church and wealth, it is a misconception that the Church is rich.

Wearing purple and Red (Rev 17:4): The anti-Catholic sites that describe the Catholic Church as the whore will include pictures of the pope and cardinals dressed in purple and red, pointing to Revelation 17:4 as proof that wearing these colors is a mark of the Whore. Consider how far-fetched it is that, if wearing these colors really indicates the whore, it's never occurred to anyone in the Catholic Church to raise his hand at a brainstorming meeting to suggest wearing, say, green and orange instead. However, not only are these colors meant to be *symbolic*, but they are prescribed for liturgical worship by God (Lev 14:4, 6, 49–52; Num 19:6) (Ex. 28:4–8, 15, 33, 39:1–8, 24, 29). When the pope and other Church leaders wear purple and red, they do so in order to symbolize repentance (purple) and martyrdom (red).

Babylon (Rev 17:5) – "Babylon" was used as a code word for Rome in the early Church (1 Pet 5:13). Some speculate that it might also refer to Jerusalem since a later passage tells us that this city is the location "where their Lord was crucified" (11:8). However, there is no reason to be threatened by a reference to Rome, as the city and its Pagan rulers, not the Catholic Church, were harsh in their persecution of Christians.

Drunk with the blood of Saints (Rev 17:6) – The Catholic

Church, having existed for 2,000 years, has been the victim of persecution from the days of pagan Rome to the martyrdom in Christians in third world countries today. The writings of the early Christians, those persecuted by the pagans, show that they were indeed Catholic.

Seven Hills (Rev 17:9) – Because Rome is known for its seven hills, some draw the conclusion that the Whore must be the Church headquartered in Rome. Since the Lateran Treaty in 1929, the Holy See is actually headquartered in Vatican City, which is across the Tiber River from Rome, proper. Most likely, the seven hills refer to pagan Rome, which persecuted the early Christians. Some also point to Jerusalem, which went apostate in the first century and contains seven noted hills. Jerusalem cooperated with pagan Rome in persecuting Christians.

Reigns over kings (Rev 17:18) – While it could be argued that, at one time, the Catholic Church intermingled too much with politics and royalty, the same could be said of Protestant groups, especially during the Reformation and the break of the Church of England. The Pope does have temporal power, even though he does not exercise it in the same way he did previously in history. However, even if the Church did chose to claim for herself authority over secular rulers, this authority would come from Christ, and it would be a bit desperate to argue that the Whore of Babylon has any authority from Christ, himself.

The Little Horn (Daniel 7) – Cassie, whom I mentioned earlier, was less obsessed with the book of *Revelation*, and more focused on Daniel 7, specifically the mention of the "little horn," a kingdom that would rise up and be responsible for great evil. The passage mentions 10 other horns, which are meant to be ten tribes, three of which are uprooted by the little horn. Adventists claim that this "little horn" is the Catholic Church, rising from among the ten tribes that existed in Rome. However, there were not ten tribes when the Catholic Church was established, but almost twenty.

Daniel was not writing about the future Catholic Church, but rather expressing the plight of a people under persecution. The ten horns represent the divided Greek empire, and the little horn stands for the oppression from Antiochus IV Epiphanes, a Seleucid king. As with much of prophetic writing, the goal may include some insight into future events, but very often the purpose was to express, in symbolic language, God's Word regarding the current events that the prophet and his people are experiencing.

Summary:

- **Prophetic books such as Daniel and Revelation use apocalyptic imagery;**
- **While this imagery can have implications for future generations, it primarily addresses the persecution faced by the author and other Christians of the era;**
- **Descriptions of the Whore of Babylon most likely refer to Pagan Rome or Jerusalem, which cooperated in this persecution;**
- **Any similarities to the Catholic Church are results of faulty interpretation, rather than the actual intent of the inspired author.**

18

WHEN THE DOORBELL RINGS:
ANSWERING JEHOVAH'S WITNESSES

"Therefore, we may confidently expect that 1925 will mark the return of Abraham, Isaac, Jacob, and the faithful prophets of old."
-"Millions Now Living Will Never Die," Watchtower Publication, 1918.

Several years ago I agreed to do a talk on how to dialogue with the Jehovah's Witness and Mormon missionaries who might come knocking. I spent several weeks doing research, including reading a great deal of literature from these two groups.

Even though I was starting to feel intellectually prepared, I realized that my preparation to talk about these two groups had one serious deficiency – I hadn't ever chatted with a Jehovah's Witness missionary and it had been a few years since I encountered the Mormon boys. So I did the only logical next step and visited the websites of these two groups to request visits.

If I failed in anything during my visit with the Jehovah's Witnesses, it was that I was too aggressive. We chatted in my basement, and my wife later summed it up this way: "I heard you talking, and then them, and then you, and then them. Then it was you, and you, and you." Successful apologetics rarely involves the onslaught of arguments that I had employed.

The two sections in this chapter will reflect on my subsequent (and more calm) visits and give the most effective strategies that I have found in years since for planting Catholic seeds. This chapter will highlight some key teachings of the Witnesses, as many people are not aware of how distinct the doctrines of this group are.

Sometimes people reject the Jehovah's Witnesses because of their doctrines, such as the prohibition on blood transfusions (an extension of their restrictions on consuming blood). Rejecting the Witnesses solely on this basis would be inappropriate, for Christians are also criticized for teachings that others see as absurd (such as the idea of a virgin giving birth to God). Any doctrine should be judged upon its foundation. As repulsive as the idea of refusing one's child a blood transfusion might be, the real question is whether or not God has commanded this. So this chapter will not give a detailed rebuttal to each teaching, but rather demonstrate how to challenge the foundation upon which they are based.

Distinctive beliefs of the Jehovah's Witnesses

In the 1993 movie, *A Perfect World.*, Kevin Costner plays an escaped convict who befriends a boy who happens to be a Jehovah's Witness. Through the movie, Costner discovers that the child has not been allowed to participate in holidays and has missed out on other childhood joys due to the doctrines of the group. He takes it upon himself to introduce these forbidden pleasures.

In addition to a refusal to acknowledge birthdays or holidays, such as Christmas, there are several other beliefs that the Witnesses hold that are different from those of Christianity:

- Christ is not "God," but really the archangel Michael, and he is in every way inferior to Jehovah-God;

- Christ was crucified on a "torture stake," not a cross, and was raised from the dead as an immortal spirit person;

- Traditional Christianity has been corrupted by Paganism and has many erroneous doctrines;

- The Holy Spirit is not a person, but an energy, like divine electricity. The Holy Spirit emanates from God and is the conduit of his work, but is not a conscious force itself;

- There is no Hell. The unsaved are simply annihilated;

- There is no such thing as an immortal soul - the human soul ceases to exist at death;

- Only 144,000 will enter Heaven, born again as spiritual sons of God, to rule with Christ. The remainder of those saved will reside on an earthly paradise;

- True Christians should accept no job with the federal government because of its involvement in wars;

- Jehovah's Witnesses should not interact or engage in interfaith activities with other religious groups (this is followed to the point of ostracizing any family members who are outside the Witness community);

- We are in the end-of-times right now. A Protestant friend shared a story of a JW missionary who visited her in the 80's. During one of those conversations, she asked this young man (in his early 20's) if he was planning on going to college. He explained that the end of the world was so immediate that going to college would be a waste of time.

Who are the Jehovah's Witnesses?

The JW church is very new, founded by Charles Taze Russell, an 19th century Congregationalist preacher who challenged an atheist to a debate ... and lost. The experience did much to send Russell into a crisis of faith, which drew him away from his church at the time. Eventually Russell fell in with the Seventh Day Adventists, which have a reputation for being unapologetically anti-Catholic and are fueled by speculation on end-of-the-world dates. From his exposure to this group, as well as others that he interacted with in his journey from traditional Protestantism, Russell eventually developed the Jehovah's Witnesses.

Encounters with the Jehovah's Witnesses generally begin when a couple of missionaries visit and offer a copy of Watchtower magazine[22] or one of their other publications. They will move on quickly to the next house. Within the next few weeks, possibly months, new missionaries will drop by to see if you have had a chance to read the material. You will be invited to take part in a personal Bible study in your own home. If you agree, you will eventually be asked to participate in a neighborhood Bible study (which will be more of a study of Watchtower publications) and to worship at the local Kingdom Hall.

When I first set up my meeting with the Witnesses, I was somewhat nervous, though my wife assured me that I was too stubborn to let anyone convert me, and it turns out she was right. However, the missionaries come very prepared for a game of Scriptural tennis, especially when discussing the divinity of Christ. The best approach is to focus, instead, on the issue of authority. Several points are worth bringing up in conversation

New World Translation of the Bible

Many of the publications of the Watchtower Society are written anonymously. Credit will be given to "A Doctor in Missouri" or "A Housewife in Nevada." Witnesses will claim they

---

[22] The Watchtower Society is the official publishing arm of the Witnesses and, whether the missionaries admit it or not, has served in a prophetic role for the group.

want their *New World* translation judged on its own merits, keeping the identities of the translators secret, but when one discovers the background of the translators, the reason for secrecy is obvious. A good translation team would have an excellent grasp of the original languages. Yet of the six individuals responsible for the original translation of *New World Bible*, only Fred Franz had any knowledge of Greek and Hebrew. But he certainly couldn't brag about it – Franz was self-taught in Hebrew and had only two years of Greek … modern Greek, that is, not the much different biblical Greek.

The committee also acted with great bias. In order to deny the divinity of Christ, several verses have been altered from what one would find in reputable Catholic and Protestant Bibles. For instance, in John 1, the *New World* Bible tells us that "In [the] beginning the Word was, and the Word was with God, and the Word was *a* god." Technically speaking, there are no indefinite articles ("a") in Greek, so it is academic opinion where to put them in translations, but Catholic and Protestant scholars overwhelmingly disagree with the Witness's decision to put an "a" in this verse.

However, I've never focused on John 1 in my discussions with the Witnesses, but rather a more obvious issue of biased translation. In Greek, the word for "lord" is *kurios*.[23] However, Jehovah's Witnesses believe that the personal name for God is Jehovah, so each time the translators encountered the word *kurios*, they translated it as *Jehovah*. However, because they are intent to show that Christ is not God, if the word *kurios* refers to Jesus, they translate it with the literal meaning of "lord" (Rom 10:9; 1 Cor 12:3; Phil 2:11; 2 Thes 2:1 and Rev 22:21).[24] So, the same word is translated two different ways in order to fit their theology.

The same is true for the word *proskune*. When the translators

---

[23] This is a transliteration, using English letters instead of Greek.
[24] "Stumpers for the Jehovah's Witnesses." www.catholic.com.

encountered it, they translate it with the traditional "worship." However, since they do not believe Christ is God, they translate the very same word as "do obeisance to" when it refers to Jesus (Luke 24:52, John 9:38 and Heb 1:6).[25]

Guided by the Watchtower Society

The Watchtower Bible and Tract Society is the official legal entity and publishing arm of the Jehovah's Witnesses. Whether or not your missionary visitors admit it, the organization and its various publications serve a prophetic role for the Witnesses. This is problematic for a couple of reasons.

For one, traditional Christianity has long understood that the time of public revelation has ended, with the deposit of faith completed during the apostolic period. As Catholics, for instance, although we believe in private revelations, such as an apparition of Mary or Christ, the messages of these visions cannot be new doctrine and are not binding upon the faithful.

Second, the Watchtower Society has made a number of predictions about the end of the world or other significant events. 1914, 1918, 1925 and 1972 have been given as the target dates, yet those years have come to pass in rather benign ways.

Scripture tells us that nobody can know the date or time of Christ's second coming, so it is suspect that the Watchtower Society has attempted to do so (Matt 24:36; Mark 13:32). Even more so, their failed prophesies are an undeniable indication that the organization is a false prophet (2 Pet 2:1-3).

The Great Apostasy

Because of their rejection of the Trinity and the divinity of Christ, the Witnesses are not Christian. However, apologists for the

---

[25] Ibid.

group will say that they are the original Christians and that Protestants and Catholic today belong to a Christianity that has been stained by pagan influence.

They will refer to an apostasy, or falling away, that swept through the Church at about the time of Constantine. Their belief is that a hidden remnant of true Christians remained as faithful and discreet servants through the years of corrupted Christianity.

One of the ways that the Witnesses will approach this in conversation is to show a picture of a three-headed Egyptian God and claim it is the inspiration for the teaching of the Trinity.

There are several problems here. As the chapter on the Trinity explained, we do not believe in a God with three parts or (especially) three heads. Second, as the chapter on fallacies explores, similarities between two religions does not mean one necessarily caused the other. Finally, traditional Christian beliefs can be seen clearly in the writings of those Christians who lived long before Constantine. Yet the unique beliefs of the Witnesses cannot. If they are the original Christians, why did nobody in the first or second century believe as they do?

References to apostasy in the Bible never refer to a full falling away of the Church. Rather, the gates of Hell will never prevail against the Church (Matt 16:19), which is the pillar and foundation of truth (1 Tim 3:15). The New Testament Church that our Lord built is perpetual and indefectible (Dan 7:13-14).

The personal name of God?

In conversations with the Witnesses, one will notice their use of the name *Jehovah God.* Jehovah comes from a less accepted translation of the name for God in the Old Testament, which most Christians translate as Yahweh. Because Hebrew did not contain vowels, we can give the Witnesses some slack here.

However, they believe that the name "Jehovah" is the personal name of God that he desires all Christians to use. However, the word "Jehovah" does not appear even once in the New Testament. If this were the preferred personal name of God, wouldn't Jesus or the apostles have used it at least one time?

The flawed *New World Translation,* as noted above, sprinkles the name Jehovah throughout, but this is because the translators use it in place of the word "lord," the accurate translation of *kurios.*

Questions for the Witness missionaries

After listening to the carefully scripted J.W. approach for a short while, the Christian must respectfully take control of the conversation. The Christian should also be prepared to give a personal testimony of the joy that exists within him as a Christian. Finally, the conversation should avoid too much discussion of specific doctrines, and instead zero in on the subject of authority:

How do members of the Jehovah's Witness faith explain the selection of each individual book of the Bible, particularly in the New Testament? In other words, by what means can we know that individual books, such as *Philemon* and *3 John,* were correctly included in Scripture, while writings such as *The Didache* and the *Epistles of Clement* were correctly excluded?

Why are there inconsistencies in the translation of the New World Bible? The same Greek words *Kurios* and *proskune,* appear to be translated, not according to a literal reading, but to fit a preconceived theology. The *New World* treatment of Philippians 2:10-11 is an excellent example of this.

When two Christians disagree on Scriptural interpretation, how should this conflict be resolved? This forces the missionaries to struggle with the Bible-alone problem introduced in the chapters on Scripture, or to admit that they have no infallible interpretation to support their beliefs.

Why, if God desires us to know him by "Jehovah," does the actual name "Jehovah" not appear even one time in the Greek original of the New Testament? The New Testament was written by individuals guided by the Holy Spirit. Surely the personal name of God would be the name by which they would have referred to the divine author.

What are the criteria for determining a false prophet? Would not the failed predictions from the Watchtower Society qualify it to be a false prophet?

Summary:

- The Jehovah's Witnesses have many beliefs that are different from Christianity, especially a rejection of the Trinity and the divinity of Christ;
- The erroneous beliefs of the Witnesses come from a flawed authority, such as a biased translation of the Bible, the failed prophesies of their parent organization, and a Scripture-alone approach to forming theology;
- According to the Witnesses, "Jehovah" is the personal name of God, even though this name appears nowhere in the New Testament;
- Focusing on authority is the best way to approach conversation with Jehovah's Witness missionaries.

19

WHAT ARE MORMON-STYLE CREAM PIES?

"*All men have heard of the Mormon Bible, but few except the 'elect' have seen it, or, at least, taken the trouble to read it. I brought away a copy from Salt Lake. The book is a curiosity to me, it is such a pretentious affair, and yet so 'slow,' so sleepy; such an insipid mess of inspiration. It is chloroform in print. If Joseph Smith composed this book, the act was a miracle — keeping awake while he did it was, at any rate. If he, according to tradition, merely translated it from certain ancient and mysteriously-engraved plates of copper, which he declares he found under a stone, in an out-of-the-way locality, the work of translating was equally a miracle, for the same reason.*

The book seems to be merely a prosy detail of imaginary history, with the Old Testament for a model; followed by a tedious plagiarism of the New Testament. The author labored to give his words and phrases the quaint, old-fashioned sound and structure of our King James's translation of the Scriptures; and the result is a mongrel — half modern glibness, and half ancient simplicity and gravity. The latter is awkward and constrained; the former natural, but grotesque by the contrast.

Whenever he found his speech growing too modern — which was about every sentence or two — he ladled in a few such Scriptural phrases as 'exceeding sore,' 'and it came to pass,' etc., and made things satisfactory again. 'And it came to pass' was his Pet If he had left that out, his Bible would have been only a pamphlet."

-*Mark Twain*, Roughing It – *Chapter 16.*

As mentioned in the last chapter, to prepare for a talk on door-to-door missionaries, I requested a visit from the Church of Jesus Christ of Latter Day Saints, more commonly known as the Mormons. The young men who visited were very pleasant, and I was already familiar with most of what the missionaries told me (and most of what they didn't) from my studies. Just to lighten up the conversation, I brought up the book *The Executioner's Song* by Norman Mailer (1979), which centers on the execution of a man named Gary Gilmore. The book takes place in Utah, and there are a couple references to family gatherings, where "Mormon-style cream pies" are served.

"So what's the deal?" I asked. "Do Mormons just like cream pies, or do you have some special type of cream pie you aren't letting the rest of us know about?"

The history of the Latter Day Saints

Mormons believe that around 600 B.C., two of the "lost tribes" of Israel, the Nephites and the Lamanites, crossed the Atlantic and settled here in North America (originally inhabited by the Jaredites, who came here after the Tower of Babel incident). After a series of great battles, the Lamanites all but eliminated the other inhabitants and are the ancestors of Native Americans. One surviving member of the Nephite tribe, Mormon, recorded the history of this period on golden tablets, which God then instructed him to hide in a nearby hillside.

Sometime later, after his persecution and crucifixion,

Mormons teach that Christ appeared in the Americas and brought his message of salvation to the people there. Mormons believe that salvation history is made up of a series of apostasies, followed by a time of prophets and repentance, and then another apostasy. They insist that the Christianity that Christ preached was identical to the Mormon faith of today. Shortly after Christ ascended, the last great apostasy began, perverting Christianity.

After that point, in the early 19th century, a disenchanted Christian named Joseph Smith claims to have been visited by God and Christ, who informed him that all of Christianity was in error. He was to restore the true church (this time for good, with no further apostasies) and begin a world-wide conversion. Smith next claimed a visited by the angel Moroni, who appeared to show him the location of the gold tablets. Though these tablets were written in an unrecognizable language, Smith claims to have translated them with the assistance of God. John the Baptist supposedly then appeared to validly baptize Smith and his initial followers.

This small group evolved into the large group we know today, which is headed by a modern-day prophet, who Mormons believe receives direct revelation from God. Directly underneath this prophet are twelve "apostles." Men in the Mormon church become "Aaronic priests" at 12 and priest in the "Melchizedek order" at 18, which is how they earn the title "Elder."

Other distinctive beliefs of the Latter Day Saints

Plurality of Gods – This subject will not come up during early conversations with Missionaries, who are taught that it is much too complex to discuss in initial encounters with others. However, the Latter Day Saints teach that the highest level of eternal salvation offers the reward that a faithful Mormon can become a God, himself, overseeing his own planet of spiritual children. Joseph Smith spoke about this in his sermons, such as the *King Follett Discourse* and the Sermon on the *Plurality of Gods*. God, as we know him, had a father, according to LDS teaching, and the cycle extends backward in time from there.

Jesus Christ – The LDS teaches that Christ and Satan are spiritual brothers. Both presented a plan for salvation to the Father, and when Christ's plan was accepted, Satan rebelled.

Baptism for the Dead – Many Christians are aware that the LDS organization has a unique interest in genealogy, and their research is often utilized by other groups seeking to put together familial timelines. This interest springs from the LDS teaching that, if one dies before being baptized, he will be preached to in the afterlife. To ensure that this individual receives salvation, a Mormon in good standing is baptized on his behalf.

A while back the LDS was criticized after it was revealed that they had performed this ceremony on behalf of several victims of the Holocaust, possibly including Anne Frank. Spokespersons for the organization apologized and promised not to include Holocaust victims in future ceremonies. This was an interesting response. If the LDS truly believes that baptism for the dead leads to eternal life, what do they have to apologize for? Is the possibility of offending others a higher concern than the salvation of so many?

Celestial Marriage – the LDS teaches that there are three levels of reward in the afterlife (almost nobody ends up in Hell), the telestial, terrestrial, and the celestial. Non LDS Christians would most likely end up in the terrestrial level, with greater sinners in the telestial. For those Mormons who achieve the celestial level, a man and woman are offered the opportunity to be "sealed" in their covenant, which means their marriage will extend into eternity. A man may only be sealed to one woman at a time, but if his wife dies, for instance, he may be sealed to another woman and will spend eternity with both of them. Women, however, are not allowed to be sealed to more than one man for eternity.

The Lost Tribes – As described earlier, the LDS teach that the indigenous population of North America comes from three groups, two of which are the "lost tribes" of Israel. This theory worked fine until DNA science came along.

After an analysis of Native American DNA, the claims in the Book of Mormon are at odds with the scientific consensus on the origins of the early North American population. Mormon apologists have attempted several sidesteps to reconcile this, such as claiming that the Lost Tribes actually migrated to very specific areas of North America and that the DNA examination was not specific enough. This drastic revision reveals a great flaw in the supposed authority of the LDS prophets and apostles. I personally avoid getting into this too deeply as intelligent discussion means dipping into scientific discussions that non-scientists would be irresponsible in undertaking.

What to expect from Mormon missionaries:

The missionaries will seem very impressive in their knowledge of Scripture. Sunday worship within the Church of Jesus Christ of Latter Day Saints is an all-morning affair, with classes during the week for many of the youth. In addition, the missionaries go through extensive training in preparation. One way to prepare for your Mormon visitors is to spend some time online looking up the verses that they will use to support such ideas as "baptism for the dead" and "the great apostasy." An effective form of persuasion is demonstrating a knowledge of another man's arguments.

The missionaries will attempt to control the conversation - The missionaries have a lot of houses to hit and very little time to do it. To make the most of each visit, they are trained to use one of several loosely-scripted approaches. Your goal should be to politely maintain control of the conversation.

Mormon missionaries will use words like "Trinity" and will describe Christ as a "savior." Make no mistake, though, the Mormon definitions for many of these "Christian" terms is vastly different from the definitions used by Christians. Make sure to ask for clarification when it appears, on the surface, that your Mormon guests agree with your beliefs.

They will rely on a subjective "burning in the bosom" - Far from providing objective support for their faith, they will rely on strong emotional proof. They will often ask you to read from selections of the *Book of Mormon*. In addition, they will ask you to pray for guidance and to wait for that "burning in the bosom" that God sends to verify that one has discovered the truth. However, in reality, all religions claim to provide "good feelings," and the chapter on faith explores the problems with this more thoroughly. Continue to ask for objective support to avoid false assurance. Continue to emphasize the euphoria that you feel when receiving the Eucharist or when engaged in adoration.

Problems with authority

When speaking with the Mormon missionaries, one should focus less on the peripheral doctrines and more on the issue of authority. I have found the following questions to be effective:

Was Christ lying or mistaken when he promised that the gates of Hell wouldn't prevail against his church (Matt 16)? This question is a good one for anyone who believes in an apostasy. If the Catholic Church brought corruption upon Christianity until Joseph Smith came along over a thousand years later, doesn't this imply that the gates of Hell had prevailed for some time and that the Holy Spirit failed in guiding the Church (John 16)?

How does one identify a false prophet? LDS teachings have changed substantially over the years. In addition, the prophesies are often in direct contrast with the Book of Mormon. For instance, while the Book of Mormon insists that there is only one God, the prophesies of Joseph Smith indicate differently.

How does one tell the difference between a burning in the bosom and false assurance? Always bring this conversation back to religious groups that claim similar emotional assurance. They can't all be correct.

Why does Joseph Smith trump Christ? Mormons admit that Christ, while not "God" in the sense that we define it, was a very special individual and more than a mere prophet. Yet, they also claim that his church began to fall into apostasy immediately after his death. However, the church was restored permanently by Joseph Smith. The World Series is the *most important* series in a baseball season – no regular season games come after it. The Super Bowl is the *most important* game in football, which is why no regular season games come after it. Yet Mormons teach that, even though Christ was the *most important* individual ever to be born, he was just another link in the chain of prophets. Why was a simple man like Smith chosen to lead a more permanent restoration than that which Christ, the Messiah, was capable?

Where are the ideas of baptism for the dead, plurality of Gods, etc. in early Christian writings? Even if the church began falling into apostasy early, wouldn't there have been at least some early writings about these distinct beliefs of the Mormons (as there are with many Catholic beliefs)? These writings are available online for examination and study.

Where is the archeological proof of the Lamanites and the Nephites? These groups supposedly built great civilizations and had great battles. Yet, archeology has turned up none of it, as it has for much of the history of the Bible. If a missionary tries to claim that some of these civilizations have been found, ask him for verification. There are Mormon "archeological" tours, in which current excavations are claimed to "possibly" be the sight of some battle or the other, but no actual proof beyond that.

The Mormon missionaries are usually very pleasant, and I've always enjoyed visiting with these young men, who are engaging in an adventurous journey into adulthood. However, this doesn't mean that any Catholic should shy away from challenging the missionaries on their beliefs and putting up a respectful defense of the Catholic Church. Remember, they came knocking on your door, not the other way around.

Summary:

- Mormon version of salvation history has the "lost tribes" of Israel migrating to North America, becoming the ancestors of Native Americans;
- LDS teaches that Christ appeared and preached in North America after his resurrection;
- A supposed revelation to Joseph Smith provided this text of the Book of Mormon;
- LDS beliefs regarding the Trinity and Christ discredit them from being called "Christian" in the traditional sense;
- Mormons believe that a great apostasy corrupted Christianity, and that Joseph Smith restored it by establishing the LDS;
- Dialoguing with Mormon missionaries calls for a discussion of authority.

Salvation

20

THE END OF THE WORLD
AS WE KNOW IT

"What the caterpillar calls the end of the world, the master calls a butterfly."
-Richard Bach

Thank goodness for the premillennialists, without whom we wouldn't have any good rapture jokes when we walk into a nearly empty room.

The rapture is the belief, mostly among fundamentalists, that at some point in the future, Christ will come down from Heaven and take all of the believers with him, leaving everyone else behind for a period of tribulation. This belief was brought into the mainstream by a series of poorly written books and an equally poorly made movie called *Left Behind*. This series feeds upon our society's anxiety over an apparent deterioration of culture and speculation over the end of the world. This chapter explores what actually will happen at the end of time.

Do Catholics believe in a rapture?

The opening chapter of the *Left Behind* series finds the main character on a plane just as he and a number of other passengers realize that several people on the plane, including the pilots, have inexplicably disappeared, leaving behind their clothes and personal belongings. What seems like the start of a science fiction novel is actually the opening scene in a work of Christian fiction meant to popularize the doctrine of the rapture.

Catholics actually do believe in a rapture event, just not the way that Fundamentalists often portray it. To begin, there are three schools of thought on the one-thousand year reign of Christ described in Revelation (20:1-3,7-8). Postmillennialists believe that Christ is presently reigning in a symbolic one-thousand years, during which the world will be almost entirely converted to Christianity. Amillennialists also believe that the one-thousand years are symbolic, but do not hold to a complete conversion of humanity. Premillennialists believe that Christ will return to earth and rule, physically and visibly, for one-thousand years.

Premillennialists have a timeline in which, before Christ returns, there is a *secret* rapture of true believers, and *then* a period of tribulation, after which the second coming occurs. Catholics, as do most Christians, believe that the rapture happens during the second coming, and Scripture supports this. One of the staple proof-texts for the rapture, from Matthew, states that "as in the days of Noah ... so shall also the coming of the Son of man be" (Matt 24:36-42). The verse goes on to describe that two will be in a field and one will be taken, then other left. Two will be grinding at the mill, with one taken and the other left.

The problem is that, with the Great Flood, the sinners were taken by the flood and the righteous left behind. Fundamentalists generally believe that the righteous will be taken and sinners left behind, exactly the opposite of the analogy Matthew uses.

As Catholics, we too wait for the second coming of Christ, when the dead shall rise and those who are alive will be taken up into the clouds with him (1 Thes 4:16-17), and that we will all be changed "in the twinkling of an eye," putting on immortality (1 Cor 15:51-53). We agree that this event will follow a period of tribulation and persecution (2 Thes 2:1-4). However, we recognize that the rapture is not a separate event, but one mentioned by Scripture as happening together with the tribulation, not before it (Mark 13:24–27; Matt 24:26–31; 2 Thes 2:1–12).

Some additional problems with the rapture remain:

- No Christians believed in a pre-tribulation rapture until the belief was invented by John Nelson Darby in the 1800's;
- The verses that indicate Christ's one-thousand year rule do not mention him ruling from earth;
- Scripture does not indicate one-thousand years between Christ's return and judgment, but rather an immediate judgment with his second coming (Matt 25:31-32, 46);
- A pre-tribulation rapture requires that Christ visits the earth secretly to bring up believers, which means that his "second" coming is really a "third" coming.

The Catholic perspective on the end of times

The events at the end of time are outlined nicely in the *Catechism of the Catholic Church*. These passages are included below, with the footnote notations replaced with the actual Bible verses to which they correspond:

The kingdom of God is present on earth right now through the body of Christ:

CCC No. 669   As Lord, Christ is also head of the Church, which is his Body (Eph 1:22). Taken up to heaven and glorified after he had thus fully accomplished his mission, Christ dwells on earth in his Church. The redemption is the source of the authority that Christ, by virtue of the Holy Spirit, exercises over the Church. "The kingdom of Christ [is] already present in mystery," "on earth, the seed and the beginning of the kingdom" (Eph 4:11-13).

The Church is currently undergoing tribulation and trial:

CCC No. 672   Before his Ascension Christ affirmed that the hour had not yet come for the glorious establishment of the messianic kingdom awaited by Israel (Acts 1:6-7) which, according to the prophets, was to bring all men the definitive order of justice, love, and peace (Isa 11:1-9). According to the Lord, the present time is the time of the Spirit and of witness, but also a time still marked by "distress" and the trial of evil which does not spare the Church (Acts 1:8; 1 Cor 7:26; Eph 5:16; 1 Pet 4:17) and ushers in the struggles of the last days. It is a time of waiting and watching (Matt 25:1, 13; Mark 13:33-37; 1 John 2:18; 4:3; 1 Tim 4:1.).

The actual date of the return of Christ cannot be known, so attempts to "calculate" the date are futile:

CCC No. 673   Since the Ascension Christ's coming in glory has been imminent (Rev 22:20), even though "it is not for you to know times or seasons which the Father has fixed by his own authority" (Acts 1:7). This eschatological coming could be accomplished at any moment, even if both it and the final trial that will precede it are "delayed" (Matt 24:44; 1 Thes 5:2; 2 Thes 2:3-12).

The full number of Gentiles will come into the Church, followed by the full inclusion of the Jews, with both of these things happening before Christ returns:

CCC No. 674   The glorious Messiah's coming is suspended at every moment of history until his recognition by "all Israel," for "a hardening has come upon part of Israel" in their "unbelief" toward Jesus (Rom 11:20-26; cf. Matt 23:39). St. Peter says to the Jews of Jerusalem after Pentecost: "Repent therefore, and turn again, that your sins may be blotted out, that times of refreshing may come from the presence of the Lord, and that he may send the Christ appointed for you, Jesus, whom heaven must receive until the time for establishing all that God spoke by the mouth of his holy prophets from of old" (Acts 3:19-21). St. Paul echoes him: "For if their rejection means the reconciliation of the world, what will their acceptance mean but life from the dead? (Rom 11:15)" The "full inclusion" of the Jews in the Messiah's salvation, in the wake of "the full number of the Gentiles, (Rom 11:12, 25; cf. Luke 21:24)" will enable the People of God to achieve "the measure of the stature of the fullness of Christ," in which "God may be all in all" (Eph 4:13; 1 Cor 15:28).

There will be a final trial of the Church through the deception of the antichrist; he will offer solutions to mankind's problems that comes at the cost of religious truth:

CCC No. 675   Before Christ's second coming the Church must pass through a final trial that will shake the faith of many believers (Luke 18:8; Matt 24:12). The persecution that accompanies her pilgrimage on earth (Luke 21:12; John 15:19-20) will unveil the "mystery of iniquity" in the form of a religious deception offering men an apparent solution to their problems at the price of apostasy from the truth. The supreme religious deception is that of the Antichrist, a pseudo-messianism by which man glorifies himself in place of God and of his Messiah come in the flesh (2 Thes 2:4-12; 1 Thes 5:2-3; 2 John 7; 1 John 2:18, 22.).

There will be a final "revolt of evil," over which Christ will triumph when he returns for the Last Judgment:

CCC No. 677 The Church will enter the glory of the kingdom only through this final Passover, when she will follow her Lord in his death and Resurrection (Rev 19:1-9). The kingdom will be fulfilled, then, not by a historic triumph of the Church through a progressive ascendancy, but only by God's victory over the final unleashing of evil, which will cause his Bride to come down from heaven. (Rev 13:8; 20:7-10; 21:2-4) God's triumph over the revolt of evil will take the form of the Last Judgment after the final cosmic upheaval of this passing world (Rev 20:12; 2 Pet 3:12-13).

Who is the antichrist?

Since the early days of the Church the antichrist has been identified as someone who will deny the role of Christ as the messiah and take upon himself a claim to that role.

In a general way, anyone who opposes the Father or does not acknowledge Jesus is the antichrist (1 John 2:22; 1 John 4:3). However, the antichrist is also a real individual (John 2:18). There is no Scriptural evidence to believe that the antichrist is Satan or a demonic force. Some have speculated he will be of Jewish origin, and possibly of the tribe of Dan based on Genesis 49:17, which calls Dan a viper along the roadside. The tribe of Dan is also noticeably missing from Revelation's list of tribes from whom the twelve-thousand will be chosen.

Whatever the actual identity of this figure, the *Catechism* points out that the Antichrist's "deception already begins to take shape in the world every time the claim" is made that hope offered through the Messiah can be found by some other path than Jesus Christ.[26]

Summary:

- Outside of Catholicism, various groups differ in their interpretation of how the end of time will take place;
- Catholics reject the idea that there will be a literal 1,000 year reign of Christ on earth, as Christ is reigning now through his Church;
- The "rapture" of Christians will take place at the time of the second coming, not at some point before that;
- Nobody can know the date nor hour of Christ's return;
- The Church outlines the events leading up to the final judgment, and these events include a conversion of the full number of Gentiles, a conversion of Israel, and a time of trial and apostasy.

---

[26] *Catechism of the Catholic Church,* No. 676

21

LAST THINGS:
DEATH, JUDGMENT,
HEAVEN AND HELL

"The true object of all human life is play. Earth is a task garden; Heaven is a playground."
Gilbert K. Chesterton

The *Four Last Things* refers to the events that happen at the end of our lives: death, judgment, Heaven or Hell. Especially because some groups rely on their own interpretation of Scripture, there is some confusion over what exactly happens after our death.

Particular judgment - As Scripture tells us, our death marks the solidification of our acceptance or rejection of Christ, so our particular, or individual, judgment comes immediately after our death. At this point, we learn whether we will spend eternity in Heaven or in Hell. The author of Hebrews explains this: "It is appointed for men to die once, and after that comes judgment" (9:27). Men die *once*, which eliminates the possibility of reincarnation, which seems to intrigue some Christians.

Heaven or Hell – Those who die having rejected Christ will immediately find themselves in Hell. Those who die with sanctifying grace will be judged as worthy, by the merits of Christ's death, of entering Heaven. They share in his merits because they are co-heirs with Christ through adoption as children of God (Rom 8: 15-17), allowing participation in the divine nature (2 Pet 1:4). There are many who are going to Heaven, though forgiven of their sins, who still face temporal consequences for them. Before entering into Heaven, they will be cleansed through Purgatory (1 Cor 3:15).

General judgment – While Scripture indicates an immediate judgment after our death, it also speaks of the great judgment at the end of time, when Christ comes in glory, with his angels. He will sit upon his throne and separate the sheep from the goats (Matt 25:31-32). At this point our sins will be publically revealed (Luke 12). At this time, the bodies of the dead will be resurrected and glorified (1 Cor 15:35-44, 1 John 3:2).

Does Hell really exist?

Some groups, such as the Jehovah's Witnesses, reject the idea of Hell. Others think Hell is not a permanent state, but that sinners will be released after a period of punishment. Both ideas are false, as is any claim to know definitively who is in Hell.

The Church has the authority to canonize saints, which means to name those who definitely obtained Heaven. This is done through the observance of miracles performed in that saint's name and an examination of his life. However, the Church does not declare any specific individual to be in Hell, as much as one might be inclined to say that Hitler is there. The closest we have to a resident is Judas, of whom Christ says, "For the Son of Man goes as it is written of Him; but woe to that man by whom the Son of Man is betrayed! It would have been better for that man if he had not been born" (Mark 14:21). This verse appears to indicate Judas, and it is difficult to reason how Heaven could be the state that is "worse" than never having been born.

However, not knowing who is in Hell is not the same as saying that we don't know for sure if *anyone* is there. Jesus said the road is narrow and the gate small that leads to eternal life (Matthew 7:14). There have been some creative attempts to define *few* among different Christians. Philosophy professor and author Peter Kreeft looks at it from a parent's perspective and explains that if even one person doesn't make it to Heaven then the number of saved is too few. One thing is certain, though, which is that Hell is not empty.

While we are not bound by private revelation, Sister Faustina Kowalska was given a vision of Hell so that she could tell of its existence. She wrote, "I, Sister Faustina Kowalska, by the order of God, have visited the Abysses of Hell so that I might tell souls about it and testify to its existence...the devils were full of hatred for me, but they had to obey me at the command of God, What I have written is but a pale shadow of the things I saw. But I noticed one thing: That most of the souls there are those who disbelieved that there is a hell" (Diary 741).

And as to whether or not Hell is permanent, Scripture again leaves no doubt. Christ refers to an *eternal* punishment (Matt 25:46) and to a fire that is not quenched (Mark 9:47-78). The smoke of the Hell's torment goes up forever and ever (Rev 14:11).

But won't Heaven be really boring?

The Simpsons has an episode where Homer and Bart have converted to Catholicism. Marge has a vision, then, of their eternal reward as she is greeted by Peter and shown Protestant Heaven and Catholic Heaven. The former is a subdued mix of croquet and badminton, while the Catholic Heaven is dancing, beer, piñatas and Irish brawls. Jesus spends most of his time at the Catholic party.

At funerals, grieving family members often console each other with assurances that Grandpa Joe is now an angel in Heaven, looking over them. However, people do not turn into angels in Heaven. Angels are a different type of creature entirely; they are beings of pure spirit. The idea that humans turn into angels is like suggesting that dogs turn into people when they die. Instead, in Heaven humans remain humans and achieve perfect sainthood, so it is not only equally reassuring, but also more correct, to say that Grandpa Joe is a *saint* in Heaven looking over us.

The problem of *what* we will do in Heaven is a good one to contemplate. Knowing how we will spend eternity gives us some insight into how we should be occupying ourselves in this life.

First and foremost, we will be engaged in direct worship of God; our Alleluias and Holy, Holy, Holy exclamations will come as an automatic response to the great joy we will feel in having our longing for unity with our creator fulfilled.

God is perfect beauty and truth, and so we will be very occupied in admiration of the highest experience of that which we sought on earth. Beyond that, our time in Heaven can be summed up by understanding that God is also perfect knowledge, perfect justice and perfect love.

Perfect knowledge – God is knowledge, and we share in this to an extent on earth, but because of the limits of our imaginations and the influence of original sin over our intellects, mankind sees things though "a glass, dimly" (1 Cor 13:12). Once we are in the immediate presence of God, those limitations will be lifted. We will share in God's divine knowledge (1 Cor 13:9-12), his divine glory (Rom 8:16-17 & 2 Cor 3:18), his divine life (1 John 5:11,20), and the fullness of God (Eph 3:19; 1 John 3:2). This doesn't mean, of course, that once we die we will know *everything*, as that would mean that our knowledge is equal to God's. However, we will be able to more fully understand God's nature and his divine plan, an experience that is called the "beatific vision." Our intellects are driven by a pursuit to know things, and in Heaven we will be eternally satisfied by an infinite well of knowledge.

Perfect justice – That God is eternal does not mean he lives for a very long time, but that he is outside of time. God watches all events, as they happen, as if they were playing simultaneously on millions of screens around him. By sharing in this, we will also be able to watch the events in our own lives and the lives of those we care about, and we will do so with a perspective that shares in God's divine authority and power (2 Tim 2:12, Rev 22:5, and Rev 2:26-28). We will see, through God's eyes, how our sins affected others. We will grow in understanding of how the tragedies in our lives were used for greater good and how even our simplest acts of charity built up the body of Christ.

A share in God's divine knowledge and justice also means that we will be aware of those whose fate is eternal separation from God (Isa 66:23-24). The knowledge of who is in Hell will be complemented by an understanding of their decision to reject Christ, and we will rejoice in the triumph of God's justice over the emptiness of sin (Prov 21:15; Rev 16:5-7; 18:20; 19:1-3).

Perfect love – Knowing, as we will, the fate of those who are in Heaven seems to us now to be something over which we would mourn, especially if these individuals are those we knew and loved previously. This is certainly something that is difficult to understand with our frail human emotions. However, Scripture tells us that in Heaven our tears are wiped away, and there is no mourning or pain (21:4). Those who are in Hell are there because they have chosen an eternity away from God. Our instincts tell us that we would miss these individuals so much as to lessen our joy in Heaven; however, the love we feel in our relationships on earth are just traces of our desire for perfect love and union with God.

When we reach Heaven, God's love has been made complete

in us (1 John 4:12). Even though husbands and wives will probably have special relationships in Heaven, even marriage no longer serves a purpose when we are in the presence of the divine bridegroom (Matt 22:30). So to argue that we will be lonely for anyone while in the presence of God is like suggesting that someone is hungry for an afternoon snack, minutes after he has just filled himself at an all-you-can-eat buffet.

Summary:

- When we die, we will go through our particular judgment and know our eternal fate;
- Some of us will go to Hell, and some to Heaven, while some will be cleansed in Purgatory before entering Heaven;
- At the end of time, we will undergo a general judgment, where the works of all mankind are revealed;
- Hell is a real place of eternal separation from God, and those there will undergo a torment caused by their own burning rejection of God;
- In Heaven, we will worship God and share in his divine knowledge, judgment and love.

22

HOW YOU LIKE DEM APPLES?
ORIGINAL SIN

"Man too was created without corruption ... But when it came about that he transgressed the commandment, he suffered a terrible and destructive fall and was reduced to a state of death. The Lord says that it was on this account that He Himself came down from heaven to the world, taking leave of the ranks and armies of the angels. ... It was to this end that the Word put on humanity. that he might overcome the serpent, and that He might Himself put down the condemnation which had first come into being when man was ruined."
-*St. Methodius of Philippi, "The Banquet of the Ten Virgins"*

Several years ago, I helped work with confirmation candidates. A list of questions had been prepared, with which I was to guide conversation with a few students who seemed less than excited to be participating. When I asked what the term "original sin" means, one girl volunteered, "It mean that babies are born, like, evil or with demons in them."

"Um ... not quite," I answered. Many misunderstand the teaching on original sin, thinking that the Church is implying that even infants are culpable for sin against God. Understanding this doctrine properly is key to explaining the reason for Christ's incarnation and death, as well as key doctrines like infant baptism.

Adam and Eve and the forbidden fruit

The Church teaches that some aspects of the story of Adam and Eve can be understood figuratively.[27] Maybe their names were actually Adam and Eve, and maybe not. Maybe the first sin actually involved eating a piece of fruit, and maybe the fruit is symbolic for a spiritual rebellion. What is *certain* is that there were two original parents to the human race – two individual creatures who were unique among all other life in that they possessed an immortal and rational soul.

These two parents lived in a unique state of harmony with God, with creation and with one another. The story in Genesis emphasizes this by explaining that the man and woman were naked and without shame (2:25).

Adam and Eve ate of the *Tree of the Knowledge of Good and Evil*, which the serpent claimed would open their eyes, making them "like God, knowing good and evil" (Gen 3:5).

In other words, the original sin of Adam and Eve was to attempt to reject God as the law maker in their lives and to take for themselves the authority to decide what is right and what is wrong.

The consequences of sin

Sin is not a *thing*, it is the absence of a thing (called *privation*), just like cold is the absence of heat and darkness is the absence of light. In the first chapter of *Genesis*, God took chaos and brought it

---

[27] *Catechism of the Catholic Church* No. 390.

into order and harmony, so to reject God is to embrace chaos and emptiness.

Our first parents, then, consciously reject God and the paradise of a close communion with him. Moving from harmony toward chaos resulted in several consequences:

- Men and women began regarding their bodies in a shameful way (3:7);
- Women experience suffering in childbirth (3:16);
- Husbands and wives would experience conflict (3:16);
- Work and sweat are required to produce food (3:17-19);
- Mankind experiences death (Rom 5:12; Cor 15:219).

Most significantly, by consciously rejecting God, our original parents also rejected the sanctifying grace that allows man to spend eternity with God. The consequence for eating of the Tree was that they would surely die on "that day" (Gen 3:3). Since Adam and Eve did not die physically *on that day*, we know the implied death was a spiritual one.

One thing that my kids can probably count on, when my wife and I die, is that they will not inherit millions of dollars. Parents cannot pass on to their children what they, themselves, do not possess. Christ, through his death, gives us the sanctifying grace that allows for the redemption of our souls. Even a man adopted into Christ suffers from the temporal consequences of original sin, including suffering and death. All that our children receive from us is our human nature, which remains in a fallen state. As Paul explains in Romans, our bodies are not yet redeemed (8:23). This means that, even after sanctifying grace is infused into our soul, it is not an inherent part of human nature, so even the children of two baptized parents cannot inherit it. Psalm 51:5 echoes this: "I was born guilty, a sinner, even as my mother conceived me."

Because our bodies are not yet redeemed, even a baptized Christian will still experience the physical consequences of original sin, such as suffering and death. In addition, our state of living apart from God results in man having *concupiscence*, a disordered desire for bodily goods. This makes us more vulnerable to the temptation to sin. Without the grace of God, man lives according to the passions of the flesh (Eph 2:1-4; Rom 3:9-12).

In the state of original sin, then, none of us can have hope of Heaven. Our own efforts, no matter how *good* we attempt to be, do not make us worthy. However, in his great mercy, God desires for each of us to spend eternity with him. It is through Christ that he rescues us from our state of spiritual separation by filling our souls with sanctifying grace, which is necessary for eternal life.

Summary:
- **Sin is the absence of good;**
- **"Original sin" does not mean that infants are responsible for personal sin;**
- **Our original parents rebelled against God and lost the original state of harmony they experienced in the garden;**
- **Because our original parents did not have sanctifying grace, they could not pass it onto their descendants, including us today;**
- **Justification is a restoration to grace from a state of original sin.**

23

ARE YOU SAVED?
AND OTHER SILLY QUESTIONS

"And as many of them, he added as have repented, shall have their dwelling in the tower. And those of them who have been slower in repenting shall dwell within the walls. And as many as do not repent at all, but abide in their deeds, shall utterly perish ... Yet they also, being naturally good, on hearing my commandments, purified themselves, and soon repented. Their dwelling, accordingly, was in the tower. But if any one relapse into strife, he will be cast out of the tower, and will lose his life."

-Hermas, The Shepherd, 3:8:7 (AD 155)

Are you saved? Do you have assurance of salvation? Catholics are often scolded for not being able to speak with complete confidence about their eternal future when posed with questions like these. Despite the title, it isn't as though these questions are, in and of themselves, silly. However, when a Catholic is asked about salvation from a Protestant, both individuals usually mean something different, even if using the same words. The same is true of questions about being "born

169

again" or "accepting Christ as his personal Lord and savior."

Can we have eternal assurance of salvation?

If a Catholic were to say that he does not have assurance of salvation, he is in pretty good company, as it was Paul who wrote, "I am not aware of anything against myself, but I am *not* thereby justified. It is the Lord who judges me" (1 Cor 4:4).

Paul understood that it was not our place to declare our salvation eternally assured. Catholics can have what is called "moral assurance," meaning a practical knowledge of whether or not we are, right now, in a state of grace with the intent to stay that way, though this is far from a certitude.[28] However, as much as a woman in her twenties might feel she has a great relationship with Christ, can she speak with absolutely confidence about whether she will feel that way years later?

The story of our relationship with Christ is the story of marriage (Eph 5), and if there is anything that marriage teaches, it is that the emotional high one feels on his wedding day isn't guaranteed to be the same feeling he wakes to each morning of the rest of his life. Husbands and wives sometimes struggle to get along. Sometimes, sadly, the relationship just falls apart.

Marriage is a journey of ebb and flow. It requires effort to stay in love and persevere when the heart sometimes seems to be running on empty.

Scripture tells us that our relationship with Christ is that of a bride to a bridegroom. The good news for us is that our divine bridegroom will never turn cold to our affection. The bad news is that believers are not always as faithful to Christ as he is to us. Just

---

[28] *Catechism of the Catholic Church* No. 2005.

as a spouse might neglect to say "I love you," the Christian grows lazy in his prayers. Just as lovers allow life to get too busy to enjoy each other's company, a Christian might exclude Mass from his weekend schedule. A husband can forget how to apologize to his bride, just as a Christian might avoid going to confession.

And eventually, like the adulterous wife in *Hosea*, the lukewarm Christian might allow her wandering eyes to turn from Christ to worldly pursuits.

Some Christians disagree with the notion that a believer can lose his salvation. They point to verses that claim that *nothing*, not even angels, will take us from the Father's hand (John 10:27-30; Rom 8:28-39). Christians are adopted into divine sonship with the Father. And no Father, they argue, would send his children away.

Catholics should have no issue with these verses. It is true that no power will ever *take us* from the Father's hand. However, we can still walk away of our own free will. An all-good, almighty father might not turn his children away, but he also won't chain them within his house if they decide to abandon him.

After all, the parable of the prodigal son shows a young man who was fully in his Father's kingdom and had an inheritance waiting for him. According to the once-saved-always-saved philosophy, nothing should have endangered that. Yet, the prodigal son still left his father and squandered his inheritance, finding himself starving and living among swine (Luke 15:11-32).

The lost son eventually returned, but only because he repented and asked for forgiveness and mercy. He would have died among swine had he not.

A Christian does not enter Heaven because, once upon a time, he accepted Christ as Lord and Savior. Rather, "he who *endures* to the end will be saved" (Matt 24:13).

Some Christians point to verses that refer to being "saved", in the past tense, to show that the act is complete in the life of a believer, but Scripture also talks about salvation as something that is currently happening (1 Cor 1:18, 2 Cor 2:15, Phil 2:12) and will continue happening in the faith journey (Rom 5:9-10; 1 Cor 3:12-15). Salvation is a process.

Like Paul, we realize that we might be "disqualified" and must "pummel" and "subdue" our bodies against temptations (1 Cor 9:27). The twelve-year-old girl who accepts Christ with tears of joy at summer camp is misled if told that her salvation is now certain. Who knows what temptations or challenges lay before her?

How is a person saved?

The chapter on Original Sin explained how, as descendants of Adam and Eve, we are born into a state of separation from God. At baptism, which is discussed in a later chapter, an individual is regenerated. He is *justified*, which means that his sins are forgiven and he is given a new nature (2 Cor 5:17; Gal. 6:15), as the Holy Spirit dwells within him and infuses righteousness into his soul. At this point, an individual has "sanctifying grace," which is the type of grace necessary to get into Heaven.

Some Protestants believe justification is merely a legal declaration – that our sinful nature is only covered. Martin Luther compared this wayward nature to snow covering a pile of dung.

Were those who lose their faith really saved in the first place?

Believers in OSAS (once saved, always saved) have a problem when attempting to explain individuals, including some preachers, who give every appearance of being saved, but later fall into a life of sin or rejection of God.

When asked to pinpoint specifically how one can know for sure if he is saved, they point to "evidence," such as whether good works exist in the life of a supposed believer. Yet many who fall away have led lives that were filled with naturally good works. Even atheists can volunteer at soup kitchens and donate to charity.

OSAS Christians must conclude that someone who falls away was never truly saved in the first place. They point to James' use of the phrase "dead" to describe the faith of such an individual.

But the problem here is that "dead" is not a synonym for "false" (Jas 2:17). By definition, something that is now dead must have once been alive. The analogy James uses is a man who once looked at himself in the mirror, but walks away and forgets what he looked like (Jas 1:23-24).

The message that true Christians cannot lose salvation runs contrary to Scripture. A number of verses illustrate this clearly:

Romans 11:13-22 explains that real Christians, those who "stand fast only through faith," can be cut off again.

Hebrews 10:26-31 explains that real Christians, those who "received the knowledge of truth" and are sanctified by the "blood of the covenant," can "sin deliberately" and face "a fury of fire."

2 Peter 2:20-21 explains that real Christians, those who have a knowledge of Jesus, can lose their salvation by entangling themselves in the worldly defilements from which they escaped.

Verses which refer to predestination

Many Catholics are not aware that our Church, like all Christian groups, has a teaching on predestination. Romans 8:29-30 affirms that God, through his omnipotence and omniscience, does predestine some of us as members of the elect. What Catholics rightfully reject is called *double*-predestination, wherein some are marked for Hell and some for Heaven. Rather, God desires to see all attain Heaven (1 Tim 2:4).

However, through our free will, some of us will accept God's grace and some will not. Those who will accept that gift, called the *elect*, are given the additional grace of final perseverance, which means it strengthens Christians further in their ability to respond to his invitation to eternal life, ensuring that they persevere until the end, even if there might be some slips and the need for repentance until then. A member of the elect may fall into mortal sin, but will be moved to repentance before his death.

The teachings on predestination are much more complicated and nuanced than this chapter allows, but it is important to discuss that this teaching *does* exist for both Catholics and Protestants (even if we have different understandings). While some verses appear to argue that all *believers* will be saved, those verses are actually saying that all of the *elect* will be saved. All cats are animals, but not all animals are cats. So, too, all of the elect become believers, but not all believers are from among the elect. Some believe for a little while, and then fall away (Luke 8:13).

What about verses that indicate salvation cannot be lost?

Despite the above explanation, OSAS Christians will still find verses that appear to show that salvation cannot be lost. The following guidelines explain how to analyze verses which appear to support a OSAS reading of Scripture.

Always read the verse in context. Sometimes OSAS advocates use Romans 8:1 and 28-39, to argue that there is "no condemnation to those who are in Christ Jesus" or that no person or power "will be able to separate us from the love of God in Christ Jesus our Lord." However, just a few chapters later, Paul writes this to the Gentiles: "But if some of the branches were broken off, and you, a wild olive tree, were grafted in their place .... They were broken off because of their unbelief, but you stand fast only through faith. So do not become proud, but stand in awe. For if God did not spare the natural branches, **neither will he spare you**" (11:17-22). Only by ignoring parts of Paul's letter can the earlier verses be twisted to support eternal assurance of salvation.

Recognize that the New Testament authors often wrote with the assumption of completion. A former Catholic once argued from John 3:18 that "He who believes in Him is *not* condemned." However, as the other New Testament authors do, John is writing "believes" to mean "believes at the point of his death." But my former Catholic acquaintance read it to mean that anyone who, at any point, decides to believe has officially been acquitted for the rest of his existence. But if this were true, then he would have a hard time explaining the rest of that same verse: "but he who does not believe *is condemned already*." So, if believing once acquits a Christian for good, then not believing would condemn them for good, which is bad news for any Christian who, because of childhood or youthful rebellion, had even a moment of disbelief.

Be familiar with the biblical teachings on predestination. Some verses, such as John 6:39 and John 10:27-30, suggest that those who are "given" to Christ will never perish. However, as explained above, these verses are referring to the elect, but not every specific person who believes at some point in his life.

Recognize that, while God will not cast us away, we still retain our free will: Another common verses for the OSAS position reads: "For I am sure that neither death, nor life, nor angels, nor principalities, nor things present, nor things to come, nor powers, nor height, nor depth, nor anything else in all creation, will be able to separate us from the love of God in Christ Jesus our Lord" (Rom 8:38-39). As Paul explains, nothing including death or angels, can pull us from God. However, this verse says nothing to preclude us from simply walking away.

Understand that Greek grammar works differently than English: Something is lost in translation, especially when going from the grammatical structure of Greek to English. John 3:16 is such a popular OSAS verse that we're used to seeing people hold this verse up on signs at football games. It reads: "For God so loved the world that He gave His only-begotten Son, that whoever believes in Him should *not perish but have everlasting life.*"

However, the verbs "believes" and "have," in the original Greek, are in a tense that means they are undefined actions, without boundaries in time. Look at this same sentence with different nouns inserted: "For God so loved the world that He gave us citrus trees, that whoever eats of them should not get scurvy but have healthy bodies." The moment we stop eating citrus, we risk again developing scurvy.

In other words, John is saying that as long as one believes, he has eternal life. The one is attached to the other.

Summary:

- **Questions that some Protestants ask about salvation are based on unproved assumptions;**
- **Salvation is an ongoing process, and individuals' can fall through sin;**
- **Being saved means being justified through baptism and receiving sanctifying grace;**
- **Someone who is justified retains free will;**
- **Not all believers are members of the elect;**
- **Verses on salvation must be read in context and with an understanding that English translations do not accurately reflect Greek grammar.**

24

IF THEY JUST WEREN'T SO MUCH FUN! MORTAL SIN

"Some offences are light, some heavy. It is one thing to owe ten thousand talents, another to owe a farthing … if we entreat for smaller offences, we obtain pardon: if for greater ones, it is difficult to obtain our request: and that there is a great difference between sins."'
Jerome, Against Jovianus, 2:30 (AD 393).

Once I was visiting a fourth grade religion class at the school where I am principal. The teacher had just asked the students what it feels like to sin, and several students answered, "It feels really bad."

This is when I cut in. "You guys are such big liars," I laughed. "Sin doesn't feel bad. Sin is a lot of fun! That's why we keep doing it all the time."

Hopefully, if our conscience is well-formed, we do eventually

177

feel bad for our sins, but if felt bad during the act of sinning, each of us would be perfect saints.

Degrees of sin

One of the reasons that sin appeals to us is that every sin takes some good and then manipulates it. Sex, for instance, is a good thing, a gift from God that builds up the unity of marriage and brings children into the world for the honor and worship of God. But sin takes sex and turns it into pornography, one-night stands and homosexual acts.

These disordered acts offend God by opposing his will. If sins are serious enough, they can endanger our salvation by emptying us of sanctifying grace.

Our relationship to Christ is that of a bride to a bridegroom (Eph 5). As with any marriage, one spouse is not chained to the other against her will. And just as a spouse, who was once ecstatic in love, might chose to walk away from marriage, Christians can also choose to walk away from the love and grace of Christ.

To be clear, earthly marriage is a metaphor of heavenly marriage to Christ, not the other way around. By understanding marriage properly, it reveals to us truths about eternal reality.

A sin of lesser degree is called a venial sin. Venial sins are not severe enough to kill sanctifying grace. Similarly, in marriage, there are things a spouse could do, such as neglecting to take out the trash, which would be "venial" offenses, and which would not end a relationship between two rational adults.

And so it is with our salvation. Taking some office supplies home from work or being boastful are sinful acts, but they will probably not endanger our sanctifying grace. Venial sins do weaken the effects of sanctifying grace, making it easier to commit mortal sin. John, in his first epistle, writes that "there is sin which is deadly," and that "all wrongdoing is sin, but there is sin that is not deadly" (5:15-17).

Mortal sin is the name for an act of such a serious nature that one's relationship with Christ ends and his soul is emptied of sanctifying grace, which is necessary to enter Heaven. Sometimes people feel it is unfair that it only takes one mortal sin to lose salvation, but this is like arguing that it is unfair that it only takes one step off the roof of a sky-scrapper to lose one's life.

Conditions for mortal sin

The Catechism of the Catholic Church explains that three conditions must be present for a sin to be mortal: full knowledge, deliberate consent and grave matter.[29]

Full Knowledge: In order for someone to be guilty of a mortal sin, he must know that a certain act is grave matter. Someone who has never been told that we are to avoid meat on Fridays during Lent cannot be faulted for eating a cheeseburger. A woman might skip Mass because her parents never catechized her.

Deliberate Consent: One is not held accountable for sins that he did not willingly commit. A ten-year-old who cannot drive himself to Mass is not guilty of sin if his parents refuse to take him. If someone stole money because his family was starving, it would be a different matter than someone stealing money to buy a new stereo. Other factors influencing one's culpability for sin include acts committed during a bout of depression, mental or physical illness, addiction, or through force of habit.

Grave matter: Directly rejecting what Christ has asked of us is often grave matter, but rejecting what the Church has taught often is, too. In Luke 10:16, Christ tells us that whoever rejects the

---

[29] *Catechism of the Catholic Church*, No. 1857-1861

leaders of the Church rejects him, as well.

A more specific guide to what make a sin "grave" are found in Christ's words to the rich young man, which correspond to the ten commandments: "Do not kill, Do not commit adultery, Do not steal, Do not bear false witness, Do not defraud, Honor your father and your mother" (Mark 10:19). Obviously, some sins are more serious than others. Murder is a more serious matter than theft. Stealing six dollars from a hungry beggar is more serious than taking the same amount from petty cash, though both are sinful.

Many Catholics are unaware of many of the acts that are *mortal* sins if committed with full knowledge and consent:

- Skipping a Sunday Mass or a Holy Day of Obligation without a reason such as severe or contagious illness (being on vacation or at a sports tournament does not trump Christ's command to "do this in memory of me");
- Intentionally becoming intoxicated, thus handicapping our ability to avoid other sins;
- Participating in murder, including abortion or supporting abortion advocacy;
- Participating in sexual sins, such as viewing pornography, acting "impure" with oneself, having sex outside of marriage, or by using contraception in the marital act.

The third section of the *Catechism of the Catholic Church* discusses many of these sins in greater detail. Grave sins, if done with full knowledge and consent, sever one's relationship with Christ.

For those who reject the idea of mortal sin, one of the main objections is that it seems so legalistic that because of one sin, an otherwise faithful Christian would suddenly be damned to Hell for eternity. Returning to the marriage analogy would help here. In marriage, a deal-breaker sin would be adultery. Imagine, then, a spouse who is unfaithful *in front of* his own wife.

Mortal sins involve those moments when a Christian chooses another love as more important than our commitment to him, committing adultery on Christ, who is aware of our every act. When an individual is tempted by such sin, it might be helpful for him to picture himself committing that same sin on Calvary, as our broken and bloody Lord watches from his cross.

To commit a mortal sin and then attempt to receive our Lord in the Eucharist doubles the insult just the same as if that adulterous husband never asked his wife for forgiveness, but instead tried to cuddle up in bed with her the night after his affair.

This is why the Church, following the instructions of St. Paul, instructs that anyone who is aware of a mortal sin must refrain from going to Holy Communion. Our bridegroom Christ is aware if we have been "gravely" unfaithful to him, and to then expect to receive him into our bodies in the Eucharist would be "profaning the body and blood of the Lord" (1 Cor 11:27).

The good news is that Christ is always willing to extend forgiveness, even for the worst sin. The fallen Christian, however, must be ready to ask for forgiveness in the way Christ intended, which is through the sacrament of reconciliation. He has also provided the sources of grace by which we can avoid sin and firm up our salvation. Christ is unconditionally forgiving, but we must be ready to ask him for pardon before we can hope to receive it.

Summary:

- Christians can lose their salvation through serious sin, which serves as a rejection of Christ;
- Sin that does not remove sanctifying grace is called venial sin;
- Grave sins are those which involve serious matter, including missing Mass;
- Mortal sins can only be forgiven through the sacrament of reconciliation.

25

WORKIN' NINE-TO-FIVE,
WHAT A WAY TO EARN SALVATION

"If anyone says that man can be justified before God by his own works,
whether done by his own natural powers or through the teaching of the
law, without divine grace through Jesus Christ, let him be anathema."
-Council of Trent, Session VI, Decree Concerning Justification,
Canon 1

hen my dad died, I was the one who discovered his body. Diabetes, heart disease and the stress of life on the fringes of poverty had taken their toll on him.

I found him slumped over in his recliner, and I sat for a moment in the desk chair next to him, digesting the moment before picking up the telephone to start the business of moving on.

The relationship between body and spirit

When Adam was created, God took the body he had molded and breathed life into it. So it is when we die, the body remains, but the spirit leaves. James reflects on this in his epistle when he is writing about faith and works.

I've pointed out this passage to Christians, even pastors, who criticize the Catholic understanding of works, claiming that works are merely the products of our faith, the demonstration of it. Faith, they claim, enlivens our works, not the other way around.

But not according to James. He parallels faith with the body, that part of my father that remained after the spirit left. Works, the inspired author writes, are like the spirit:

> For as the **body** apart from the _spirit_ is dead,
> So **faith** apart from _works_ is dead (2:26).

It is true that works are a demonstration of a true faith, but this doesn't mean that this is the only purpose of works. James writes that one's faith is also "completed" by his works (2:22).

Judged by our works

Catholics are often wrongly criticized for believing that one can "earn" salvation through good works. To the contrary, it was the Catholic Church which condemned heresies, such as Pelagianism, which taught that good works and man's own effort can get him into Heaven independent of the grace of God.

The other extreme, however, is the belief that works have no role whatsoever in our salvation. Even though many Christians claim that we are saved by _faith alone_, these words only appear once in all of Scripture, and this is when James rejects the idea: "You see that a man is justified by works and _not_ by faith alone" (2:24).

Scripture tells us that we will actually be judged by our good works (Matt 16:27; Rom 2:5-13; 2 Cor 5:10; 1 Pet 1:17; and Rev 22:12). We are urged to use our talents wisely if God is to reward us (Matt 14:30). And, just before the parable of the wise and foolish builders, Jesus says that only he "who does the will of my Father" will enter the kingdom of heaven (Matt 7:21).

When an individual first becomes a Christian, he is *justified*. This means he is adopted as a son of God and has sin wiped from his soul. This justification is a free gift and no amount of work can earn it. This justification comes by way of the gift of faith to the believer: "For by grace you have been saved, through faith; and this is not your own doing, it is a gift of God – not because of works, lest any man should boast" (Eph 2:8-10).

However, even after being justified, a Christian still has free will and can commit a mortal sin, walking away from his Father, as the prodigal son did. To help us stay in a state of grace, God's grace also "sanctifies" us, which means that it allows us to participate in God's divine life and prepares our souls for Heaven.

Does Paul contradict James?

In the book of Romans and Galatians, Paul writes things which appear to directly contradict James, such as this passage from Romans 5:1: "Therefore, since we are justified by faith, we have peace with God through our Lord Jesus Christ."

However, when Paul is writing about faith apart from works in these passages, he is referring to "works of the law," as he specifically explains in Romans 3:21. At the time of Christ, there were individuals known as Judaizers who insisted that in addition to accepting Christ, one still had to follow Old Covenant rituals like as circumcision and ritual cleansing. These rituals are not part of the New Covenant.

In addition, Paul is writing specifically about how works have no role at the point of initial justification, when an individual first becomes "saved". Catholics agree with this. Here is what the Church stated on the matter at the Council of Trent: "[N]one of those things which precede justification, whether faith or works, merit the grace of justification; for if [justification] is by grace, it is not now by works; otherwise, as the Apostle says, grace is no more grace" (*Decree on Justification* 8, citing Rom 11:6).

However, justification is a life-long process, and after the point when we are initially justified, we must persevere in the faith. Returning to the analogy of marriage is helpful here. The initial justification of a Christian is paralleled in the wedding vows that a husband and wife take. However, *marriage* is a life-long process. If spouses lived together based on love alone, the marriage would fall apart. A marriage is kept together by two people expressing an active love, filled with kisses and kind acts and legs entangled on the couch during late night movies.

Without *works* of affection, the marital love dries up. So, too, our marriage to the bridegroom Christ is kept alive through our works. Christians are to be "doers of the word and not hearers only," and an individual who neglects this "is like a man who observes his natural face in a mirror; for he observes himself and goes away and at once forgets what he was like" (Jas 1:22-24).

James writes in his epistle about *continuing* in justification, whereas the earlier verses from Paul refer to *initial* justification. Martin Luther was so bothered by what James wrote about works that, in his preface to the New Testament, he called his letter an "epistle of straw" and argued for its removal from the Bible.

This still does not mean that our works are our own, separate from God's grace. Man is only capable of good works because God sends the actual graces necessary, and we must chose to cooperate.

When was Abraham justified?

Scripture identifies several points at which Abraham is justified. The text that Fundamentalists will use against Catholics is this one: "For if Abraham was justified by works, he has something to boast about, but not before God. For what does the scripture says? 'Abraham believed God, and it was reckoned to him as righteousness" (Rom 4:3). Paul, here, references Genesis 15:6, where God promises Abraham countless descendants.

However, Hebrews 11:8 explains that Abraham was *already* justified by this point when he responded to God's command to relocate in Canaan (Gen 12).

So at this point, we have an initial justification and a point later in Abraham's spiritual life where his justification is renewed because of something he did, which was to believe God.

But the New Testament's treatment of Abraham is not finished yet. In Genesis 22:15-17, Abraham is justified yet again, this time for the *work* of offering Isaac as a sacrifice. James writes, "Was not Abraham our father justified by works, when he offered his son Isaac upon the altar? You see that faith was active along with his works, and faith was *completed* by works ... You see that a man is justified by works and not by faith alone" (2:21-24).

Co-workers with Christ

The idea of cooperating with God's grace is not one that any Christian should shy from. Paul goes so far as to call himself God's co-worker in evangelization (2 Cor 6:1), so how much of a stretch is it to say we are his co-workers in our own salvation?

While the marriage analogy is helpful in understanding our salvation, Christians are also adopted into divine sonship.

My kids have chores to do around the house, from unloading the dishwasher to pulling weeds in the flower garden. By participating in the upkeep of our house, they grow into a deeper respect and attachment to our household and family. They might even merit rewards, such as video games or an allowance. My wife and I provided the kids with the opportunity to help and the instruction necessary to do it. We fixed their errors, and even the rewards existed, in the first place, because our salaries had purchased the video games and paid the electric bill needed to enjoy them. The allowance was nothing more than our gift to them from our own paychecks, which we decided to apply to the specific acts they had performed around the house.

Catholics cannot "earn" God's grace, but God wills that our works actually do *merit* a spiritual reward (Rom 2:6-11). Paul clarifies that this reward is Heaven, in addition to whatever other rewards might await us (Gal 6:7-10), and as with the rewards my kids enjoyed from their chores around the house, salvation cannot be earned independent of God's benevolence.

It doesn't take away from the perfect act of Christ to say that God desires us to participate with his grace. Paul demonstrates this in Colossians 1:24, when he writes, "Now I rejoice in my sufferings for your sake, and in my flesh I complete what is lacking in Christ' afflictions for the sake of his body, that is, the Church ..." Is Paul trying to say that Christ' sacrifice was imperfect? Of course not. But just as Christ called Paul and others to be active participants in his mission of salvation, he wills that each of us be active participants in our salvation, coming to spiritual maturity through the good works that he offers us.

Summary:

- **Justification is a free gift from God, and no good work on the part of man can earn it;**
- **Justification initially comes by faith, but continues as an life-long process, and is tied to sanctification, which is the process by which one becomes more holy;**
- **Sanctification is furthered by our works, which themselves are free gifts of God's grace;**
- **Good works are products and demonstrations of our faith, but they also "complete" it;**
- **Our supernaturally pleasing good works *merit* grace and glory.**

26

GOD'S DOORMAT: PURGATORY

""Our souls demand Purgatory, don't they? Would it not break the heart if God said to us, 'It is true, my son, that your breath smells and your rags drip with mud and slime, but we are charitable here and no one will upbraid you with these things, nor draw away from you. Enter into the joy'? Should we not reply, 'With submission, sir, and if there is no objection, I'd rather be cleaned first.' 'It may hurt, you know' - 'Even so, sir.'"

-C.S. Lewis, Letters to Malcolm

A new bride and her groom are standing before the priest, and as he is asking the bride for her vows, she seems distracted and distant. After the wedding, the groom asks her about this. "Hank," she tells him, "You asked me to be your wife and I accepted. I will love you until death do us part ... but I just can't get my old boyfriend David off my mind."

Ouch.

Christ is our bridegroom, but when we become Christians, many of us still cling to earthly things, loving them more than him on occasion. Perhaps we love sleeping in more than we love Mass on some Sunday. Perhaps we love TV more than prayer. Yet, for a marriage to be truly perfect, we must be "purged" of these distractions to our faith. Purgatory is the place where God's grace allows us to break from our earthly desires and sinful attachments before entering into his glory. After all, nothing unclean will enter into Heaven (Rev 21:27).

Purgatory is not, as many believe, a second chance. Anyone who goes there is already destined for Heaven and is simply being purified before entrance. Purgatory is also not a place where mortal sins are forgiven – this must happen *before* an individual's death.

Is Purgatory in the Bible?

Sometimes Catholics are challenged to explain why they believe in Purgatory, when that word does not appear in the Bible. The simple answer is that the words "Trinity" and "Bible" also appear nowhere in Scripture, but the concepts do.

"Purgatory," after all, is just a useful word to describe a concept that is real enough and undeniably present in Scripture, as well as in the belief system of the early Christians.

In Luke's gospel, Christ speaks of those who fail to be reconciled with others when they reach the judge: "I tell you, you will never get out till you have paid the very last copper" (12:59). Our own meeting with the judge comes at the moment of our deaths, when we have our particular judgment and learn our eternal fate. What place is it from which we will not escape until we have paid a debt? Surely not Hell, which is eternal.

The two books of Maccabees were removed from the Old Testament during the Reformation, so Protestants do not consider them inspired. However, writings do not need to be inspired to be good historical testimonies; one might, for example, read the uninspired personal notes of George Washington to learn of his life. So it is important to note what we learn about Jewish culture in second Maccabees, where prayers are offered for some dead soldiers, so that they might be "loosed from their sins" (12:43-45).

Finally, in 1 Cor 3:15, Paul discusses how we must build on the foundation of Christ. Those who don't will go to Hell, of course. Of those who do, some will build with valuable metals, while others will chose more common materials. Paul writes that each man's work will be tested with fire, and "If any man's work is burned up, he will suffer loss, though he himself will be saved, but only as through fire." Now, consider this - we are not saved in Hell, yet we suffer no loss in Heaven, so there must be some other place or event after death in which we suffer loss but are saved.

Will there be suffering in Purgatory?

Sometimes people are intimidated by the idea of Purgatorial suffering, but any suffering one feels in Purgatory will be much different from the torment in Hell.

There is suffering any time we break ourselves of something unhealthy. My body aches when I start an exercise routine, but it is a good pain because I know I am toning those muscles and reducing that fat. A drug addict sweats and shakes in a rehabilitation center, but this is a good suffering because it is a sign of the body purging itself of the poison. Any discomfort or pain we feel in Purgatory will be the consequence of stripping from ourselves all that is distracting us from our love of Christ.

Scripture attests to the cleansing effect of suffering:

"My son, do not regard lightly the discipline of the Lord, nor lose courage when you are punished by him. For the Lord disciplines him whom he loves, and chastises every son whom he receives" (Heb 12:5-6).

"[W]however has suffered in the flesh has ceased from sin" (1 Pet 4:1).

"Blows that wound cleanse away evil; strokes make clean the innermost parts" (Prov 20:30).

Through Scripture, God's intense love takes the form of cleansing fire: the fire pot and flaming torch (Gen 15); the burning bush and Moses (Ex 3); the pillar of fire leading the Israelites (Num 9); the heavenly altar-sacrifice consuming fire with Solomon and Elijah (1 Kings 8:18); Tongues of fire (Acts 2); and God's description as a consuming fire (Heb 12:29). Even the name "Seraphim," for the powerful angels, means "burning ones."

Not all of us will need to experience Purgatory. Surely some of us are working out our suffering here on Earth, such as might have been the case for the good thief who confessed belief in Christ before his crucifixion. Others of us, those true saints, might have completely stripped ourselves of earthly attachments and will have no need for this purging.

Is Purgatory compatible with Christ's perfect sacrifice?

Many make the mistake of assuming that Purgatory is supplemental to Christ's work - something in addition. Rather, Purgatory is a manifestation of Christ's work - it owes its very existence to his redemptive act.

The interesting thing is that many Protestants, while recoiling at the very Catholic word "Purgatory" see verses such as the passage from 1 Corinthians 3 and agree that some sort of purification happens between death and entrance into Heaven so that we won't be unclean. They reject the idea, however, that Purgatory is a place or some period of time.

Actually, while Catholics are bound to believe in Purgatory, the Church has never actually defined it as a place. It is perfectly permissible for Catholics to believe that Purgatory might be, rather than a place, an instantaneous event, though more or less intense depending on the individual.

One thing we do know is that the prayers of a righteous man are powerful (Jas 5:16), and that God accepts our prayers for those in Purgatory because he wills it that the body of Christ is built up through acts such as this.

It is even possible that the New Testament records Paul's prayers on behalf of a recently deceased friend, Onesiphorus. In 2 Timothy, Paul prays that the Lord grant mercy to his household on behalf of Onesiphorus' service (1:16). Two verses later, he asks for the Lord to grant him to find mercy "on that day." While there is no hard evidence that Paul's friend was indeed dead, the language seems to suggest this.

Most of us have been to funerals where, to console the grieving family, well-meaning friends will assure them that "your dad is in Heaven now, looking down upon you." However, it is very possible – actually, it is probable – that most of us will pass through a purification before entering God's throne room, and we will surely want our friends and family praying for us, rather than assuming our instant sainthood.

Other objections

Objection: 2 Corinthians 5:8 indicates that when we are absent from the body, we are present with the Lord, leaving no space for Purgatory. The Catholic response: While this objection is commonly used to refute Purgatory, there is one serious problem – this is not what 2 Corinthians 5:8 says. Rather, Paul writes, "we would rather be away from the body and at home with the Lord." He is stating his preference for the eternal life over the temporal, but not at all saying we are immediately with God once we die. Similarly, a man might say, "I would rather be away from work and at the beach." This doesn't mean that anytime someone is away from work he is also at the beach.

Objection: The thief on the cross in Luke 23:43 was told that "today" he will be with Christ in paradise. Why didn't he go to Purgatory first? The Catholic response: The chapter on authority explored how, with no commas in the original Greek, we cannot be sure if the translation is accurate. However, it really doesn't matter to the question of Purgatory. Christ did not ascend to Heaven until forty-two days later, so it would be improbable for him to have meant that he and the thief would be together in Heaven on that day. It is also possible that the thief's suffering on the cross served as his Purgatory or that, as explained in this chapter, Purgatory is an instantaneous process.

Summary:

- Purgatory is a name given to our purification, through the grace earned by Christ, before we enter Heaven;
- This purification has nothing to do with forgiveness for sins, but rather detaches us from our love of anything besides God;
- This detachment will result in suffering, but it will be a suffering that we know is healing us;
- The prayers of other Christians are helpful to those in Purgatory.

27

A CUP THAT RUNNETH OVER:
INDULGENCES

"[T]he Church invites all its children to think over and weigh up in their minds as well as they can how the use of indulgences benefits their lives and all Christian society.... Supported by these truths, holy Mother Church again recommends the practice of indulgences to the faithful. It has been very dear to Christian people for many centuries as well as in our own day. Experience proves this."
- *Pope Paul VI*, Indulgentarium Doctrina, 9, 11

Just down the street from our home is a state-of-the-art house designed for a man who will spend the rest of his life in a wheelchair. A sniper bullet hit this soldier while he served in Afghanistan.

The house was a gift from businesses and individuals in the community who appreciated my neighbor's patriotic sacrifice. Nearly everything, from the foundation to the Christmas lights, were donated or purchased by those who recognize that their blessings in life were bought by the sacrifices of our veterans.

This Marine's house was purchased for him through the merits of others. Indulgences work much the same way. An indulgence is a remission from temporal punishment for sins that are *already* forgiven. The Church intervenes through the treasury of merit earned by Christ and the saints and applies this merit toward the temporal punishment owed by the Christian seeking the indulgence.

Many Catholics today think that indulgences are no longer part of the Church's teaching. However, the Church's teachings on indulgences are an infallible part of what Catholics believe. The Council of Trent reaffirmed this in the 16th century.[30]

Sin results in both eternal and temporal consequences

As already discussed in the chapter on Purgatory, there are both eternal and temporal consequences for sin.

Christ, by his death upon the cross, paid the spiritual debt for our sins, a debt that was beyond man's ability to pay otherwise. However, even after an individual receives forgiveness, the temporal consequences may still remain, such as when David's child had to die because of his sins, even after the Lord forgave him (2 Sam 12:13-14). Likewise, I can receive forgiveness from my friend for backing into his car, but the dent still remains and has to be repaired. We still face death and struggles despite becoming Christian because these temporal consequences remain from the original sin.

We are members of the same body

Sometimes people have a hard time understanding that no sin is private. Because we are all members of the same body, the sins

---

[30] Session 25, *Decree on Indulgences*

of one affects the whole (1 Cor 12:26). Likewise, an infection in one part of my body threatens the whole.

For the same reason, medicine that treats one part of my body can heal the whole. Reducing the infection in my arm lowers my fever and restores my energy. So, returning to Paul's passage from Corinthians, not only does the sin of one member of Christ's body affect the whole, but the graces merited by righteous individuals can be used to strengthen other members of the body of Christ.

For instance, it was because of the virtue of a few righteous men that the Lord was willing to spare the sinful people of Sodom (Gen 18:16-33; cf. 1 Kgs 11:11-13; Rom 11:28-2). In the New Testament, Jesus was willing to heal the paralytic based upon the faith of his friends (Matt 9:1-8).

Any Christian merit has its primary origin in Christ, but God desires to build up the body of Christ by having us act on behalf of one another.

The Church has the authority to remit temporal consequences

The Church is the fullness of Christ (Eph 1:22-23), and the one to whom Christ gave the authority to bind and loose on his behalf (Matt 18:18; John 20:21).

It is then through the Church that Christ works to administer grace from the treasury of merits. Just as sin damages us, righteous acts help to strengthen and sanctify us. Sometimes, though, the damage done by sin is so great that the penitential acts necessary are too overwhelming for this life, resulting in Purgatorial suffering after we die. Indulgences in this life can reduce our need for cleansing in the next.

Some confusion has come of the claim that certain indulgences knock off so many "years" of Purgatory. However, we do not know enough about Purgatory to even say if actual *years* are involved. When the Church speaks of relieving X number of years from Purgatory, it means that the reduced suffering in Purgatory would be equal to that many years of penance during earthly life. An indulgence for twenty years of Purgatory, for instance, means that the merits granted are equal to twenty years of penance.

Devotional acts are not only pleasing to God, but to engage in them has the opposite effect as that of committing sin, which tears at our soul. There are a number of opportunities for either a partial or a plenary (full) indulgence through such acts like Scripture study, saying the rosary, or mental prayer. Giving alms, which means to give charitably to the Church, is a virtuous act by which we sacrifice financially on behalf of others. While almsgiving is worthy of receiving an indulgence, this practice was once abused, prompting Luther's rebellion. Because indulgences do not gain us forgiveness of sins, one must already be in a state of grace. The intent must exist to gain the indulgence and to do it in the way the Church prescribes, such as by including a prayer for the pope's intentions.

Summary:
- Indulgences are still a part of Church teaching today;
- Sin results in eternal consequences, but also temporal consequences that remain after the sin is forgiven;
- Christians are members of Christ's mystical body. Just as the sin of one affects the whole, blessings can be given to one on behalf of another;
- The Church has the authority to remit temporal consequences of an individual through the merits of Christ and the saints.

4

Sacraments

28

THE MAGNIFICENT SEVEN: THE SACRAMENTS

"The spiritual virtue of a sacrament is like light; although it passes among the impure, it is not polluted."
-Augustine of Hippo, *Works, Vol. iii. In Johannis Evangelum, c. tr. 5, Section 15*

After spending some time away from the faith in high school and college, I met my wife, a faithful Catholic, and begin studying Catholicism again. This was a couple years past the point where I had studied my way out of atheism and discovered God's existence through philosophy, science, and history. Even though I slowly became convinced of the truth of Catholicism, there were some hold-backs.

For instance, going to confession to a priest was one of the last teachings I bought into. I remember the night I planned a return to confession after many years away from the sacrament. There was a reconciliation service for Advent at our parish, and as I prepared to go, I was jogging down the stairs, slipped and fell. The pop I heard from my ankle told me more than the pain.

Able to wiggle my toes, I decided that the ankle was not broken, but I knew it would be the size of a softball later that evening. I certainly didn't feel like making the trip to church at that point, but I had too much weighing down on me. I kidded to my wife that maybe Satan, himself, had tripped me on the way down.

The sacredness of seven

The sacraments of the Catholic Church are reconciliation (confession), and also baptism, the Eucharist, confirmation, marriage, holy orders, and the anointing of the sick. Seven is a powerfully symbolic number through Scripture:

- Seven days of creation and rest;
- From the book of Revelation, there are seven churches, seven spirits, seven stars, seven seals, seven trumpets, seven vials, and various other occurrences;
- In Rev 10:7, it was with the voice of the seventh angel that the mystery of God is finished;
- The *clean* animals taken aboard Noah's ark were by sevens (Gen 7:2), whereas the unclean were in pairs;
- The consecration of the Aaronic priesthood took place over seven days (Lev 8:31-36);
- The high priests sprinkles blood seven times on the Day of Atonement (Lev 16:14);
- The Israelites marched around Jericho seven times.

The list could literally fill a few pages, but suffice it to say that the Holy Spirit saw seven as a number signifying the great covenant between God and his people, so it shouldn't be any surprise that Christ established seven sacraments as instruments of his grace.

While various non-Catholic Christians believe in some of these sacraments (sometimes they will refer to them as ordinances), many of our seven sacraments are rejected by Christian groups who feel confession and regenerative baptism add to the all-sufficient work of Christ on the cross. They are just works, some might argue, when all a person needs to be saved is faith. Christ's grace, however, wasn't given in one big burst, but rather it is distributed throughout our lives, especially through the sacraments, and it is Christ's intent that we access this grace through them.

Mankind as both physical and spiritual

Christ, in recognizing our nature as both physical and spiritual creatures, deputized a visible Church to shepherd his flock. Likewise, Christ realizes that his grace is most powerfully received in a form that is both physical and spiritual. The definition of a sacrament is a physical sign that actually causes the spiritual reality it represents.

Through the Old and New Testament, God interacts with his people through physical signs of his presence. His message to Moses came from a burning bush (Ex 3) and King Belshazzar witnesses a giant hand inscribe upon the temple walls as his dinner guests profaned the sacred vessels (Dan 5). Our Heavenly Father leads Abraham to the very brink of having to sacrifice his own son so that the patriarch can physically experience the significance of what would happen on Good Friday (Gen 22). The most powerful example of God using physical means to bring us a spiritual reality is when Christ, the Son, came to live among us in the flesh, rather than just through prayer.

God understands that receiving *grace* can be something of an abstract experience to us and our fallible hearts and emotions make it hard to experience this abstract gift in our lives. For this reason, God chooses to give us sanctifying grace in a way that resonates with our physical beings. Sacred Tradition confirms that Christ, himself, established the seven sacraments as a gift to the Church.

These sacraments are designed to be physical signs of the spiritual reality taking place. For instance, as the waters of baptism wash our bodies clean, grace is washing our souls clean at that very moment. In marriage, we receive certain graces that draw us closer to Christ. The "symbol" of a husband and wife becoming one remind us of the reality of Christ becoming one with his bride, the Church, through the Eucharist (Eph 5:31-32). But more than this, the sacraments actually cause the grace they symbolize.

Sacraments as instruments of grace

The sacraments do not at all take away from the perfect act of Christ's death. Sacramental graces have their source in Christ's death. He just chooses to dispense these graces through the sacraments because the "signs" of the sacraments draw us closer to him through our active participation. Scripture tells us that the Church is the fullness of Christ (Eph 1:22-23), as well as his mystical body (Eph 1:22-23), so any grace that comes through the Church is a direct gift from our Savior.

Christ gave the apostles the power to administer the sacraments. They later passed this authority on to those who would succeed them as Christ's "deputies." For two-thousand years the power to administer the sacraments was passed on by a laying on of hands (1 Tim 4:14). It is through this chain of succession that the true Church today can trace its authority to herald truth and administer grace all the way back to the apostles.

Summary:
- Seven is a sacred number through Scripture, which is why Christ instituted seven sacraments;
- A sacrament is a physical sign that causes a spiritual reality;
- The graces received through sacraments are one and the same earned by Christ upon the cross;
- Only through the succession of laying on of hands in the Catholic Church does the authority to administer the sacraments exist today.

29

WHY CATHOLICS ARE ALL WET:
THE NECESSITY OF BAPTISM

"But give me now your best attention, I pray you, for I wish to go back to the fountain of life, and to view the fountain that gushes with healing. The Father of immortality sent the immortal Son and Word into the world, who came to man in order to wash him with water and the Spirit; and He, begetting us again to incorruption of soul and body, breathed into us the breath (spirit) of life, and imbued us with an incorruptible panoply. If, therefore, man has become immortal, he will also be God. And if he is made God by water and the Holy Spirit after the regeneration of the laver he is found to be also joint-heir with Christ after the resurrection from the dead. Wherefore I preach to this effect: Come, all ye kindred of the nations, to the immortality of the baptism."

-Hippolytus of Rome, Discourse on the Holy Theophany, 8 (AD 217)"

Symbols do not foreshadow symbols.

If a woman is driving and sees a sign with a picture of a curvy road, what should she expect to see ahead? Another road sign for a curvy road? Or the road itself actually curving?

Old Testament foreshadowing of baptism

One of the most important reasons for studying the Old Testament is that it is filled with signs that foreshadow things in the New Testament. Another word for such signs is "types," such as in the word "proto*type*," which is a model that represents something else. The New Testament is hidden in the Old, and the Old is fulfilled in the new, as Jerome once wrote. For instance, *types* of Jesus occur through the Old Testament. Abraham was called to sacrifice Isaac upon the altar, which foreshadows that God will offer his own son for sacrifice many years later.

Consider all the times that people are saved or washed clean by water in the Old Testament. The earth is washed clean by the flood (Gen 7:6). The Israelites pass through the Red Sea to escape from the Egyptians (Ex. 14:10). Elijah parts the Jordan before his assumption (2 Kgs 2:8). And Naaman the leper is dipped in the Jordan to be cured (2 Kgs 5:1-14). It is Peter's reference to an Old Testament *type* that provides the strongest support for baptism. Peter alludes to the great flood and writes, "Baptism, which corresponds to this, now saves you, not as a removal of dirt from the body but as an appeal to God for a clear conscience, through the resurrection of Jesus Christ ..." (1 Pet 3:21).

Baptism is the New Testament fulfillment of these types. Some claim that baptism is only symbolic, but the logic here makes as much sense as having a road sign to let drivers know there is another road sign ahead.

Christ understands that we are partly physical creatures, and out of love, he makes his offer of salvation to us in tangible forms that appeal to the five senses to help us understand, in a concrete way, the more abstract spiritual mystery at work. In baptism, for instance, the act of washing with water represents the reality that, at that moment, our souls are being washed clean. The image of being buried by the water symbolizes burial with Christ, putting to death our sinful ways. The symbol and the grace have been joined together, and so it is that we receive this grace through baptism, which makes it a necessary part of Christian initiation.

What of those who have no chance to be baptized

There are some who will point to a few rare examples in Scripture of someone dying or receiving grace without first being baptized, such as the thief who died alongside Christ. While we are bound by the sacraments, God is not. Christ, who promised paradise to the thief, certainly is within his authority to do so without demanding, that the thief climb down from his own cross and seek baptism first. In line with this the Church recognizes that there are some of us who are baptized by "desire," which means that if we have truly accepted Christ and desire communion with him through baptism, it is by virtue of our very desire that we receive his grace if obstacles are in the way to receiving the sacrament. Those who sincerely desire knowledge of God, but to whom no missionary has ever preached, are also baptized by desire. Similarly, those who profess Christ but who die as martyrs before baptism are "baptized by blood," also a teaching of the Church.

These unusual circumstances aside, however, for those of us who hear the teachings of the church and have opportunity for baptism, it is not an option, but a sacrament which must be part of our Christian initiation. Christ tells us in John 3:5, "Truly, truly, I say to you, unless one is born of water and the Spirit, he cannot enter the kingdom of God." Some Christian groups claim that being "born of water" refers to our actual birth from our mothers and that the spiritual baptism is merely an assent to faith. This reading, however, is completely foreign to the early Christians, whose writings indicate a belief in regenerative baptism.

The effects of baptism

In addition, further study of the New Testament demonstrates that Christ was truly speaking of the necessity of a water baptism. In Titus 3:5, we are told that "he saved us ... by the washing of regeneration and renewal in the Holy Spirit, which he poured out upon us richly through Jesus Christ, our Savior ..." The author of Hebrews urges us to "draw near with a true heart in full assurance of faith, with our hearts sprinkled clean from an evil conscience and our bodies washed with pure water" (10:22), and Paul writes in Romans 6:4, "We were buried therefore with him by baptism into death ..." In 1 Corinthians, he explains "But you were washed, you were sanctified, you were justified in the name of the Lord Jesus Christ in the Spirit of our God" (6:11).

There are other verses which speak to the importance of baptism, many which put it hand-and-hand with repentance and belief as a condition for receiving Christ (Mark 16:16, Acts. 2:37-39, and Acts 8:12-13). It is in baptism, after all, that we not only are forgiven of our sins, but we also receive the Holy Spirit, and with him, an infusion of sanctifying grace, restoring us fully to God's family. Returning to the Old Testament types for a moment, consider that almost every time one sees the salvific and cleansing role of water, it appears alongside a symbol for the presence of the God. During the great flood, it was a dove – a symbol of the spirit – which Noah sent to search for land. A pillar of fire and cloud leads the Israelites through the Red Sea. Joshua carries the ark, the vessel of God, as he passes through the Jordan.

Baptism "now saves you," this apostle writes, his pen inspired by the Holy Spirit. This is baptism by water of which he writes, and this is made clear by the reference to the great washing of the earth in Genesis. Just as Noah and his family, those righteous few, were lifted up as the sin upon the ground was cleaned away, so too does the water of baptism lift up our souls above those desires of the flesh into which we have been born.

Summary:

- Baptism by water is foreshadowed in several places in the Old Testament;
- The symbolic act of death and cleansing by water represent that, through baptism, we die to our former ways and are washed clean by grace;
- Generally speaking, water baptism is necessary for salvation;
- For those who die desiring to follow Christ, but who never have the opportunity to be baptized, God can act outside of the sacrament and baptize them by desire or by the blood of their martyrdom.

30

INFANT BAPTISM:
TO SUCH BELONGS THE KINGDOM OF
HEAVEN

"And they shall baptize the little children first. And if they can answer
for themselves, let them answer. But if they cannot, let their parents
answer or someone from their family."
-Hippolytus of Rome, Apostolic Tradition, 21 (c. AD 215).

Sometimes, when I discuss Catholic schools with others, it
sounds at first as if I am trying to talk myself out of a job. I
point out that, in the Bible, we do not see Christ and the
apostles going from town to town, setting up elementary schools.
They do not use their ministry to start youth programs or Sunday
school classes. In fact, interaction with children seems so odd to
the apostles that they attempt to hold the young ones back as they
were brought to Jesus (Mark 10:13-14). I make this point, not to
argue for shutting down Catholic schools, but to emphasize that
the primary catechists in the lives of our youth are their parents.

Christ asked that the children be brought to him, of course,
but the point remains that the ministry of our Lord and his apostles

was to adults. These men and women, then, brought their families into the faith.

Arguments against infant baptism

The argument *against* infant baptism rests upon a few basic foundations: A) rejection of the doctrine of original sin by certain groups, such as the Church of Christ, B) the absence of any direct mention of infant baptism in Scripture, and C) the idea that baptism must be preceded by *repentance* (Acts 2:38), *belief* (Mark 16:16), and *confession of faith* (Romans 10:9), which are surely actions which are beyond the ability of a newborn.

Original sin is discussed in an earlier chapter, so moving on to the second point, it is true that there are no direct references to infant baptism in Scripture. There are *indirect* references, to be discussed later, and there are certainly no places where Scripture directly forbids the baptism of infants and children. It shouldn't be any surprise to us, though, that in the early Church the overwhelming majority of the Christians baptized were adults, or that Scripture only directly mentions the baptism of adults. After all, if Christians were to team up to convert all Muslims, for example, *would we show up at the daycares?* Of course not. Even if we all came to an agreement that infant baptism was necessary, we would still aim our efforts at the heads of the households, those who steered the faith of the entire family. Our efforts would look strikingly similar to the efforts one sees in the New Testament.

Still, how could one justify infant baptism if Scripture makes clear that baptism must be preceded by repentance, belief, and confession of faith? The simple answer is that forgiveness of sins is not the *only* effect of baptism. This sacramental act accomplishes three things:

- Baptism removes the stain of original sin through burial with Christ (Romans 6:4) an infusion of sanctifying grace

209

(1 Cor 6:11) and an indwelling of the Holy Spirit (John 1:33, 3:5, Matthew 3:11);

* Baptism cleans an individual of actual sin Acts 2:37-38;
* Baptism serves as a mark of initiation into Christian faith.

The baptisms that we witness in the New Testament appear to be performed on adults. This means, of course, that the baptized have come from non-Christian backgrounds. For these individuals, *repentance* was necessary because of the sinful lives they lead apart from the guidance of the Holy Spirit. *Belief* was essential to establish a break from the false gods of their pagan (in many cases) background or from a superficial devotedness to worldly things. And, of course, *confession of belief* was a testimony to the completeness and whole-heartedness of the conversion.

For adults.

Children below the age of reason, however, would have no need of repentance or of a rejection of a former beliefs. However, even with children, baptism is necessary for removing original sin, infusing sanctifying grace and initiating them into the Christian faith. After all, by claiming that one must be of the age of reason to be baptized, aren't we putting salvation in our hands, instead of in the sovereign hands of God? In Jeremiah 31:33, under the New Covenant, God would write his law "in their inward parts, and write it in their hearts." *Does God need us at the age of reason for this?* John the Baptist was filled with the Holy Spirit while he still remained in his mother's womb (Luke 1:15).

The circumcision of the heart

To truly understand Christian baptism, one must put himself into the mind of a first century Jew. After all, the New Testament was largely written to a Jewish audience (and also to a first-century Gentile audience, which would have understood the culture and customs of the Jews). In doing so, one verse in particular would stand out glaringly in a study of baptism. In Col 2:11-12, Paul writes, "In him also you were circumcised with a circumcision made without hands, by putting off the body of flesh in the circumcision of Christ; and you were buried with him in baptism, in which you were also raised with him through faith in the working of God, who raised him from the dead."

Paul, therefore, draws a sharp parallel between baptism and circumcision (the circumcision of the heart). At first glance, this makes absolutely no sense. After all, circumcision is a surgical removal of part of the body (a very sensitive part) as an initiation into the faith. Wouldn't an introduction into Christianity be better described as a "renewal" of the heart or a "washing" of the heart, as it is in other places? How does the idea of circumcision, an Old Testament ritual of mutilation, help us understand baptism? How could it capture of the idea of sanctification through baptism?

To a Jew, it would have made perfect sense.

Under the Old Covenant, circumcision was marked by four attributes: A) it was performed on males only, B) it was a mark of initiation into the covenant, C) it was performed on infants in *anticipation of the faith*, and D) it was performed on adult converts, following *repentance and belief in the Israelite God*.

Notice attribute C. Adult conversions to Judaism had to be preceded by a rejection of the sinful and false lifestyle from which the convert had come. However, infants were also circumcised in "anticipation" of the faith, just as infants under the New Covenant are baptized in anticipation of their parents' faith. Infants were circumcised as a mark of initiation into the covenant, for the same reason Christian infants are baptized today. Remember, Christ did not come to abolish the Old Law, but to fulfill it (Matt 5:17). Given the connection that Paul draws between circumcision and baptism, we should not assume differences that are not directly spelled out in Scripture. For that reason, one might be tempted to conclude

211

that because only men were circumcised, only men would be baptized; but the New Testament makes clear that this sacrament is available to all (Acts 8:12; 14:15-16). Further, speaking of baptism, Paul writes that there is no "male and female" (Gal 3:28).

The New Testament was not meant to be an exposition of Christianity "from scratch". Rather, the revelation brought by Christ Jesus builds upon and clarifies that which was revealed in the Old.

Whole families were baptized

The next step in understanding infant baptism is to visit Paul and Silas as they pray and sing hymns among the jailors in Acts 16. After a great earthquake, which opened the doors to the prison, the jailor woke and prepared to kill himself, thinking the prisoners had escaped. Upon hearing Paul's voice, however, he fell before them and asked, "Men, what must I do to be saved?" The answer is remarkable. "Believe in the Lord Jesus," Paul and Silas tell him, "And you will be saved, you *and your household.*" Now, as it turns out, everyone in the jailor's family appears to have been old enough to appreciate the message preached by the two disciples.

Yet Paul and Silas did not know this. They did not ask him how old his family was. They didn't even tell him that his family had to believe before being saved. The faith of the jailor, the head of the household, would have been sufficient to bring the entire family into the faith. It is a nice coincidence that everyone in his family was of the age of reason, but Paul and Silas were apparently not working on this assumption when they made the promise of salvation to the jailor's entire family. It was through *his* belief that they would be saved.

Entire households were baptized during the first century: 1 Cor 1:16 (Stephanas), Acts 14:15-16 (Lydia), Acts 18:8 (Crispus), and Acts 10:47-48 (Cornelius). In biblical times, a "household" included one's spouse and children, as well as any servants and their children.

For those who believe that baptism should be reserved to those who are of the age of reason, one of the most commonly cited proof-texts is Acts 8:12, which reads, "But when they [Samarians] believed Philip as he preached good news about the kingdom of God and the name of Jesus Christ, they were baptized, both men and women." On face value, this seems to support adult baptism. However, just as in the case of similar verses (Acts 2:41), where many adults were baptized, we have to remember that the *primary* objective of the apostles was to convert the heads of the households, who would then return and have their families baptized at the newly established local churches.

What of children who die before baptism?

If baptism is necessary for salvation, then what happens to infants who die before receiving this sacrament? Christians who intend to raise their children in Christ have an obligation to see them baptized, equipping them fully to mature into acceptance of Christ and a life of sanctification.

Of those who do not get baptized, revelation has not been given, but we can make some guesses based on what we know about salvation. For one, infants are not guilty of personal sin, so they have not earned eternity in Hell. Some conclude that God simply has mercy on the unbaptized children, bringing them into Heaven. Others have speculated of a location called "Limbo," which is a state of natural happiness, but different from the supernatural happiness in Heaven. Limbo was never a doctrine, but a theory, so Catholics are not bound to believe in it. Another possibility is that, at the moment of death, God gives the infant soul a mature intellect and understanding of his plan for salvation and offers him the chance to accept or reject it.

But for those infants who have the opportunity for baptism, there is no age limit on the infusion of grace and the indwelling of the Holy Spirit. This gift is not restricted by some arbitrary age of reason. "Repent and be baptized, every one of you, in the name of Jesus Christ for the forgiveness of your sins; and you will receive the gift of the Holy Spirit," Peter proclaims in Acts 2:38-39. "For the promise is made to you *and to your children* and to all those far off, whomever the Lord our God will call."

Summary:

- Infant baptism is rejected by groups who do not believe in original sin, and also because no direct examples of infant baptism appear in Scripture;
- Scripture seems to indicate that one must be able to repent and believe before being able to be baptized, but this applied only to adult converts;
- Baptism is the circumcision of the heart, so we can learn about baptism by studying the way circumcision was administered;
- In the New Testament, whole families were baptized, as parents brought their children into the faith;
- God's mercy offers hope for children who die before being baptized.

31

BAPTISM BY POURING
AND SPRINKLING

"Concerning baptism, baptize in this manner: Having said all these things beforehand, baptize in the name of the Father and of the Son and of the Holy Spirit in living water [that is, in running water, as in a river]. If there is no living water, baptize in other water; and, if you are not able to use cold water, use warm. If you have neither, pour water three times upon the head in the name of the Father, Son, and Holy Spirit."
-Didache, 70 AD

There are some Christian groups that insist that baptism is only valid if it is through a full immersion in water, and they reject baptism by pouring or sprinkling.

There is one primary reason for the strict immersion-only rule in some churches. Baptism symbolizes our death and burial with Christ (Rom 6:3-5; Col 2:12), from which we are born again, so some Protestant groups insist that it must resemble an actual burial in that the water completely swallows us, as would the earth when we are finally laid to rest. Outside of this reasoning, there is actually little Scriptural evidence to support the idea that full immersion is the only valid way to baptize. Some groups point to Scripture that appears to indicate examples of immersion baptism. For instance, after Jesus was baptized in the Jordan, he went "up straightway out of the water" (Matt 3:16), which some groups take to imply that he had gone "down" into the water to begin with. When Philip baptized the Ethiopian "they went down both into the water" and then came "up out of the water" (Acts 8:38-39).

Other arguments for immersion-only baptism include the claim that the very word baptism (from the Greek *baptizo*) means, according to those who reject pouring and sprinkling, "to dip, to plunge, or to immerse."

Now, especially considering how weak the Scriptural evidence is for immersion, there are some fundamental problems with the immersion-only philosophy. First, as Catholics we absolutely accept immersion as valid. Indeed, the above verses support immersion and many of our Catholic church buildings have pools designed for this. We also accept as valid any baptism from another church as long as it meets two criteria: it must involve water and it must be done in the Trinitarian formula (Matt 28:19). Mormons and Oneness Pentecostals, for instance, do not believe in the Trinity, so their baptisms are not validly done in the name of the Father, Son and Holy Spirit.

What are the objections?

That said, we need to examine the Scriptural evidence and address the three main points in the immersion-only argument:

Objection: Baptism must model a burial with Christ. Catholic response: We are indeed buried with Christ in baptism, but that is not the only thing that baptism accomplishes. In addition, the Holy Spirit is "poured" upon us (Acts 2:17, 18, 33), resulting in an infusion of sanctifying grace. In Matthew 3:16, the Holy Spirit descends upon Jesus' head like a dove and upon Mary and the apostles in Acts 2:3-4, fulfilling Joel's prophecy that the

Lord will pour out his Spirit upon us (2:28). In an Old Testament "type" of baptism, the Lord "pours" water on the thirsty land and "pours" his Spirit upon our descendants (Isa 44:3). If baptism through immersion symbolizes burial with Christ, does not the pouring of water appropriately express the pouring of the Spirit?

Sprinkling is not practiced as much in the Roman rite of the Catholic Church, but some of the Eastern rites practice it. Either way, the Scriptural support is just as strong. In Ezekiel 36:25, Ezekiel prophesies that God will "sprinkle" clean water on you and you shall be clean. This is reaffirmed in the New Testament, where the author of Hebrews (10:22) writes, "with our hearts sprinkled clean from an evil conscience."

Sure, baptism is a burial with Christ, but it is also a pouring upon us of the Holy Spirit, and sprinkling of God's cleansing grace. Scripture nowhere tells us that immersion is the only form of baptism, but instead supports all three modes of water purification.

Objection: "Baptizo" means "to dip, to plunge, or to immerse." Catholic response: Actually, this is just untrue. "Baptizo" also means a ritual cleansing. For instance, in Numbers 19:18, the verbs for dipping and sprinkling are "baptisantes" and "bapsei." Concrete examples can be seen in Mark 7:3, where the Pharisees do not eat unless they wash ("baptizo") their hands, which did not mean immersion, but a pouring of water over the hands. The Jews also washed ("bapto") cups, pitchers, and vessels (Mark 7:4); some manuscripts say the Jews washed ("bapto") couches, yet this surely did not mean dragging a couch to the Jordan and dunking it. Finally, Jesus washed ("ebaptishthe") his hands before dinner (Luke 11:38), which would have been a pouring of water and wiping clean. To have fully immersed, without indoor plumbing, would have contaminated an entire container of water. The trips to the River or well would never end.

Objection: Scripture refers to people going "down into" the water or coming "up from" it. Catholic response: This only indicates (and Catholics would agree) that baptism by immersion is valid. However, there is evidence to indicate that baptism by pouring or sprinkling also took place. For instance, the book of Acts gives numerous examples that appear to describe people being baptized in houses: Paul in the house of Ananias (Acts 9:18), Peter baptizing in the house of Cornelius (Acts 10:47-48). As there were no hot tubs, swimming pools, or bathtubs in these houses, pouring and sprinkling are the only explanations. In addition, in Acts 2:41, at Peter's first sermon, 3,000 were baptized. Immersion would have been impossible in this area, especially for so many people. Most likely, a baptism of sprinkling took place.

The evidence for baptism by pouring and sprinkling is just as strong as that for immersion. In addition, one only needs to ask the question: if baptism is only valid through immersion, does this mean that people confined to hospital beds or to life-support systems are to be deprived of this wonderful source of grace? God would never have designed so necessary a sacrament if the least among us would have faced such limitations in accessing it.

Whether by immersion, sprinkling or pouring, the grace of God is abound in the cleansing waters of baptism.

Summary:

- **Since the early Church, baptism has been valid through immersion, sprinkling and pouring;**
- **While baptism through immersion represents being buried with Christ, sprinkling and pouring also have biblical symbolism attached to them;**
- **Practical limitations would have prevented baptism by immersion in many biblical examples.**

32

SORRY DOESN'T HAVE TO BE
THE HARDEST WORD:
CONFESSION

*"Such are the words and deeds by which, in our own district of the Rome,
they have deluded many women, who have their consciences seared as with
a hot iron. Some of them, indeed, make a public confession of their sins;
but others of them are ashamed to do this, and in a tacit kind of way,
despairing of [attaining to] the life of God, have, some of them,
apostatized altogether; while others hesitate between the two courses, and
incur that which is implied in the proverb, 'neither without nor within',
possessing this as the fruit from the seed of the children of knowledge."*
-Irenaeus, Against Heresies, 1:13 (AD 180)

Peter denied Christ three times, with apparent impunity. Then his Savior laid eyes on him through the crowd, and at that point, Peter wept (Luke 22:61).

The last few chapters have looked at how the sacraments are physical signs that effect a spiritual reality. In baptism, for instance, God uses the symbolism of being washed to actually cause our souls to be washed clean. Likewise, when we go to confession, Christ understood that our human nature responds best to actually hearing another human voice tell us, on Christ's behalf, that we are forgiven. Peter was able to deny Christ very easily until he made eye contact with him. As Peter experienced, there is something about interaction with another human being that bring us to a level of humility and repentance that we otherwise do not experience.

Sometimes a Christian can convince himself that his sins are too awful to tell another person, or are too trivial to bother with at all. But whatever the secret reasons one might stay away from the confessional, the universal excuse is one we have all heard, if not used ourselves: *why should I confess to some man when I can confess straight to God, Himself?*

The simple answer is *because God wants us to do it that way.*

Scripture is filled with calls to repentance (Luke 13:3-5; Acts 2:38), and Paul warns that to receive the Eucharist without acknowledging one's wrongdoings is to eat and drink damnation (1 Cor 11:27-29). In other words, to receive the body and blood of Christ as Mass, without first confessing our sins in the way Christ instituted, is to go more deeply into sin.

If we acknowledge our sins, our faithful and just God will forgive them and cleanse us (1 John 1:9). A Catholic can and should confess "straight to God," but Scripture affirms that a necessary part of that process is to articulate mortal sins to a priest.

To begin, the Old Testament set the precedent that individuals must confess their sins and receive absolution through a priest (Lev 5:5-6). In the New Testament, Christ took this practice and elevated it with a sacramental character. In the Gospel of John, Christ breathes into His disciples. It is one of only two times that God breathes the Holy Spirit into man, the first time being at the creation of human life. Jesus then tells the apostles that those sins which they forgive are forgiven and those sins which they retain are retained (20:23). Many Christians wonder where confession is in the Bible, but it couldn't be more clear than in this passage, where Christ prepares to go to Heaven by giving his apostles the power to forgive on his behalf.

As the apostles were not granted the ability to read minds, it logically follows that in order to decide what sins to forgive or retain, they would need those sins confessed to them, and from the earliest days of the Church, for 2,000 years, Christians have confessed their sins in a Church.

Christ gave man the power to forgive sins. Paul refers to this gift as the "ministry of reconciliation" (2 Cor 5:18). There is only one mediator between God and man, which is the standard objection that is used against this sacrament. However, Paul and others who administer grace act "in the person of Christ" when pardoning others, allowing God to work through them, not replacing him as a mediator.

In addition, when an individual sins, even privately, damage is done to the entire body of Christ. The priest stands, therefore, in the person of Christ, but also as a representative of all of mankind so that we can fully follow the instructions in James to confess our sins to one another (Jas 5:16).

Objections to the sacrament of Confession

Despite the strong Scriptural support for this sacrament, many objections remain for why individuals neglect confession:

The priest is a sinner just like I. Who is he to offer forgiveness for my sins? Even a chain-smoking, overweight doctor can prescribe the medicine and lifestyle that heals, even if he doesn't follow his own advice. The grace of reconciliation comes from God, and works through the priest, despite his personal sins.

Christ earned forgiveness for all of our sins on the cross. However, the prayer He taught in the gospels teaches the faithful disciple to continue *asking* for forgiveness (Matt 6:9-13). That forgiveness, though Christ's one-time act, is given throughout the life of an individuals as long as he remains receptive.

God already knows my sins, so it seems silly to have to confess them. The act of articulating one's sins is not done for God's sake, but ours. The sacraments give a confidence of God's grace that we would not otherwise find isolated from them. In addition, Christ created this sacrament because he understood that, as a creature that is spiritual *and* physical, mankind needs a physical sign by which to interact with a spiritual gift. When a man tells another about the worst of what he has done, there is a powerful humility and a moment of spiritual clarity. Through the priest, a Christian has the opportunity to weep with Peter as he makes amends with Christ and hears the soft words of forgiveness in the quiet interruption of a busy and hectic world.

Penance is required for sins

When an individual sins, he incurs both an eternal and temporal consequence. David's baby died because of adultery even after he was forgiven (2 Sam 12:11-14); God forgave Moses, but refused him entry into promised land after Moses doubted him (Num 20:12, Deut 34:4).

Once of the temporal consequences is that the sinner forms attachments to those sins and his resistance to them breaks down. Someone who shoplifts once or twice finds it easier to do it again. Those who have neglected prayer for television eventually find it harder to break from their favorite shows for a moment with God.

Breaking from these attachments to temporal things calls for training ourselves in righteousness, which is the work of penance. Sometimes this might even be uncomfortable, but this is only a sign that we are being cleansed (Prov 20:30; Heb 12:5-6; 1 Peter 4:1). The good acts one does after the sacrament of reconciliation has nothing to do with forgiveness – that was already given in the confessional. Rather, penance helps us "drive and train" ourselves so that we are not disqualified (1 Cor 9:27). Because sin has caused us to form an attachment to the vices in our life, penance is designed to help us form attachments to virtues to replace them.

Summary:

- Forgiveness ultimately comes from God, but he authorized the leaders of his Church to forgive in his name;

- The power of the sacrament is effective regardless of the worth of the individual man administering it;

- Forgiveness through a priest does not set up another mediator instead of Christ, who often uses human instruments to distribute his grace;

- Penance is the means by which, after receiving forgiveness, we work to train ourselves to break from these sins.

33

ONWARD CHRISTIAN SOLDIER: CONFIRMATION

"And about your laughing at me and calling me 'Christian,' you know not what you are saying. First, because that which is anointed is sweet and serviceable, and far from contemptible. For what ship can be serviceable and seaworthy, unless it be first caulked [anointed]? Or what castle or house is beautiful and serviceable when it has not been anointed? And what man, when he enters into this life or into the gymnasium, is not anointed with oil? And what work has either ornament or beauty unless it be anointed and burnished? Then the air and all that is under heaven is in a certain sort anointed by light and spirit; and are you unwilling to be anointed with the oil of God? Wherefore we are called Christians on this account, because we are anointed with the oil of God."
-Theophilus of Antioch, To Autolycus, I:12 (AD 181) ."

We live in a society that values independence and personal accountability. Personal freedom is a frequent rally cry in politics, so it isn't surprising to see a similar trend in religious thought. Sometimes parents will make the decision that they will not force their child into one religion or another, but let him decide for himself. And if parents do not hold this attitude, society certainly does, to the extent that many young men and women raised in the Catholic faith choose not to partake in the sacrament of confirmation.

I was one of these teens who, when time for confirmation came in 11th grade, decided that I did not want to be a Catholic, so I had no intention of *confirming* myself as a Catholic. Now, as an adult involved in Catholic education, not a year goes by that I do not hear of a number of teens making the same decision.

Confirmation is a strengthening of the Spirit within us

As adults, parents and teachers, we have dropped the ball here. Confirmation actually has nothing to do with an individual "confirming" whether or not he wants to be Catholic, though adults often explain the sacrament this way. Rather, confirmation refers to God *confirming* the gifts of the Holy Spirit within us.

The gifts of the Holy Spirit are wisdom, understanding, counsel, fortitude, knowledge, piety, and fear of the Lord.[31] When a teen decides he doesn't want to be confirmed, what he is really rejecting are these seven free gifts from God, gifts that will surely equip him to more fully face the challenges of life. Reflecting upon my own teen years, I see the spiritual harm that came to me as I entered into adulthood without a fullness of the gifts that God intended for me.

At baptism, one enters into the family of God and receives sanctifying grace through the Holy Spirit. Some Christians do not recognize confirmation as a sacrament because, if the Holy Spirit comes at baptism, how could we again receive the Spirit at a later time. However, Scripture offers specific examples of individuals who had already been baptized receiving the Holy Spirit through a

---

[31] *Catechism of the Catholic Church*, No. 1831.

laying on of hands (Acts 8:14-17).

This laying on of hands is listed alongside repentance and baptism as an elementary Christian doctrine in Hebrews 6:2. At confirmation one receives a special anointing, bringing him into even more full conformity with Christ. The word *Messiah* means "anointed one." Christ, in reading from Isaiah, recognized himself to have received a special anointing from the Spirit: "The Spirit of the Lord is upon me, because he has anointed me to preach good news to the poor." … And he closed the book, and gave it back to the attendant, and sat down; and the eyes of all in the synagogue were fixed on him. And he began to say to them, "Today this scripture has been fulfilled in your hearing" (Luke 4:14-21).

Christ then promised his believers, the members of his body, an anointing similar to his: "He who believes in me, as the scripture has said, 'Out of his heart shall flow rivers of living water.' Now this he said about the Spirit, which those who believed in him were to receive; for as yet the Spirit had not been given, because Jesus was not yet glorified" (John 7:38-39).

Preparing for battle

At baptism we receive, through the Spirit, entrance into the family of God. At confirmation, we are then given the gifts that allow us to, not only remain in God's favor, but to bring others into faith as well. When a Christian was confirmed decades ago, he received a light slap on the cheek from the bishop as a reminder that the newly confirmed needed to toughen up for the spiritual battle that lay ahead.

Hebrews reminds us that we are in battle with spiritual forces that set out for our destruction, and that we are to arm ourselves with the shield of faith, the armor of God, and the breastplate of righteousness (6:10-17). Through confirmation God equips us for the battle for our salvation and that of others around us.

"Confirmation . . . gives us a special strength of the Holy Spirit to spread and defend the faith by word and action as true witnesses of Christ, to confess the name of Christ boldly, and never to be ashamed of the cross" (CCC 1303).

Summary:

- Confirmation has nothing to do with our "confirming" of our Catholicism, but rather the Holy Spirit confirming his gifts in us;
- Confirmation is the completion of the spiritual gifts we receive at baptism and prepares us to go forth and proclaim the Good News;
- Confirmation is administered through a laying on of hands from an individual qualified to do so, which is a bishop or a priest to whom he delegates this authority.

34

THE SACRIFICE COMPLETED:
THE EUCHARIST

"Well, toward morning the conversation turned on the Eucharist, which I, being the Catholic, was obviously supposed to defend. Mrs. Broadwater said ... she thought of [the Eucharist] as a symbol and implied that it was a pretty good one. I then said, in a very shaky voice, Well, if it's a symbol, to hell with it."

-Flannery O'Connor, The Habit of Being: Letters of Flannery O'Connor

Two disciples on the road to Emmaus encountered a man they did not recognize. They discussed with him the recent death of the Messiah, as well as the reports of his resurrection. It was Christ, himself, who visited with them, but their eyes were prevented from recognizing him in his glorified form. Later, these disciples would report that their hearts burned within them as they read from Scripture. However, as important as Scripture is in the life of a Christian, it was not until Christ broke bread and they ate of it that "their eyes were opened" and they recognized who sat before them (Luke 24:13-35).

What to do with a hard teaching?

Several years ago, I went to visit an Evangelical church where a friend of mine was an associate pastor. In preparation for the Lord's supper, he read the Bread of Life discourse from the sixth chapter of John.

In this passage, after recalling the manna that the Israelites ate in the desert, Christ says of himself, "This is the bread which comes down from heaven; if anyone eats of this bread, he will live forever; and the bread which I shall give for the life of the world is my flesh." . . ." (50-51).

As my friend finished the with the passage, he then addressed the congregation and said, "I have to believe that the disciples listening to Christ back then would have understood that he was speaking figuratively."

I wish he would have kept reading, as John describes exactly what the disciples believed about his strange words: "The Jews then disputed among themselves, saying, 'How can this man give us his flesh to eat?'" (52).

The Jews were obviously taking him literally, so if Christ meant these words to be figurative, he should have clarified at this point. Rather, he continues, "Truly, truly, I say to you, unless you eat the flesh of the Son of man and drink his blood, you have no life in you; he who eats my flesh and drinks my blood has eternal life, and I will raise him up at the last day" (53-54).

Finally, the disciples complain that his words are "hard teaching," which makes no sense if he is speaking figuratively. In addition, in verse 66 John tells us that many "drew back" and stopped following Christ.

Over a symbol? If Christ were speaking figuratively, why didn't he stop them? Why didn't he call out, "Hey, it's just a metaphor, come back." Rather, he lets them walk away because they have chosen not to accept his clear teaching.

Earlier in John 6, Christ multiplies the loaves, showing the power that God has over a few pieces of bread, and then he walks on water, showing he can do anything with his own body, both of which introduce the beautiful teaching that Christ give us his own body, transformed through the consecration of the bread, to consume, that we might have eternal life through him.

As Catholics, the term we use for the transformation from bread and wine to body and blood is "transubstantiation." By transubstantiation, we mean that the substance of the bread and wine changes, becoming the body of Christ, but that the "accidents," which is a word that refers to the appearance and physical properties of the bread and wine, remain the same. That is, even examined under a microscope, the body and blood would retain the appearance of bread and wine, just as they retain the taste. God understands that the Eucharist needs to be presented to us in a way that would be acceptable for us to receive orally. Second, while the Eucharist is not merely a symbol, its form serves a symbolic purpose. By receiving Christ in the appearance of bread and wine, we remember that he is the true source of nourishment. Sacraments are spiritual realities presented through physical signs.

Some non-Catholics point out that in verse 63, Christ says that "it is the spirit that gives life, the flesh is of no avail ..." They use this verse to argue that Christ is saying that he is present in spirit, not flesh, in the Eucharist. However, if Christ really meant that *his* flesh were of no avail, then his death upon the cross would have been meaningless. All he was saying here is that *our* flesh alone can accomplish nothing, as he clarifies in John 3:5 by saying that anything "born of flesh is flesh, and that which is born of Spirit is spirit." In both instances, Christ is contrasting the natural with the supernatural.

Christ's words in John 6 are echoed strongly by Paul, who writes to the Corinthians, "The cup of blessing that we bless, is it not a participation in the blood of Christ? The bread that we break, is it not a participation in the body of Christ?" (10:16-17). In the next chapter, verse 27, Paul shows us just how important it is that we recognize that Christ is present in the Eucharistic meal: "For anyone who eats and drinks without discerning the body eats and drinks judgment upon himself." Paul goes on to write that many are sick and some have died because of their casual attitude toward the Eucharist (30).

Throughout Scripture Christ fulfills the "type" (or symbol) of the paschal lamb, which the Israelites offered during Passover. Just as the lamb was sacrificed as a sin offering, Christ was sacrificed for our sins. The lamb's bones could not be broken, and Christ died before the soldiers could break his bones. The lamb's blood was spread on the doorposts so that the angel of death would "pass over" the homes of the Israelites, and Christ's blood was shed on the "post" so that we would not die spiritually. Of course, to conclude the Passover meal, the lamb had to be consumed. Likewise, Christ offers his body and blood for our consumption through the Eucharist.

The marriage analogy

While the paschal mystery helps explain the Eucharist, the analogy of marriage, which explains much of salvation, can be applied powerfully here. Paul writes about the role of Christ as our bridegroom in Ephesians:

Husbands, love your wives, as Christ loved the church and gave himself up for her, that he might sanctify her, having cleansed her by the washing of water with the word, that he might present the Church to himself in splendor, without spot or wrinkle or any such thing, that she might be holy and without blemish. Even so husbands should love their wives as

231

their own bodies. He who loves his wife loves himself. For no man ever hates his own flesh, but nourishes and cherishes it, as Christ does the Church, because we are members of his body. "For this reason a man shall leave his father and mother and be joined to his wife, and the two shall become one flesh." This is a great mystery, and I mean in reference to Christ and the Church (5:25-33).

Through his death upon the cross, Christ gave himself fully to his Church, and each of us is made without stain or wrinkle through the process of sanctification. Paul specifically brings in the language of Genesis to emphasize that, through marriage, a man and women become one flesh. This happens most perfectly in the marital act, when the husband physically joins with his spouse. Sexual interaction between spouses is a temporal thing – a way that physical creatures model the unity of God. We shouldn't think of our relationship with Christ in those terms. However, he *does* unite himself most completely with a Christian through the Eucharist by entering into the body of the believer.

Oftentimes Catholics are asked, "Have you received Christ as your personal Lord and Savior?" Understanding, now, the gift that Christ has offered through the Eucharist, we can answer, "Yes! But more than that, I receive my Lord and Savior, body, blood, soul, and divinity each and every time I partake of the holy Eucharist."

Was Christ just being figurative?

One of the things that non-Catholics are most surprised about when they really begin studying our faith is how literally Catholics take much of Scripture. In three of the Gospels, Christ is recorded to have said of the bread, "This IS my body, which will be given up for you ..." (Luke 22:19, Matt 26:26, and Mark 14:22). Notice that Christ does not say, "This represents my body." Modern scholars have found over three dozen ways Jesus could have expressed that his words were symbolic, but he chose to speak in very direct terms.

Often, however, when Catholics bring these verses to the attention to someone who does not believe in the true presence of Christ in the Eucharist, the conversation goes something like this:

Catholic: "Christ says, 'This is my body'. Why can't we take him at his word?

Non-Catholic: "Because Christ also calls himself a vine (John 15:1) and a door (John 10:7), among other things. Are we to believe he is actually a plant or a thing on hinges?

It's interesting to see how an otherwise literalist student of the Bible suddenly turns figurative when it comes to reconciling his rejection of a distinctly Catholic doctrine.

The point such a person would be making, of course, is that Christ often spoke in metaphors to help his followers understand the full scope of his being. Why, the non-Catholic might ask, should we believe that the Last Supper discourse is any different?

To give fair consideration to this perspective, here are several more "things" that God (in the person of Christ or otherwise) compares himself to through inspired Scripture:

The Branch (Zech. 3:8)
The Bright and Morning Star (Rev 22:16)
The Chief Corner Stone (Eph 2:20; 1Pet 2:7)
An Eagle (Deut 32:11)
A Fountain (Zech. 13:1)
The Lamb (John 1:29; Rev 5:6)
The Rock (1 Cor 10:4)

There's something of a verbal sleight-of-hand trick happening when non-Catholics try to equate the institution of the Eucharist to

Christ's many metaphorical statements about himself.

A metaphor works this way: the subject of the sentence is joined by a linking verb to a seemingly different predicate nominative, which reflectively describes something unique about the subject. A literal truth about the predicate nominative describes a figurative truth about the subject. For instance, in the sentence, "My dad is an ox," the subject (dad) is probably big and hairy, given his resemblance to the predicate nominative (ox). It is important to note that, given the structure of a metaphor, "ox" is describing "dad," not the other way around. The ox weighs nearly a thousand pounds and is covered from head to foot with fur; my dad is only figuratively an ox in that his size and hair exceed that of the average person. To understand it more clearly, one can take the metaphor and turn it into a simile by adding "like" or "as": My dad is like an ox.

The simile approach emphasizes that it is impossible to flip the comparison around without changing the meaning outright. "My dad is like an ox" becomes weird when we flip it to say, "An ox is like my dad."

Let's take the metaphors of Scripture and state them in simple declarative sentences (using the generic "God" to simplify the process):

God is a vine.
God is a door.
God is the branch.
God is the bright and morning star.
God is the chief corner stone.
God is an eagle.
God is a fountain.
God is the lamb.
God is the rock.

Now, notice the problem when we look at the institution of

the Eucharist:

This [bread] is my body.

Or, to make the comparison easier, substitute the word "God" for the words "my body":

This [bread] is God.

Or, to be specific:

This [bread] is Jesus.

It would make no sense to flip the comparison (unless one's grammar resembles that of Yoda):

A vine is God.
A door is God.
A rock is God.
A lamb is God.

These last four don't make sense because, in the figurative examples above, God is always the subject. The predicate nominatives describe qualities of God. God is a source of life, like a vine. He is our entrance into Heaven, like a door. He is the foundation of our faith, like a "rock" or "cornerstone." He was sacrificed for us, like a lamb.

This is how metaphors work, which is why it is silly to claim that Christ is speaking figuratively in the last supper narrative, when "God" or "my body" becomes the predicate nominative. To do so would mean that we are using the divine figuratively to describe a literal truth about the bread. How is this possible? Is the bread in anyway omniscient? Omnipotent? Omnipresent? To illustrate, let's turn our "metaphors" into similes:

God is like a rock. Makes sense.
God is like a lamb. Makes sense.

God is like a vine. Makes sense.
God is like a door. Makes sense.
This bread is like God. Huh?

Even the original text would fail this test (This [bread] is like my body). The reason? By putting God as the predicate nominative, the metaphor serves to exalt bread to something divine by comparison. This makes no sense and has no place in the unity of Scripture unless

Unless it wasn't meant to be figurative ...

Which would mean it was literal ...

Which would mean that the bread isn't bread anymore.

Summary:

- Christ tells us that the host is his body and we are to eat of it to receive eternal life;
- Some disciples rejected Christ's teaching as being too hard to accept, but he did not water it down to prevent them from walking away;
- Christ's death was a fulfillment of the Old Testament sacrifice, which called for the victim to be consumed;
- Christians take Christ into their bodies to become one with him much as a husband becomes one with his wife;
- Christ's words cannot be interpreted figuratively without having to twist the meaning of what he said.

35

TWO BECOME ONE: MARRIAGE

"Marriage is an act of will that signifies and involves a mutual gift, which unites the spouses and binds them to their eventual souls, with whom they make up a sole family - a domestic church."
-John Paul II Love and Responsibility, *1981*

There was this girl I dated when I was just out of high school. It would be fair to say we had ... *different* views on what should happen between two people who were dating. I remember intentionally popping a CD of "Only the Good Die Young" into my car CD play, hoping that, if I couldn't convince her, maybe Billy Joel could: *Come on, Virginia, don't make me wait. You Catholic girls start much too late.*

Eventually the values of this girl, now my wife, won out over that of a young man whose creed was indifference and whose understanding of marriage was formed by a culture of self-interest.

In *Genesis*, the creation story explains how God, in order to give man companionship, removed Adam's rib and formed woman, to which Adam responded, "This one, at last, is bone of my bones and flesh of my flesh" (2:23). The Church acknowledges that some details of the creation story can be taken figuratively, but the account of Adam and Eve makes clear that man and woman are different, yet complimentary.

God provided companionship for man because we have a deep longing within us. Marriage is a partial answer to this. Ultimately, however, our hearts are really calling out for our eternal unity with God, which is why even the best of marriages do not completely elevate us above occasional loneliness or temptations.

Within a culture that has lost sight of God as our final end, many are confused by the longing and desires they feel within themselves and try to answer them through pornography, extramarital relationships or Billy Joel CDs.

Paul emphasized that marriage and sex helped individuals overcome lack of self-control (1 Cor 7:5). This is true, but even more than that, Christ elevated marriage to the level of a sacrament. As discussed earlier, the sacraments are physical signs that communicate and cause spiritual realities. Too many think of marriage as just a way that two people who love each other decide to spend the rest of their lives together. The problem with this is that when the love appears to have faded, there often doesn't seem to be reason to continue being married.

True marriage must be viewed as a way for two people to grow closer to God through a sacrament. Scripture tells us that Christ is the bridegroom and is *married* to the Church (Eph 5:25-27). When a husband and wife get married, they should do so with the intent to model Christ and his Church. God sees it as pleasing that individuals would model their lives after Christ and the Church, so when a couple marries, he gives them certain graces that help them to grow closer to Christ. Marriage provides spiritual assistance that does not come when two people just sleep together.

Is marriage only between a man and a woman?

Christ instituted marriage very specifically to be between a man and a woman as a model of his marriage to the Church. So, anything other than that is a counterfeit that distorts the model. This is one of the reasons that homosexual relationships cannot be sacramental marriages – it would offend God to create a symbol that suggests that Christ is married to himself, as would happen in the case of two men in a relationship.

Another important component of marriage is the physical intimacy between a husband and wife, the means by which "two become one." An analogy would be taking a chair and cutting it in half. The two halves, taken from one whole, form a unity when combined. However, taking the left side from two different chairs does not produce a unity at all. In forming this unity, a man and woman model the creative aspect of God by loving each other so intensely that this love actually becomes another human life. Sexual relationships outside of marriage, homosexual or heterosexual, are sinful because they take a component of Christ's sacrament and try to use it for purely carnal or emotional reasons.

The Church is labeled as "homophobic" for articulating her traditional teachings on marriage. Many Catholics have gone so far as to reject these teachings, concluding that the Church just needs to catch up with the times.

There are plenty of verses condemning homosexuality (Lev 18:22, 20:13; Rom 1:26–28, 32; 1 Cor 6:9–10). But Catholics can take a different approach, one that introduces a much more respectful dialogue with others.

Rather than engaging in a scavenger hunt for the verse that tells us what marriage isn't, the much more powerful approach is to see what Scripture tells us marriage *is*, understanding that everything else is a counterfeit.

Should wives submit to their husbands?

My own favorite verse in the Bible is Ephesians 5:22, which commands wives to submit to their husbands. This means, of course, that if I wake up at two in the morning and am hungry, my wife has to fix me something to eat or she goes to Hell!

Of course, this isn't what Paul was saying, but many reject this verse without really trying to dig into the meaning of an otherwise beautiful passage. In the previous verse, Paul actually begins by saying that husbands and wives should submit to one another. When he does ask wives, specifically, to give submission to their husbands, he writes that a husband is head of the household in the same way that Christ is the head of the Church.

So, far from being able to command his wife to obey his every command, a husband is to exercise his headship in the model of Christ. Christ did not order those around him to tend to his every need. Rather, he served others (John 13:1-17), protected the helpless (John 7:53-8:11), and sacrificed himself for those he loves.

Husbands, too, are called to serve, protect and sacrifice themselves for their families, and their wives are called to submit to that. The word "submission" implies that a woman is to put herself under ("sub") the mission of her husband as a Christ-figure.

Divorce and annulments

Tragically the divorce rate among Catholics is comparable to the rate among secular society. The Church recognizes legitimate reasons to divorce, such as abuse, addition and infidelity, but these reasons make up only a fraction of the broken marriages in our culture today, and none of these situations, in and of themselves, give a green light to remarriage. It is one thing to say that, for her safety, a woman should leave an abusive husband. It is another to say that by doing so she has dissolved the sacramental bond.

Scripture is very clear that marriage is a union joined by God, not man. It lasts until the death of at least one spouse. For this reason, man has no authority to dissolve it (Matt 19:6). Man and woman become "one" flesh (Gen 2:20-24), and God uses his prophet Malachi to state his hatred for divorce (2:16).

Those who secure a civil divorce have done nothing to dissolve the sacramental bond, which means that they are still married in the eyes of God. This is why Christ and the inspired authors make clear that to divorce and then remarry another is adultery (Matt 19:9; Mark 10:11-12; Luke 16:18; Rom 7:2-3).

Some Protestant groups permit divorce based on Matthew 5:31-32, which permits it in the case of "*porneia*," the Greek word which some interpret as unchastity. However, the word is usually used in reference to incest, but in either case there is no mentioned allowance for remarriage. In his first letter to the Corinthians, Paul does permit remarriage in the case of two unbaptized people, if one of them becomes baptized (7:12-15).

While the Catholic Church does not allow divorce and remarriage (following the biblical example), some refer to annulments as "Catholic divorces," as if Catholics have simply created a loophole that isn't supported by Scripture.

However, an annulment is not a divorce at all. In what is properly called "declarations of nullity," the Church investigates a relationship to see if the conditions were present for the couple to have been validly married in the first place. For instance, if either of the couple was not fully consenting to the marriage (because of youth or intoxication, for instance), then the marriage was not valid. Other reasons a marriage might be declared null include one of the spouses misleading the other or the couple lying before God, such as promising to bring children into the relationship, with no intent to do so.

The idea of annulment should not really confuse people as

much as it does. Our society understands contracts. I could not enter into a contract with someone who is legally prohibited from doing so, such as trying to hire a lawyer who already represents my opponent or attempting to hire a minor. I would not be legally bound by a contract to someone who deceives me as to his identity or who is mentally incompetent.

Note that an annulment cannot be granted because of something that happens later in the marriage. There must be a reason that the bond never came into existence. While some claim that annulments are just a money-making scam for the Church, many dioceses do not charge for this service, and when they do, the money is used to pay for the expense of the investigation into the claims of the couple, or to fund payroll for the staff of the marriage tribunal, itself. In fact, far from using annulments as a money-making scheme, every diocese loses money on this process.

It may seem to some today that annulments are granted rather flippantly. However, the more likely explanation is that, in today's culture, fewer couples take the sacrament of marriage seriously, so it is much more likely that a greater number of marriages had some impediment to their sacramental nature to begin with.

Summary:
- **God created marriage as a means by which men and women experience unity and bring children into the world;**
- **Christ raised marriage to the level of a sacrament, which means that it is a source of grace and sanctification for the spouses;**
- **Two individuals of the same sex cannot be married, as defined by God;**
- **Divorce does not separate what God has joined together through a sacrament;**
- **Annulments are declarations that no valid marriage took place.**

36

A PRIEST FOREVER:
HOLY ORDERS

"Take care to do all things in harmony with God, with the bishop presiding in the place of God, and with the presbyters in the place of the council of the apostles, and with the deacons, who are most dear to me, entrusted with the business of Jesus Christ, who was with the Father from the beginning and is at last made manifest"
-Ignatius of Antioch, Letter to the Magnesians 2 6:1 (AD 110)

Afew years back I read about a daycare in Stockholm that promoted a genderless environment, where the language, books, and activities were designed to promote complete neutrality in a culture that has long identified a difference between slugs and snails, in little boys, and sugar and spice, in girls.

This overboard political correctness sometimes finds its way into religion, with crusaders for androgyny attempting to revise the "sexism" out of Scripture. But God purposefully created inherent differences in males and females, and not just externally. There is something about being a *husband* that is different from what it means to be a *wife*, and something inherent in masculinity that is suited for fatherhood and that is complementary to the feminine character of motherhood.

And while God is neither male nor female, he very clearly inspired the authors of Scripture to use "he" and "him" as a reference for our "Father," the title that Christ gave us in the model prayer (Matt 6:9-13). Something about fatherhood symbolized what God wanted us to understand about his relationship to us. Christ himself was incarnated as a male and selected males as his apostles, and the Church has always ordained only men to the offices of deacon, priest, and bishop.

In a culture that finds the emergence of gender-neutral daycares, it is no surprise that the Church is often called sexist for only ordaining men. This is certainly an odd claim, considering our view of the *mother* of Christ as worthy of honor greater than any other living person aside from Jesus.

The doctrine that holy orders are reserved for men is far from sexism. Rather, it is the recognition that Christ established the sacraments to have certain form, matter, and ministers. The Eucharist is not celebrated with pizza and chocolate milk, but wheat bread and grape wine. Marriage is between a man and a woman, not two men. Baptism takes place with the pouring of water, not olive oil.

The Church has definitively declared that, because Christ established that holy orders would only be conferred on men, the Church does not have the authority to act otherwise, so women will never be ordained to the priesthood in the Catholic Church.[32]

And, in establishing the priesthood, Christ desired for ministers of his Church to represent him. The maleness of a priest or bishop serves to remind us of Christ, through whom the graces of the Church are earned.

---

[32] *Ordinatio Sacerdotalis*

The New Testament priesthood

In the Old Testament, there were many priests whose offices were temporary, but through the New Covenant, we have a permanent priesthood established in Christ (Heb 7:22-25). And, while Christ is the one mediator of our salvation, he established a ministerial priesthood that participates in the one priesthood of Christ as a body (Rom 12:5; 1 Cor 12:12-27) with Christ as the head (Eph 1:22-23). Fatherhood is a natural priesthood (Jdg 17:10), but the ministerial priesthood is supernatural fatherhood as the ordained priests are fathers in Jesus Christ, as instruments of his grace and truth, for the family of the Church (1 Cor 4:15).

Christ appointed certain men to act as ministers in his place (Jas 5:14; Eph 4:11; 1 Tim 3:1), and gave them the power to administer the sacraments in his place, such as by forgiving sins for him (John. 20:21-23). In the book of James, it is the "elders," or priests, of the Church who anoint and pray over a sick man to forgive his sins (5:13-17).

The authority of the apostles is given first and foremost to the bishops, who are the successors to the apostles. However, as the Church grew, the bishops appointed priests to share in that ministry and to stand in the place of Christ during the Mass. In a bit more limited role, deacons are also anointed to assist bishops and priests in continuing the sacraments as Christ initiated them.

The authority of holy orders has been passed on, through 2,000 years, by the laying on of hands (1 Tim 4:14). A bishop only has sacramental and teaching authority in so far as he has received the laying-on-of hands from other bishops, who in turn received their ordination from other bishops. The line of ordination must be traceable all the way back to the apostles. Likewise, a priest only has authority in so far as he has received it from a properly ordained bishop. In other words, no matter how much an individual might feel as though God is calling him (or her) to the priesthood, simply starting a church and declaring oneself a pastor does not grant the authority that only comes through holy orders.

Celibacy for the Kingdom

It is a sight that has probably confused a few of our parents at the school where I am principal. A man who appears to be a priest, with his black clothes and white color, picks up two kids every day after school.

Those who haven't seen the articles in our diocesan newspaper wouldn't know that our diocese has marked its first ordination of a married man under the "pastoral provision," which allows priests from the Anglican or Episcopalian tradition to receive holy orders after conversion to Catholicism.

The chapter on church disciplines explained that, unlike a male-only priesthood, celibacy is a discipline, not a dogma. This doesn't mean that the practice will universally change anytime soon, or that it should, but it does explain how exceptions like the pastoral provision can exist. The Catholic Church has had married priests for centuries within the Eastern Catholic Churches, which are in full communion with the pope, but who have worship and some disciplines that are shaped by cultural considerations.

Celibacy has a strong biblical foundation. From the Old Testament, when soldiers would refrain from intercourse while at war (1 Sam 21:4) to the new, which reaffirms that a good soldier does not get entangled in civilian pursuits (2 Tim 2:3-4).

We are involved in spiritual warfare, and the leaders of our Church are on the frontlines, which is why Paul recommends celibacy for full-time ministers, as married men would be anxious about things of the world (1 Cor 7:32-35). In addition, the discipline of celibacy allows for a clear sign of spiritual fatherhood over all.

Also in 1 Corinthians, Paul upholds celibacy as the higher vocation (7:38), echoing what the other apostles have concluded (Matt 19:10). Jesus refers to those who remain celibate for the kingdom (Matt 19:11-12). The apostles also appear to have ceased living normal family lives (Matt 19:27-29).

A Protestant friend of mine once commented on her church's search for a new head pastor. They specifically required that, for any applicant to be considered, he must be married and have children. I pointed out that, with those conditions, Jesus and Paul would not be considered!

Does the Bible warn against the celibate priesthood?

Peter was married, as Mark mentions his mother-in-law and Paul seems to indicate that Peter took a wife along with him when he traveled (1 Cor 9:5). But as mentioned, celibacy is a discipline, so this is no threat to the Catholic position. For the great majority of Christianity, bishops and priests have chosen the celibate life.

Another objection to priestly celibacy is that line in 1 Timothy that indicates that a bishop must be the husband of one wife (4:4-5). However, coming from Paul, who was a celibate leader in the Church, we know that he was not commanding that a bishop be married, but that he be married *only* once. It was a restriction, not a command, to prevent bishops from remarrying later in life. Even today, in the eastern rite communities, if a priest's wife dies, he does not remarry.

The final common objection to priestly celibacy is also from Timothy, where Paul warns against groups that forbid marriage. In this instance, Paul was specifically referring to gnostic groups who taught that the flesh was evil, as was marriage. The Church does not believe marriage is evil or restrict anyone from marrying. Rather, priests are generally selected from among those who have already chosen a life of celibacy, those men who have decided that instead of pursuing marriage, they would embrace, in this life, the marriage of Christ to his Church, for which marriage is just a preparation (Matt 22:23-29).

Summary:

- There are distinct differences between males and females;
- In instituting holy orders, Christ saw it as fitting that only men should fill this role;
- Men stand in the person of Christ as the bridegroom of the Church;
- Holy orders include bishops (who are the successors of the apostles), as well as priests and deacons to assist them with local administration;
- Unlike the male-only priesthood, which is doctrine, celibacy is a discipline in the Church;
- Paul and other writers encouraged celibacy, especially for ministers in the Church.

37

OBJECTIONS TO THE CATHOLIC PRIESTHOOD

"Not fornication only, but even marriages make us unfit for ecclesiastical honors; for neither a bishop, nor a presbyter, nor a deacon, nor a widow is able to be twice married"
-Origen, Homilies on Luke (AD 234).

Imagine what the greeting cards would look like if Christ had been speaking literally: *Happy Male Parent's Day!*

In Matthew's gospel, Christ warns not to call any man "your father on earth, for you have one Father, who is in Heaven" (23:9). This is the smoking gun, to many, of the illegitimacy of Catholicism. After all, not only do Catholics call our priests "Father," but even the word "pope" comes from the word *papa*.

Does the Bible forbid calling priests "Father"?

A proof-text taken out of context is a pretext: The Bible is composed of 73 books that make up one whole, with one divine author, the Holy Spirit. When verses are taken out of context, Scripture can be used to support just about anything one desires for it to support. If, after all, it is sinful and offensive to God for individuals to give others the term "father," then the inspired authors are committing this same offense. St. Stephen calls the Jewish leaders "fathers" (Acts 7:2), and St. Paul applies the term to the Jerusalem Jews (Acts 21:40, 22:1). In Romans, Abraham is called "the father of us all" (Rom 4:16-17). In his first epistle, John writes to the elders of the local communities (most likely priests), calling them "fathers" (1 John 2:13-14).

Paul appears to be the worst offender by writing to the Corinthians to tell them that he became their "father in Christ Jesus through the gospel" (1 Cor 4:14-15). In addition to forbidding the use of the term "father," Christ also forbids the terms "master" and "rabbi," which means "teacher." However, both terms are very common in Protestant communities. "Doctor" means "teacher" and the word "mister" is a form of the word "master'. In addition, Sunday school "teachers" are common in many groups. If, then, Catholics are wrong in applying the term "father" to spiritual leaders, we are in pretty good company.

Christ often used hyperbole in making a point: Earlier in Matthew's gospel, he tells sinners that if their right eye is the cause of their acts, they are to pluck it out, and if their right hand is the culprit, they are to cut it off (5:29-30). Obviously, his point is not that Christians are to become amputees to avoid sin, but that one is to try to remove the source of our temptations. For instance, a man tempted to view pornography should reconsider the private placement of his computer. Luke also recorded where Christ insisted that one must hate the members of our family in order to follow him (14:26). However, the God of love was surely using the strong word "hate" to emphasize that, while we should love our family, we must love God first and foremost.

Likewise, even the most hardened anti-Catholic would agree that Christ does not forbid us from addressing our male parent as "father." Nor do we hear protests against using phrases like

"Father of our Country" for George Washington.

So what did Christ mean? In Matthew 23, the context of the passage shows that Christ is criticizing the scribes and Pharisees because their actions were designed to bring glory to themselves, rather than to God. It isn't that we cannot use the word "father" for earthly or spiritual leaders, but rather we should never use that term to indicate that some mere man, alone, is responsible for our salvation and growth in Christ.

As documented in the article "Are Mother and Father Appropriate Terms for Protestant Clergy," by David Holmes, the term "Father" was even commonly used among Protestant groups before the nineteenth century.[33] The article also documents that the term was actually not used widely among Catholics until the wave of Irish immigration in the 1840's, at which point the term became an almost exclusively Catholic one and American Protestants began rejecting it, showing a theology built upon culture rather than Scripture.

Priesthood of the people?

Of all the challenges thrown almost exclusively at Catholics, the oldest objection in the Book comes when Protestants object that because we are all priests, there is no place for a ministerial priesthood in Christianity. This charge is based upon 1 Peter 2:5, 9, which calls Christians a royal priesthood.

Catholics agree that each individual Christian is a member of the common priesthood. We are all priests in that we offer prayers and personal sacrifices (time, money, luxuries) to the Lord. Does this mean, however, that a sacramental priesthood does not exist?

The opening comment, that this is the "oldest objection in the

---

[33] *The Christian Century*, December 4, 1985.

Book," comes from the recognition that people were objecting to a special priesthood as far back as Exodus 19:6, which reads, "And you should be to me a kingdom of priests and a holy nation ..."

So, the idea of a common priesthood is not some New Testament institution; it existed throughout salvation history. But 1 Tim 5:17; Jas 5:14-15 shows priests (presbyters, elders) tending to the flock through preaching and by administering the sacraments. Exodus 19:21-22 reads: "And the Lord said to Moses, 'Go down and warn the people, lest they break through to the Lord to gaze and many of them perish. And also let the priests who come near to the Lord consecrate themselves, lest the Lord break out upon them.'" This verse shows that, among the common priesthood, there was a special "priestly" group, the Levites. In the same way, the New Testament "common priesthood" still allows for a sacramental priesthood.

Yet, today many non-Catholics complain about a set of men set apart as "priests" in the Catholic Church, as if they are somehow exalted above the rest of us. This charge usually extends to include the bishops and the pope. However, if any of them would carefully read Numbers 16:3, they would see a prophetic foreshadowing of their charge as the Israelites grumbled against Moses and Aaron: "You have gone too far! For all the congregation are holy, every one of them, and the Lord is among them; why then do you exalt yourselves above the assembly of the Lord?"

All through salvation history God has called for his church to have a select priesthood among the faithful. This isn't some new "Catholic invention." Rather, its roots extend all the way through the history of Israel. Unfortunately, so does the grumbling.

Summary:

- **When Jesus condemned calling any man "father," he was not issuing a blanket condemnation of the word, but rather expressing** that no man should take credit for another's salvation;

- Several of the inspired authors and apostles referred to spiritual leaders as "father," as Catholics do today;
- The New Testament expresses that we are all members of a royal priesthood, which is by virtue of our belonging to the body of Christ, our high priest;
- There was a priesthood of the people in the Old Testament, but a ministerial priesthood existed, as well;
- The New Testament also has a ministerial priesthood in addition to the priesthood of the people.

38

ANOINTING OF THE SICK

"In the seventeenth prayer of this work is a form for consecrating the oil of the sick, in the course of which God is besought to impart to the oil a supernatural efficacy for good grace and remission of sins, for a medicine of life and salvation, for health and soundness of soul, body, spirit, for perfect strengthening."
-Serapion of Thmuis, Anaphora, 29:1 (AD 350)

My wife and I have now hosted four baptism receptions, one for first reconciliation, and a party for first Communion. We've recently been to gatherings following confirmations and ordinations. Our own wedding was followed by a dinner and dance.

The sacraments are generally times for celebration, except of course for the anointing of the sick. Nobody puts out punch and cookies to commemorate the prayers over a man in his eleventh hour. Hallmark does not publish a "Happy Anointing" card.

I've been present at a couple anointings, including one for my mother, who recovered, and one for my wife's mother, who did not. It is a sober, solemn experience to sit beside the bed of a family member as a priest traces a cross onto her forehead.

The chapter on atheism answered the objection that God doesn't heal amputees. As explained there, Christ had something in mind other than delivering universal health care. He is a physician of the soul, as were the apostles and the men who followed after them through the sacrament of holy orders.

As with all of the sacraments, Christ instituted the anointing of the sick. Just as the sanctifying power of baptism comes from the graces earned by Christ on the cross, so too does the healing of a priest's anointing come through the power of the one who came to take our infirmities and bear our diseases (Matt 8:17).

The apostles anointed many who were sick during their ministry (Mark 6:13), and James wrote instructions to call an elder (i.e. priest) to anoint the sick, that the Lord will raise him up and forgive his sins (Jas 5:14-15).

The verse from James is key. For one, it shows Scriptural evidence that God intended for mere men, specifically priests, to have the power to forgive sins through their actions. Secondly, it emphasizes that the primary intent of the anointing of the sick is not a physical healing, but a spiritual one.

Often the sick or their concerned family call upon a priest's anointing in hopes that it will shrivel a cancer or strengthen a heart. These things may very well happen, but our "days are like grass" and each of us has an appointed time to die, which does not mean that the sacrament has failed. As the *Catechism* explains, the effect of the anointing is to unite us to the passion of Christ, to strengthen us in courage and peace, and to forgive our sins.[34]

---

[34] *Catechism of the Catholic Church*, No. 1532

Only if it is "conducive to the salvation of his soul," the *Catechism* continues, does the sacrament also bring physical healing. There are reasons that God may very well permit continued suffering, as hard as that may be to accept. The redemptive power of suffering is covered later, in its own chapter.

Or it could be that God desires our restored health and continued life. In his omniscience, he may foresee a turn toward grace that awaits a man in the days beyond the hospital room, so it is "conducive" to that man's salvation that his body regains strength and shuts down disease.

Either way, the message of the anointing of the sick is the same as the message of Scriptural healings, which is that when God heals (and even when he doesn't), he acts with a purpose.

Summary:
- God does not will that prayer for the sick will result in healing for every individual;
- Anointing of the sick can only be administered by those who have received the sacrament of holy orders;
- Unless it is against our personal will, our sins are forgiven through the actions of the priest at the time of holy orders;
- God may have specific purposes for not healing the sick, including redemptive suffering.

5

Prayer and Devotion

39

IS THERE AN ECHO IN HERE?
CATHOLIC PRAYER

"Prayer is not an old woman's idle amusement. Properly understood and applied, it is the most potent instrument of action. "
-Mahatma Gandhi

Over the years, I've tried to find ways to engage my own kids in prayer. We have our routine prayers, such as the one before meals. We bring in a number of traditional prayers, such as during November, when the *Eternal Rest* replaces our regular bedtime prayer. Catholics sometimes struggle with the extemporaneous prayers that Protestants are often so practiced at, and we've experimented with this at home, too, with mixed results.

The art of talking with God is one that must be developed and nurtured. So often prayer is reduced to a list of requests for God, and a neglect of praise, contemplation, and thanksgiving. While there are many good resources to help Christians develop their spiritual lives, the focus of this chapter is not to offer a guide to prayer. Rather, it focuses on the distinct characteristics of

Catholic prayer that seem so foreign, manufactured and even unbiblical to those who do not understand the richness of our spirituality or the significance of our traditions, resulting in many misconceptions.

Repetitive prayer and the rosary

The rosary has always been a difficult prayer for me. My mind wanders often, especially at meetings or during presentations. So when attempting a rosary, I sometimes find myself on autopilot by about the fourth *Hail Mary*, thinking about something that has been weighing me down or some problem at work I've been trying to solve. My inability to focus fully on the mysteries of Christ used to bother me, but then I realized that God was guiding my thoughts to those things I needed to pray about.

If I, as an adult, had difficulty keeping focus through five decades of the rosary, I knew that it was unreasonable to expect my kids to connect to this devotion. One of the ways we've found to help with this is to pull upon the interest my kids have taken in art. We put the rosary CD in the computer and pull up an internet image representing one of the five mysteries of that evening's set. For instance, one of the Glorious Mysteries is the descent of the Holy Spirit, so while reciting the prayers along with the CD, we all sketched a picture of the Spirit in the form of a dove.

Some Protestants cite Matthew 6:7 in order to criticize Catholics repetitive prayer: "And in praying do not heap up empty phrases as the Gentiles do; for they think that they will be heard for their many words." Some translations refer to vain repetition, which is what non-Catholics see in the Catholic rosary, the Divine Mercy chaplet and other such prayers, where the same phrase is repeated several times. In the rosary, for instance, there are ten *Hail Mary* prayers for every single *Our Father*.

But notice that the verse doesn't condemn repetition, but *vain* repetition and *empty* words. Repetition in prayer, itself, is found all through the Bible. Jesus prayed three times, "saying the same words" (Mark 14:39). The four living creatures in Revelation pray without ceasing day and night, "Holy, holy, holy, is the Lord God Almighty, who was and is and is to come!" (4:8), and the psalmist assures us, over and over, that God's "steadfast love endures forever" (Psa 136).

For sure it would be empty if someone were to pray the same thing repetitively simply because he believed that piling those prayers up would convince God or wear him out somehow, and there have surely been Catholics who are guilty of this, just as there are undoubtedly Protestant who mumble extemporaneous prayers without putting heart into it. But sincerity in our repeated prayers is not just pleasing to God, it is also edifying for ourselves, as our repetition helps to imprint the message of the prayer into the lens by which we view our lives.

The rosary is probably *the* prayer that people think of when accusing Catholics of repetition, but this is only because this beautiful prayer is misunderstood. The rosary is a devotional designed to help focus one's mind on the mysteries of Christ, including his birth, ministry, death and resurrection.

The ten *Hail Mary* prayers that occur within each decade are not acts of worship directed at Mary, but requests for her intercession: *Pray for us sinners, now and at the hour of our deaths.*

Catholics ask Mary to pray for us as we contemplate the amazing events that happened because God became flesh and entered the world. The chant-like repetition serve the very practical purpose of diverting our mind from the distractions of life. The rosary is a Christ-centered prayer, but one for which we ask the partnership of his mother and ours.

Does Scripture forbid graven images?

We have pictures of our family on the walls and shelves

throughout our house. My kids and my wife are framed on my desk, and there are countless more photos on our electronic devices. For each of our kids, we have plaster hands and feet from when they were infants. None of these items replace the real thing, of course – I cannot hug a picture of my son. However, they serve as reminders of the people most special to us in our lives. Sometimes, on a busy and stressful day, I take a moment or two just to look at the pictures on my desk.

The listing of the Ten Commandments include the prohibition against making images of anything in Heaven or earth and bowing to or worshiping them (Ex 20:4-5; Deut 5:9).

Catholics seem in gross violation of this with our churches filled with statues and the (I'll admit it) superstitious act of burying poor St. Joseph upside down in the front yard to sell a house. While the tradition with St. Joseph is a bit silly, there is nothing offensive to God with having statues of the great men and women who have modeled the ideal in Christian living.

Protestants seem to understand that simply having statues is not, itself, problematic, as there are no protests from Southern Baptists over statues of our nation's forefathers. However, the standards appear to be different when it comes to houses of worship. Protestant buildings generally have no statues, and their crosses are bare. Catholics join Paul in preaching "Christ crucified," as our crucifixes have the body of Christ on them (1 Cor 1:23).

If making graven images were a sinful act, then our God is a confused one since, just after issuing the Ten Commandments, he ordered the molding of cherubim from gold (Ex. 25:18-19). The first book of Kings shows that Solomon's temple had engraved angels, oxen, lions, and other creatures (6:23-29; 7:25-45). Ezekiel also describes graven images in the temple (41:15).

The Bible also does not prohibit focusing on graven images for the purpose of prayer. If a man, traveling out of state, looked at a picture of his wife while he chatted with her on the phone, he would not be guilty of cheating on her with a photograph. He would just be using a visual reminder of her, as Catholics do when they look at a picture of a saint while asking for his intercession. God understood this full well when he asked Moses to create a bronze serpent and put it upon a pole for the Israelites to focus on when seeking healing (Num 21:8-9). In a similar way, my son Bryce likes to look at the crucifix in our living room when he says evening prayer. He knows it isn't a little metal God on the cross, but looking at the image of Christ is certainly better than staring at a fly on the wall while we pray.

If a Catholic truly believed that a statue *was* a type of god and worthy of worship, that individual would absolutely be guilty of idolatry. However, it is a safe bet that no Catholic believes that the statue of St. Francis in his garden is actually a concrete god.

Bowing before images

If making a graven image is not sinful, surely bowing down before them is, as this is mentioned specifically in the Ten Commandments.

Of course, bowing down is not by itself the same as worship, and the two are mentioned together in the listing of the Commandments. Bowing is a common gesture in our culture, from a greeting before a karate match to a man who genuflects before his girlfriend to propose. From the Old Testament, Lot bowed down to the ground in veneration before two angels in Sodom (Gen 19:1), and Joshua fell prostrate when encountering an angel (Josh 5:14). Individuals in the Old Testament bowed before other humans, such as Saul bowing before Samuel (1 Sam 28:14) and Joseph's brothers bowing before him (Gen 42:9). More examples include bowing before kings and prophets (1 Chr 21:21; 1 Kgs 1:23; 2:15; Dan 2:46; 8:17). In John's vision of Heaven, Jesus spoke of people bowing before those in the Philadelphia church (Rev

3:9).

When Catholics bow before statues, they are really directing this gesture to Christ or to the saint represented as a form of honor, much as a man bows before a king when entering his throne room.

What's the deal with Catholics digging up dead people?

An earlier chapter mentioned the incorruptibles, those saints who, upon being interred, were discovered to have been preserved from corruption. A big question that might have popped into the head of a non-Catholic at that point was *why* the Church digs up the bodies of the deceased.

The Catholic Church has long required that altars contain a relic from a known saint. There are three types, or classes, of relics: 1) actual body parts from a saint; 2) items owned by the saint or used against them, if martyred; and 3) items that have been in contact with the first or second class of relic. Having a relic in the altar recalls the image in John's vision of the souls of the martyred crying out from beneath the altar (Rev 6:9).

The idea of relics is taken from Scripture. In the second book of Kings, contact with Elisha's bones restored life (13:20-21). In two of the Gospels, a woman with hemorrhage was cured by the hem of Christ's cloak (Matt 9:21; Mark 5:28). Cures occurred for those within Peter's shadow (Acts 5:15-16) and for those who touched the face cloths that Paul had used (Acts 19:11-12).

Relics and statues are just one of the ways that Catholics recognize that prayer is rarely a solitary act. When we bring ourselves into conversation with God, whether it is to glorify him or to petition his guidance in our lives, we know that we are joined by the angels and saints who offer up their own prayers from their place directly in the presence of God. And like a spouse who never tires of hearing the words *I love you*, God accepts each heartfelt repetition of praise and adoration, whether it be through a family's evening rosary or in our eternal worship of him in Heaven.

Summary:

- Repetitive prayer is not, itself, offensive to God; rather, he does not want us to use vain repetition or pile up empty words;
- Scripture gives several examples to show that God does not outright reject graven images, but instead rejects treating them as other gods;
- Bowing is not synonymous with worship, as bowing as a sign of respect is modeled consistently in Scripture;
- Relics are used in the Catholic Church, as shown in Scripture, to be instruments of God's grace.

40

HEAVENLY WORSHIP IN THE MASS

"On the Lord's Day . . . gather together, break bread and offer the Eucharist, after confessing your transgressions so that your sacrifice may be pure."
-Didache (AD 70)

Until I met Christy, I hadn't been to Mass in a few years. Even though I started attending with her, I refrained from participating in anything until I understood and agreed with the meaning behind it. As much as I was familiar with the Mass from childhood, the experience I had when I returned was that everything seemed a bit too prescribed and mechanical.

The Mass is part of the liturgy, a word which refers to the public prayer of the Church. Other liturgical prayers include the Divine Office, which priests and deacons say each day. To take part in the liturgy is to join others saying the same prayer throughout the world.

Because of its public nature, the Mass is very uniform. One can attend Mass anywhere in the world and experience the same structure as he would find at his home parish.

The Mass *is* biblical worship

The Mass is divided into two parts, the Liturgy of the Word, during which several readings from Scripture are proclaimed, and the Liturgy of the Eucharist, which includes the consecration of bread and wine, and related prayers. This is prefigured in the encounter between Christ and the disciples on the road to Emmaus, when they first read from the Scriptures and then break bread (Luke 24:13-35).

As unfamiliar as non-Catholics claim the Mass is to their style of worship, it should actually appear very familiar to anyone who has studied the book of Revelation. The Mass models the worship of the angels and saints in Heaven.

Alleluia 19:1, 3, 4, 6	Altar 8:3-4; 11:1; 14:!8	Holy, Holy, Holy 4:8	Amen 4:8
Priests (elders) 4:4; 11:15; 14:3; 19:4	Vestments 1:13; 4:4; 6:11; 7:9; 15:6; 19:13-14	Lamb of God 5:6	Lamp stands or Menorah 1:12; 2:5
Expressions of Penitence chapters 2, 3	Incense 5:8; 8:3-5	Antiphonal chant 4:8-11; 5:9-14; 7:10-12; 18:1-8	Intercession of Angels and Saints 5:8; 6:9-10; 8:3-4
Readings from Scripture 2-3; 5; 8:2-11	Priesthood of faithful 1:6; 2-:6	Eucharistic Host 2:17	Chalices 15:7; 16; 21:9
Sign of Cross 7:3; 14:1; 22:4	Gloria 15:3-4	Silent Contemplation 8:1	Book or Scroll 5:1

There is so much going on in John's Revelation, the concluding book of the New Testament. Its pages depict God's throne room, glimpses of the great spiritual war, the judgment of mankind, and a wedding feast. Each of these elements of the author's vision are tied together by Christ, the slain lamb, who now rules triumphantly from Heaven as our judge and bridegroom.

Many Protestant services are built around a long sermon, with some worship music and possibly the Lord's supper. The Mass, however, is built around the Eucharist. The homily rarely lasts any longer than ten minutes or so, which surprises Protestant Christians who are used to forty minutes of preaching.

The Mass as a sacrifice

The Catholic Mass is more than a worship service. As signified by the altar, there is an actual sacrifice taking place. It is the same sacrifice that Christ offered on the cross at Calvary, and it is re-presented during each Mass (1 Cor 10:16).

Some Protestants accuse Catholics of sacrificing Christ over and over again, but this is not the case. Imagine a hydrant breaking somewhere at the top of a hill in a neighborhood, with the water flowing through the neighborhood through the culverts and streets. Individuals in two different locations would see the water flowing past them, and it would be silly to say that the hydrant has been broken again for each street corner the water passes. Rather, the spilling of the water has been presented to each of them at different locations. Likewise, the sacrifice of Christ flows out through time and location through each Mass. Jesus Christ, after all, is "the same yesterday and today and forever" (Heb 13:8).

The last prophet of the Old Testament, Malachi, prophesied that in every place, from sunrise to sunset, a pure offering would be brought to God's name (1:10-11); and under the New Covenant, that pure offering is Christ, who replaced the perpetual sacrifices of the Old Testament.

The sacrifice of Christ is re-presented in an unbloody manner. Some groups object to this by claiming that only a sacrifice that sheds the blood of the victim is effective in removing our sins. And it is true that Christ's death on the cross was the ultimate act that released us from our sins, but he continues to offer himself as a living sacrifice to the Father, as we are called to do (Rom 12:1). This sacrifice is present to us under the appearance of bread and wine in the manner of Melchizedek (Psa 110).

At the last supper, Christ commanded that his followers "do this in remembrance of me" (Luke 22:19), and the word *anamnesis*, which is translated as "remembrance," does not simply mean "in memory of," but often implies a commemorative sacrifice when it is used elsewhere in the Scripture. For instance, in Hebrews 10:3, the Old Testament *sacrifices* serve as reminders of sin.

Did the Catholic Church change the Sabbath Day?

The Seventh Day Adventists get a lot of traction from their claim that the Catholic Church changed the Sabbath from Saturday to Sunday. The charge fails for many reasons. For one, there has been no change in the Sabbath at all. It still falls on Saturday, as it always had. Christians do not have a new Sabbath; rather, we no longer recognize the Sabbath as our day of worship.

Observing the Sabbath was part of the Mosaic law, but as the author of Hebrews writes, with a new priesthood there is a new law (7:12), which is why Christians are not bound to circumcision and dietary restrictions, as the Jews were.

It seems strange that any group would try to claim that the Catholic Church changed the day of worship since Scripture, itself, records that the first Christians recognized Sunday as the day of worship in commemoration of Christ's resurrection (Acts 20:7, 1 Cor 16:2, Col 2:16-17, and Rev 1:10). Catholics do have the option to go to Mass on Saturday evenings. This comes from the understanding that, for the Jews, the Saturday Sabbath actually began at sundown the previous day. So, for Christians, our Sunday Eucharistic celebration begins the evening of the previous day as well.

Can I go to Hell for missing Mass?

Missing Mass, if done with full knowledge and intent, is a mortal sin (without dispensation or a grave reason). Mortal sins, if not confessed, lead to damnation.

It is a hard concept for many Christians, including a good number of Catholics, to understand this simple conclusion. The statistics tell us that most Catholic *do not* go to Mass on a regular basis.[35] To an extent this is the result of poor catechesis, as many Catholics have never had the significance of Mass properly explained to them, nor had solid reasons explained for the requirement of attendance on weekends or holy days of obligation.

Going to Mass is the *one* thing that Christ specifically asked us to do for him (Luke 22:19). Protestants emphasize the importance of weekend worship, but typically do not consider it mortally sinful to miss attending. Many Catholics have adopted the same philosophy, so much so that some are referred to as Christmas and Easter Catholics, referring to those two times a year they attend with family. My own anecdotal experience indicates that even the Christmas and Easter folks are becoming endangered species, as our Catholic culture becomes one where even those token visits are less common.

Going to Mass is more than just a nice thing to do. It is more than a prayer service or a family meal. It is substantially more than

---

[35] Lydia Saad, "Churchgoing Among US Catholics Slides to Tie Protestants," www.gallup.com, April 9, 2009.

just fellowship. Christ is our bridegroom and at Mass, we become one with him. To miss Mass is the equivalent of a husband knowingly missing an anniversary dinner his wife has prepared, leaving her at the candle-lit table with nothing more than a text message indicating that he won't be there. They went out to eat last weekend, he tells her, and he's taking a break this weekend.

The marriage would fall apart, especially if he never had the dignity to get on his knees and apologize. Mass is *the* event, the source and summit of our faith through the reception of the Eucharist, and to miss it ends our marriage with Christ as well.

Summary:
- The Mass is a liturgy, one of the public prayers of the Church;
- The structure and prayers of the Mass are strongly rooted in Scripture, especially in the model of Heavenly worship seen in *Revelation*;
- The Mass is the one sacrifice of Christ represented in an unbloody fashion as Christ offers himself as a living sacrifice to the Lord;
- The Sabbath remains on Saturday, but Sunday was recognized in Scripture as the new day of worship in commemoration of Christ's resurrection.

41

INTERCESSION OF THE SAINTS

"Then we commemorate also those who have fallen asleep before us, first Patriarchs, Prophets, Apostles, Martyrs, that at their prayers and intercessions God would receive our petition. Then on behalf also of the Holy Fathers and Bishops who have fallen asleep before us, and in a word of all who in past years have fallen asleep among us, believing that it will be a very great benefit to the souls, for whom the supplication is put up, while that holy and most awful sacrifice is set forth."
-Cyril of Jerusalem, Catechetical Lectures, 23:9 (AD 350).

"**I**f you ever get really sick, don't ask me to pray for you."

I once said this to a friend, a Protestant pastor, as we ate supper together at a local restaurant.

The look of shock on his face made it evident that he was a bit offended that I would say something so heartless. We had been discussing the Catholic practice of praying to the saints, and he had stated his objection to this. "Scripture tells us that there is just one mediator between man and God," he had told me, "so you should be praying straight to God."

"Then you shouldn't be asking me to pray for you," I explained. "There is only one mediator between man and God, and you should be going straight to Him, not me."

"But I'm not asking you to heal me," he said. "I'm just asking you to join me in prayer."

"Exactly," I told him. "And this is what we do with the saints." It took a few seconds, but the point sunk in.

The prayers of a righteous man

Of course Christians can and should often pray straight to God. However, throughout Scripture individuals intercede for others, and God often acts on one person's behalf because of the requests of another. It is "good and acceptable" to make prayers and intercessions for others (1 Tim 2:1-4; Eph 6:18). For instance, Christ helps the wedding party because of Mary's request (John. 2:3-5). Onias and Jeremiah intercede for the Jews before the resurrection (2 Mac 15:11-16). The angel Raphael speaks of interceding on behalf of Tobit and Sarah (Tob 12:12).

The prayers of a righteous man are very powerful (James 5:16), so if a woman can ask a stranger in a check-out lane to pray for her, why could she not ask the same of one who has reached eternal glory? Who is more righteous than those who are now within God's throne room?

If one listens to the words of the *Hail Mary*, for instance, we do not pray, "Mary, please save us and heal us through your power." Rather, we say, "*Pray for us ...*"

Of course I would pray for my friend if he got sick. If he really became ill, he would hopefully ask his family to pray for him, his friends to pray for him, his coworkers to pray for him, and his fellow Christians, including the ones in Heaven, to pray for him.

Many non-Catholics get confused because, to them, the word pray means "worship." However, pray traditionally means to "ask." When we pray to a saint, we are asking that individual to pray for us just as we would someone we bump into at the library.

Objections to intercession of the Saints

Though the "one mediator" objection falls apart quickly, some roadblocks still remain for many Protestant Christians:

Objection: Deuteronomy 18:11 expresses that it is offensive to the Lord to consult with the dead. The Catholic response: the full text of this passage makes it clear that God objects to attempts to necromancy, which means to seek knowledge from the dead, such as in a séance. Those who attempted this occult practice should have turned their attention, instead, to the prophets, who had the authority to speak for God (18:15) Deuteronomy is not addressing saintly intercession.

Objection: If the saints are dead, wouldn't hearing all of our prayers require omniscience? The Catholic response: ours is not a God of the dead, but of the living (Mark. 12:26-27). While our bodies might be "asleep," our spirits are very much alive in Christ. We are all parts of the body of Christ (Rom 12:5; 1 Cor 12:25-27) and of one another (Eph 4:25), even after death, and the Church refers to this mystery as the "communion of saints." When we unite in prayer, we come together in stronger spiritual union, building up that mystical body.

As far as how the saints can hear all of these prayers, Scripture tells us that the saints share in God's divine knowledge (1 Cor 13:9-12) and his divine authority and power (2 Tim 2:12, Rev 22:5; Rev 2:26-28), and in the fullness of God (Eph 3:19; 1 John 3:2). Saints can hear our prayers because God invites them into his *beatific vision*, and through his power, they have become that "great cloud of witnesses" that oversee all that we do (Heb 12:1). In Rev 5:13-14, John writes that he "heard every creature in Heaven and on earth and under the earth and in the sea" praising God. The "elders," or saints, in Heaven also heard all of this praise from earth, because they fell down and answered, "Amen!"

Objection: There are no biblical examples of saints interceding for us. The Catholic response: This is not true. In Revelation 5:8, the elders in Heaven are offering up incense. The really interesting thing about Revelation is that there is much symbolism, and Christians can disagree about what some of the vision actually means. But the vision of the elders offering up incense is one of the only times that John actually tells us what the literal meaning is. He writes that the bowls of incense "are the prayers of the saints." Since Protestant Christians agree that the biblical writers referred to all Christians as saints (Romans 15:25; Phil 1:1), then these elders in Heaven are offering up the prayers of those on earth.

When Christians invoke a saint in our prayers, they in turn offer those prayers to God directly. Those who have gone before us, as part of their heavenly worship, are praying for us now and at the hour of our death, amen.

Summary:

- **The prayers of a righteous man are very powerful;**
- **When Catholics pray to saints, we are simply asking them to pray for us;**
- **The saints are aware of our prayers because God shares his divine knowledge with them.**

42

QUEENSHIP OF MARY

*"The veneration of Mary is inscribed in the very depths of the
human heart."*
-Martin Luther

To anti-Catholics, the "pagan origins" of Catholicism couldn't be more apparent than when, throughout the world, parishes participate in an event called "May Crowning," which celebrates Mary's role as Queen of Heaven and Earth. Not only do Catholics appear to be attributing to Mary the title of a Babylonian goddess (Jer 7:18), but several young ladies in their nicest spring dresses gather to put a crown on ... a *statue*!

To assume that apparent similarities between paganism and Christianity means that one borrowed from the other is a logical fallacy. After all, if the similarity of Mary's title as Queen of Heaven to that of a Babylonian goddess is a smoking gun against Catholicism, one must also view with suspicion Christ's title as "King of Kings," which is also attributed to the pagan king Nebuchadnezzar (Dan 2:37).

This thinking is flawed, especially when discussing the supposed pagan roots of Catholicism, and not just for the obvious reason that coincidences happen.

For one, no substantial evidence exists to support the idea that most of the similar pagan beliefs and practices preceded those of Catholicism. The exact reverse could be true, and pagan religions could have borrowed from Christianity.

Second, the truth of God's nature is written on our souls, even if it has been distorted by humanity's sinful nature. Some *hints* of truth would surely have emerged in the doctrines of primitive religions.

Finally, these accusations sometimes come from non-Catholic Christians who do not realize the irony that all of Christianity, not just Catholicism, would have to be discounted because concepts such as the incarnation of a divinity, the virgin birth, and the flames of Pentecost have elements in common with Pagan mythology.

The Davidic King and the Queen Mother

The truth is that Mary's title of Queen of Heaven and Earth *does* have its origins in the Old Testament, not just in the book of Jeremiah, but also in the first book of Kings. The term typology refers to the study of Old Testament signs that reflect New Testament truths. For instance, Christ is foreshadowed by many "types" in the Old Testament, such as in the near-sacrifice of Isaac and in David's kingship.

To try to understand the Christianity of the New Testament without the Judaism of the Old is like going to graduate school to become a doctor and skipping elementary and high school. One of the reasons non-Catholics misunderstand the Church's teachings on Mary's queenship is because they do not understand how this is foreshadowed in the Old Testament.

The queen mother of the Davidic king is given great prominence in Scripture and acts as an advocate on behalf of the people to the king (1 Kgs 2:18, 20). Especially because the king often had many wives, there was a unique honor given to the queen mother, who sits at the right side of the king, a place of great honor, and to whom even the king himself bowed (1 Kgs 2:19).

Christ, the Davidic king, also has his queen mother. She intercedes on behalf of the wedding party in Cana (John 2:3-5) and, as the mother of our Lord, is blessed among women (Luke 1:42-43). Our last Scriptural image of Mary is in the image John has of Heaven, in which he sees a "woman clothed with the sun, with the moon under her feet, and on her head a crown of twelve stars" (Rev 12:1-2). Though some interpret this image of Mary as representing Israel or the Church, individuals often represent groups within Scripture, such as how Jacob represents the nation of Israel (Psalm 44:4).

All who persevere to sainthood will receive a crown of life and of glory (Jas 1:12; 1 Pet 5:4; Wis 5:16), so it should be no surprise that the greatest of the saints wears the greatest of these crowns. As all teachings about Mary are really about Christ, the tradition of May crowning celebrates the fact that Mary, to whom even the angels say "Hail," has a unique place of honor in Heaven and on earth, simply by virtue of the significance of her son, our King.

Does Christ disrespect Mary in Scripture?

Some of the language and the sayings of Christ that appear in the Gospels are used by non-Catholics to support the claim that Christ saw nothing special in his mother.

Christ calls Mary "woman" (John 2:3-4). At the wedding feast in Cana, Mary makes a request that Jesus assist the wedding party after the wine runs out. Christ, in response, calls Mary "woman," which sounds to our modern sensibilities like he is cutting her down to size. We know, however, that Christ would not disrespect his mother in this way, for this would be sinful and a violation of the commandment to honor one's parents. Christ is incapable of sin. The title *woman*, far from being an intended slight, is actually a reference to Genesis 3:15, when God curses the serpent and says that he will put enmity between the serpent and the woman. Mary is the woman prophesized in Genesis, and Jesus recognizes this by the title he uses.

Jesus says that no one born of woman is greater than John the Baptist (Matthew 11:11). This verse is used to indicate that, as special as Catholics believe Mary to be, John the Baptist is even greater, so our honor is misplaced. However, Christ is speaking in hyperbole here. If he meant this literally, then he would have just said that John the Baptist is greater even than Christ, himself, as our Lord was born of woman. However, the point of this passage is that Jesus is telling his disciples that even the greatness of John the Baptist is nothing compared to that of anyone who is received into the kingdom of Heaven, which will also include John the Baptist upon his death.

Jesus rebukes the crowd, saying that anyone who "does the will of God" is his mother (Matthew 12:48; Mark 3:33). As seen clearly by his comment on John the Baptist, Jesus often downplays temporal relationships to make points about the significance of following God's will. In Mark, a man calls him "good teacher," and Christ asks, "Why do you call me good? No one is good but God alone" (10:18). Obviously, Christ is not denying that he is good, though it appears that way as he directs the man's attention to God as the source of truth.

When the disciples tell him his mother and brothers await him, Jesus is not ignoring the importance of his family, but using the moment as an opportunity to emphasize that spiritual communion with him is much greater than family relations. As Mary "does the will of God" in a very remarkable way by saying yes to bear the Savior in her womb, so then she is surely the supreme example of what Christ asks of his disciples.

Is Mary our redeemer and mediator, too?

Though not defined infallibly by the Church, the titles of *co-redemptrix* and *co-mediatrix* are sometimes used to describe Mary. The titles are unfortunate because, even though the idea behind them is perfectly compatible with Christian doctrine, Protestants understandably feel that these titles are an attempt to elevate Mary to the level of Christ.

When the prefix "co" is used today, it often implies someone who is an equal partner in something, such as a co-founder of a company. Catholics do not believe, though, that Mary was responsible for our salvation or that she is another mediator between God and man, a role given solely to Christ (1 Tim 2:5).

Christ uses many of us as instruments in his work of salvation, such as the preacher who introduces an atheist to the faith. In that way, Christians are cooperators, or co-workers, with Christ in his mission of salvation (1 Cor 3:9). Though Christ is our high priest, we share in his priesthood (Rev 1:5-6; 1 Pet 2:5,9).

Mary did this in a primary way by saying *yes* to the invitation to bear Christ in her womb. She set the example for all of us by her consent of will. And while all of us share in Christ's sufferings (2 Cor 1:5; Phil 3:10), Mary surely did this in a substantially greater way as she stood beneath the cross and watched her child suffer and die. In this powerful way, she united herself with the work of redemption, as we are all called to do.

The role of Mary as queen-mother points to her as an intercessor for others. But even more than the simple act at the Wedding of Cana, she acts as any good mother would and intercedes for her children.

As we are all members of Christ's body, Mary is our mother and continues to petition God on our behalf. The title *co-mediatrix*, then, does not imply that Mary is another bridge to God, but that her will, and therefore her prayers, are perfectly aligned with the will of Christ in his salvific work.

Summary:

- Christ sits on the throne of David as our king;
- The queen-mother of the Davidic king interceded for her people, and Mary stands in that role today;
- Christ does not intend to disrespect Mary by referring to her as "woman," but rather is identifying her as the woman referred to in Genesis, who will have enmity with Satan;
- Mary did not cause our redemption and cannot, herself, bridge the gap between God and man, but serves as the perfect example of how one cooperates with the suffering and will of Christ.

43

THE IMMACULATE CONCEPTION AND ASSUMPTION

"Thou alone and thy Mother are in all things fair, there is no flaw in thee and no stain in thy Mother."
-Ephraem, Nisibene Hymns, 27:8 (AD 370)

When we sin, we are less than human. The idea can't be emphasized enough that God did not create the human creature with the intent that he would be a sinner by nature.

In the Garden of Eden, as it has been described in the book of Genesis, God created man and woman to live in perfect harmony with Him, with nature, and with themselves.

In creating the human race, God bestowed upon us the ability to rise above the animalistic instincts of lesser creatures. We have intellect, which comes with a sense of morality and the ability to act in accordance with that sense of morality. Because of our "flesh," we become lustful, greedy, angry, and proud. We have desires, some of which are unhealthy and destructive. But humans were created in God's image, and the image of God cannot be associated with sin.

Sin is disharmony. Sin is animalistic. When we sin, we are acting less than human.

The New Eve

Another consequence of the sin of Adam and Eve is that man lost his perfect harmony with God. Redemption comes through Christ. God could have, of course, simply "snapped his finger," so to speak, and humanity would have been saved. However, he chose another route, which was to take the consequences of sin upon himself and to make amends for them upon the cross. He chose to become human … *fully* human.

When Catholics speak of Mary's Immaculate Conception, many mistakenly assume that we place her on a pedestal, making her something *more* than human. They assume that humanity, in general, is "normal" and that Catholics perceive Mary as being above humanity, a god herself. The opposite is true. The rest of humanity acts *less* than human – animalistic – and God simply made Mary as he intended for all of us. He made her the type of parent Christ would have had if he had been born in the Garden.

From very early in the Church, Mary has been identified as the "new Eve." Through her rebellion, Eve set in motion the fall of mankind; Mary, though, reversed that trend by saying *yes* to God in such a way that the *new Adam* could bring redemption for all.

The first Scriptural indication of Mary's immaculate conception occurs in the book of Genesis, when God is cursing the serpent. He says to him, "I will put enmity between you and the woman, and between your offspring and hers" (3:15). If Christ is the offspring, then the woman can only be the mother of that seed, meaning that it is Mary, not Eve, who has enmity with the serpent.

The Ark of the New Covenant

Continuing in the Old Testament, one can see another foreshadowing of Mary in the Ark of the Covenant, which was greatly venerated among the Israelites. The box was adorned with beautiful statues, it was carried into battle, and it was kept in the Holy of Holies, where only the high priest was allowed to enter, and only on the rare occasion, once a year, when he made sin offerings on behalf of the people. Nobody was allowed to even touch the box, such as when Uzzah reached to steady it and dropped dead (2 Sam 6:7).

Nothing impure was allowed to touch the Ark of the Covenant. But why? It was just a box. Would not many modern Christians be scandalized by the type of veneration given to a material object?

The answer, of course, is that it wasn't about the box at all, but its contents. This "box" contained pieces of manna from the desert, Aaron's priestly rod, and – perhaps most importantly – the Ten Commandments, the word of God engraved on stone. This box had to be kept pure and away from defilement because it carried these holy items, which needed to be kept in only the most pure containers.

Mary is the Ark of the *New* Covenant.

The Old Testament Ark contained the manna from Heaven; Mary contained the Bread that gives eternal life. The Old Testament Ark contained the priestly rod of Aaron; Mary contained the High Priest. Finally, the Old Testament Ark contained the engraved word of God; Mary contained the Word made flesh.

This isn't just some figment of Catholic imagination - the inspired author Luke draws this same comparison early in his gospel. Notice the parallels between his narrative and the description of David's encounter with the Ark:

- Both Mary and the Ark are on a journey (Luke 1:39-52 & 2 Samuel 6:4-16);
- David dances before the Ark (2 Sam 6:9) and the infant John dances (leaps) in his mother's womb when Mary (bearing Christ) stands before Elizabeth;
- David asks, ""How shall the ark of the Lord come to me?" (2 Sam 6:9) while Elizabeth asks "Who am I, that the mother of my Lord should come to me?" (Luke 1:43);
- And the ark stayed in the house of Obededom for three months (2 Sam 6:11) while Mary stayed in Elizabeth's house for three months.

Lastly, when reading Revelation 11, the conclusion of this chapter tells us that "then God's temple in heaven was opened, and the ark of his covenant was seen within his temple ..." By this point in Jewish history, the Ark of the Covenant had disappeared. A first century Jew would have been on the edge of his seat as Revelation tells us that John sees a vision of the Ark. Anticipating that John was about to describe the Ark, imagine his surprise when the very next verse describes, not a box, but a woman: "A great portent appeared in heaven, a woman clothed with the sun, with the moon under her feet, and on her head a crown of twelve stars" (Rev 12:1). Chapter numbers were not part of the inspired text, so even though this verse appears in chapter 12, to the original audience, it would have flowed seamlessly from the verse at the end of chapter 11. For sure, this "woman" also represents Israel in a symbolic way (Revelation is a symbolic book), but all of the "symbols" also represent real people (as the four "creatures" earlier in chapter 11 represent the four gospel writers).

Mary is the Ark of the New Covenant, which means that, just as that "box" in the Old Testament needed to be kept pure, so did she because God would not have entered the world through an impure passage. He would not have resided, for nine months, in defiled flesh.

This is why, when the angel greets Mary, he says to her, "Hail, full of grace." The original Greek here is "kecharitomene," which is a perfect passive participle, implying an indwelling of grace that has existed, does exist, and will continue to exist. The angel recognized that God had filled Mary with this extraordinary grace because she would be the doorway through which Christ would enter the world.

Most people mistakenly assume that Catholic beliefs about Mary are our attempt to exalt her. On the contrary, our beliefs – properly understood – are simply a reflection of our honor of Christ. Mary was without sin because Christ was so magnificent that only the most pure vessel could contain him. Mary chose not to sin, not because of her own merits, but because God's grace is so powerful as to allow her to overcome any temptation.

Common objections

Non-Catholics generally have three objections to the idea that Mary was without sin. These are three very sincere objections, each worthy of examination.

Objection: In Romans 3:23, Paul writes that "all have sinned." He didn't say "all, except Mary." The Catholic response: To take this verse as literally as that should give every Christian some concern, not just Catholics. If we believe that "all" have sinned means each and every person, then this would imply that aborted babies and those who died as infants have sinned. It would mean that the severely mentally handicapped have sinned. It would mean that Christ had sinned. Fortunately, by reading this verse in context, the intended meaning becomes obvious. In Romans Paul writes concerning the need for salvation to be extended to the Gentiles. Many at the time tried to claim that, either salvation was just for Jews, or that Gentiles needed to be circumcised to receive this gift from God. In *Romans*, Paul adamantly denies this. Salvation is not just for Jews or just for Gentiles because *all* [groups] have sinned. It is a similar use of hyperbole as one might hear a parent use with her child: "You disobey me *all* of the time." Obviously, no child can be in a perpetual state of disobedience. One must never pull a verse out of context, and a careful reading of the context here indicates that Paul was not putting forth a judgment of each and every human, but of the need for salvation for all groups.

Objection: In Luke 1:47, Mary proclaims, "my spirit rejoices in God my savior." Why would Mary need a savior if she never sinned? The Catholic response: Catholics enthusiastically agree that Mary needed a savior. Our Church has never taught otherwise. Does this mean, though, that Mary had to have sinned? Not necessarily, as the following analogy will illustrate. Suppose that two individuals are walking through the woods. In their path lies a giant tiger pit. The first person falls into the hole and a local man comes out of the bushes, offers him a rope, and pulls him out. He would respond to that local man, "You are my savior." The second individual will also fall into the hole. However, in this case, the local man recognizes her as his mother. He steps out of the bushes early and puts his arm out to stop her from falling in. (Wouldn't we do the same for our own mother?) Relieved, she exclaims, "You are my savior!" Humanity has fallen into the hole, and through his death, Christ "pulled us out." Mary, his mother, is sinless because Christ's redemption on the cross is not bound by time. She is "pre-redeemed," so to speak. Because she is the Ark of the New Covenant, his grace (not her own efforts) affected her very conception, preventing her from falling into the hole in the first place.

Objection: Luke 2:22-24 states that Mary went to the temple for a sin offering. How could Mary have been sinless all her life when she made an offering for sin? The Catholic response: The offering, in this case, had nothing to do with personal sin. To understand the Mosaic law in this matter, examine

Leviticus 12:2,4,6-8: "If a woman conceives, and bears a male child, then she shall be unclean seven days; as at the time of her menstruation, she shall be unclean ... Then she shall continue for thirty-three days in the blood of her purifying; she shall not touch any hallowed thing, nor come into the sanctuary, until the days of her purifying are completed. ... And when the days of her purifying are completed, whether for a son or for a daughter, she shall bring to the priest at the door of the tent of meeting a lamb a year old for burnt offering and a young pigeon or a turtledove for a sin offering." So, according to Mosaic law, a woman was *legally* unclean. Mary, as an obedient Jew, would never have broken one of the laws of her faith. Neither would Christ. After all, Jesus was circumcised and baptized, although he had no need of spiritual cleansing (Rom 2:29) or showing the world he had repented of His sins (Matt 3:11). Jesus was " born under the Law" (Gal 4:4).

Mary's bodily Assumption

By being preserved from original sin, the natural question is whether or not Mary would have experienced the consequences that humanity faced since leaving the Garden.

Scripture tells us that Mary would experience suffering as she united herself with the passion of her son (Luke 2:35). However, Catholics are bound to believe in the *Assumption* of Mary. This teaching remains silent on whether or not Mary died. But at the end of her earthly life, her body was taken immediately into Heaven. We will all be reunited with our bodies in Heaven, but Mary's body was spared the corruption of death.

Of course there are biblical examples of bodies being assumed before the second coming (1 Cor 15:23, Mat 27:52-53). Enoch and Elijah were "assumed" and spared from death, so the idea of an assumption isn't foreign at all to Scripture (Gen 5:24, Heb 11:5; 2 Kgs 2:11-12; 1 Mac 2:58).

There are no direct Scriptural references to Mary being

assumed, but this shouldn't be surprising at all, considering most of the New Testament was probably written during her life.

Revelation does contain the vision of Mary in Heaven, suggesting that she now resides there bodily. But in addition to this, it is through the infallible guidance of Christ's church that we know why no historical record exists of Mary's burial place. Our Lord went to his resting place, and in fulfillment of Psalm 132:8, so did the Ark of his might.

To truly understand how Catholics view Mary, one should think about the relationship of the moon to the sun. To go out on a clear night, one can appreciate how truly beautiful the moon is – glowing so splendidly in the night. However, the moon can only glow in so much as it reflects the light from the sun. The sun burns from its own intrinsic energy, and without it, the moon is dark. Catholics believe what we do about Mary, not because we feel that she is great based on her own merits, but in that everything we understand about Mary merely *reflects* the overwhelming glory of Christ. True Marian doctrine should bring us closer to Christ, and the fact that the Ark of the New Covenant – a mere container - was created without blemish is God's way of indicating the true magnificence of the contents.

Summary:
- Original sin has taken our human nature and caused us to act in a way that is less than human;
- As the "new Eve," Mary gave the consent that helped to reverse Eve's rejection;
- As the "Ark of the New Covenant," Mary is kept pure by virtue of the contents of her womb;
- Mary needed a savior as we all did, and her salvation is dependent upon Christ;
- Because she was preserved from original sin, Mary was also sparred the consequence of deterioration through her Assumption.

44

THE PERPETUAL VIRGINITY OF MARY

"I firmly believe that Mary, according to the words of the gospel as a pure Virgin brought forth for us the Son of God and in childbirth and after childbirth forever remained a pure, intact Virgin.
-Protestant Reformer Ulrich Zwingli, Zwingli Opera, Corpus Reformatorum, Berlin, 1905, v. 1, p. 424.)

As my daughter neared fourth grade, my wife and I decided to sit down and have *the talk* with her. I knew, from working in an elementary school, that by fifth grade the students understood how the biology worked, and we preferred that she heard it explained by us.

Until that point we had done the necessary prep work, teaching our kids to use the right words for their personal areas, and explaining that babies came from the daddy putting a seed in the mommy. Still, she remained fairly innocent in her understanding of the world, and I'm pretty sure that she still believed that babies came in a bag of ready-mix from Wal-Mart.

The conversation actually came about near Christmas, when

we were reading the nativity story, and she asked what it meant that Joseph did not "know" Mary.

"How could he not know his own wife?" she wondered.

So we put the younger brothers to bed and explained what it meant for a man to "know" his wife in the biblical way.

"But it was different for Mary," I explained after the strange details of how mommies and daddies create rug-crawlers. "She remained a virgin, which means that Joseph didn't put a seed in her the way we just talked about."

"The *Virgin* Mary," she said, suddenly understanding the title. "God put the baby Jesus in her."

And with that, she summed up one of the central mysteries of Christianity, which is that Mary conceived Jesus without losing her virginity. On that point there is nearly complete agreement among all Christian groups.

As Catholics, however, we believe that Mary then remained a virgin through the rest of her life, whereas most Protestant groups hold that Mary had other children, brothers and sisters to our Lord. This is different from the belief of the Reformers, such as Luther, Calvin, and Zwingli, who agreed with the Catholic view. Modern Protestants are often unaware that their belief that Mary had other children is contrary to what the founders of their groups believed.

Objections to the perpetual virginity of Mary

It is understandable that Christians today might read the New Testament and think that Mary had other children. To properly read the Bible, one has to be familiar with the culture of the time period, as well as with the way language was used. To read text that was written to first century Jews and Gentiles means one has to read it like a first century Jew or Gentile. Words that we use today might have a different meaning than they did for Christians two-thousand years ago. Look at how words have changed in just a few hundred years, since the writings of Shakespeare. Before looking at why Catholics believe Mary remained a virgin through the rest of her life, it would be helpful to see some of the phrases that confuse modern Christians:

Objection: The evangelist Matthew says of Mary that Joseph "knew her not until she had borne a son; and he called his name Jesus" (1:25). The Catholic response: Because of the word "until," Protestants often argue that Mary was a virgin at first, but that she engaged in normal marital relations after Christ was born. Today we often use "until" in this way, such as in this sentence: "I did not eat until I got home." From this, we could assume the speaker ate once he did get home.

However, the Greek word for "until" (*heos*) implies something that is true up until a certain point but without making a statement about what happens after that point. Scriptural examples can be seen in several places, such as Matthew 28:20, where Christ promises, that he would be with us "*until*" the end of time. To use the same logic that so many apply to Mary's virginity, Christ will stick with us until the end of time, but then he will ... abandon us?

Matthew is not even trying to make a statement one way or the other about what happened after Jesus was born; he is simply emphasizing that the prophecies foretelling of the virgin birth have been fulfilled.

Objection: Luke 2:7 tells us that Jesus was Mary's "firstborn." Protestants read the word "firstborn" to imply that there would be additional children. However, throughout the Old Testament, it becomes very clear to us that "firstborn" is far from being a mere indicator of birth order among multiple children. It is a legal designation by which the child who first opens the mother's womb (regardless of whether there are subsequent children) is entitled, by law, to the main share of the inheritance.

"Firstborn" does not even have to be the one who is born first as the Old Testament also uses the term to refer to high favor bestowed upon a child. Examples of "firstborn" being used in a way that does not include additional children can be found in Ex 13:2, Nb 3:12, and Ex 34:20. With that said, would anyone argue that this legal designation does not apply to Christ? Just as God refers to Israel as his "firstborn" to denote the high favor he holds for the Israelites (Ex. 4:23, Duet. 7:6), Christ surely held high favor, not just for his Father in Heaven, but for his mother on Earth, as well, and Luke simply recognized this in his gospel. The phrase has nothing to do with whether or not he had brothers or sisters.

Objection: Scripture speaks of Jesus' "brothers" and "sisters" (Mark 3:32; Matt 13:54-56). This reading of Scripture, as with the previous examples, indicates a poor understanding of Jewish culture. In Jewish culture, the word brother (*adelphos* in Greek) included blood brothers, for sure, but also immediate family, such as cousins and step-brothers. In fact, in the language of the Jews, which was Aramaic, there does not even exist a word for cousin, as extended family were referred to as brothers and sisters. While there is a word for cousin in Greek, the New Testament contains the Jewish concept of relations.

An overwhelming number of Scripture verses show the word "brothers" used for individuals who were related, but not actually siblings (Gen 14:14; Gen 11:26-28; Gen 29:15; 1 Chro 23:21-22; Deut 23:7; Jer 34:9; 2 Kgs 10:13-14; 2 Sam 1:26; 1 Kgs 9:13, 20:30; and Amos 1:9). As with "firstborn," the word brother had an important legal implication. If an only child died, his cousins ("brothers") would be entitled to his inheritance. Jesus and his immediate followers were Jews and would have understood their relationships in a Jewish way.

The Old Testament foreshadows the perpetual virginity

As mentioned in an earlier chapter, the Old Testament foreshadows the doctrines of Christ. A saying attributed to St. Jerome, the translator of the Latin Bible, is that the New Testament is hidden in the Old, and the Old is fulfilled in the New. As an example, the sacrifice of Christ is foreshadowed by the *type* of Abraham nearly sacrificing Isaac.

In the Old Testament, a man named Uzzah was struck dead for putting his hand upon the Ark of the Covenant when it appeared that the box was about to fall (2 Sam 6:7). This simple box was set aside as unworthy of casual contact because of its contents. The last chapter explained how Mary, by bearing Christ, is the Ark of the New Covenant, and she too has been set aside for a special purpose. She had been chosen to be the womb through which Christ was born, and Ezekiel prophesied the no man would enter through the gate by which the Lord entered the world (44:2).

An ancient Jewish writing, the *Protoevangelium of James*, records that Mary was dedicated to the temple at a young age. As this dedication involved a vow of celibacy, Mary was then married to an older widower, Joseph, who would protect her from other men who might have less honorable intentions. If the history in the *Protoevangelium* is correct, it would explain why Joseph disappears so quickly from the Gospels, as he would have died long before Mary. It also offers an explanation of the "brothers" and "sisters" who might very well be Joseph's children from his previous marriage.

The *Protoevangelium* is not inspired. However, the journals of those who knew Abraham Lincoln were not inspired, but they still give a pretty good glimpse into history. Most Christians who believe that Mary had other children are not even aware of this early Christian writing.

Practical proofs that Mary remained a virgin

Even if one disregards the *Protoevangelium*, Catholics do not believe Mary remained "ever-Virgin" simply because of an early Christian document. We believe it because the Church, which is the pillar and foundation of truth (1 Tim 3:16), tells us it is so. We believe it because history tells us it is so, in that no early Christian writer identified Mary as having other children. The "brothers" of Christ are never called Mary's children. Finally, we believe Mary remained virgin because Scripture tells us so:

- At the crucifixion, as Christ prepared to die upon the cross, he handed Mary over to be cared for by the apostle John, telling him that she was now *his* mother (John 19:26-27). If Mary had other children, it would have been scandalous for Christ not to hand her over to one of them.

- When the Angel Gabriel tells Mary that she *will* conceive a child, her curious response is to ask how this could be possible, claiming "I *have* no husband" (Luke 1:31:34). This response makes no sense. The angel was speaking in future tense, so Mary should have assumed that even though she currently did not have relations with man, Gabriel was speaking about a point later in her relationship with Joseph. The present tense statement that she did not "have" relations with man implied that this was a state that would continue for her at any given point in the future.

- In the listing of the apostles, there are two men identified as James. For each, a father is given – Alphaeus is the father of James the Less, and Zebedee is given as the father of James the Greater. However, in Galatians 1:19, Paul writes, "But I did not see any other of the apostles, only James the brother of the Lord." He identifies James as the brother of the Lord *and* as an apostle. If "brother," in this passage, truly meant biological brother, the only way this would be possible is if Mary had been with another man beside Joseph (either Alphaeus or Zebedee). In order to resolve this, Protestants typically assume the existence of a *third* James who is worthy of being called an apostle.

* James and John are identified as being "brothers" of Jesus, but John 19:25 paralleled with Mark 15:40 identifies *another* Mary, the wife of Cleophas, as the mother of these two.

As the Ark of the New Covenant, Mary was chosen by the Holy Spirit for a very special purpose. Gabriel tells her that the Holy Spirit would come upon her and "overshadow" her (Luke 1:35), just as the Spirit overshadowed the Ark when it resided in the Holy of Holies in the Old Testament (Ex 24:15-16, 40:34-38, 1 Kgs 8:10). Joseph, respecting the Jewish laws on adultery, would have respected that Mary had been espoused to the Spirit in the sense that she had been chosen to bear the son of God.

Either way, Catholics believe in the perpetual virginity of Mary, not because we prefer to, but because it is the consistent witness of Scripture and Christians through two millennia. We believe it, not because it tells us something remarkable about Mary, but rather because her preservation in purity reveals everything about the Divine figure who entered the world through her womb.

Summary:
* The Old Testament prophesied that Christ would be born of a virgin, and Mary's pure state continued through the rest of her life;
* The teaching on Mary's perpetual virginity is a reflection on the greatness of Christ, that no other individual would be worthy of entering the world through the "gate" by which he entered;
* The "brothers" of Christ are either his cousins or Joseph's children from a previous marriage;
* The actual mother of two of Christ's "brothers" is identified elsewhere in Scripture.

6

Catholic Living

45

WITHHOLDING OURSELVES: CONTRACEPTION

"Another effect that gives cause for alarm is that a man who grows accustomed to the use of contraceptive methods may forget the reverence due to a woman, and, disregarding her physical and emotional equilibrium, reduce her to being a mere instrument for the satisfaction of his own desires, no longer considering her as his partner whom he should surround with care and affection."
-*Pope Paul VI* Humanae Vitae *(AD 1968)*

When Christy and I were ready to start having children, we had just planned a trip to Europe. I joked that it would be fun to conceive during our whirlwind trip and, as our child developed a personality, to guess in which country the conception had happened. If she turned out overly diplomatic, possibly Switzerland. If artsy and a high-brow, possibly France.

As it turned out, we didn't conceive on that trip, or for a while after. It wasn't until our frustration started to set in that I read the fine print for the birth control that she had been using, which had called for her to receive an injection every few months. A delay in conception, one of the listed possible side effects, could potentially last up to a year or two.

We were devastated, but it was our fault for not reading the small print earlier. However, it was just *normal*, we thought, that married couples contracepted in order to regulate family size. It was just as normal as car loans and Sunday brunch.

For a number of years, contraception has been seen by much of society as the stick-in-the mud teaching of an archaic Church – old celibate men in Rome giving relationship advice.

But the times, they are a'changin'. More Christian groups are realizing the sinful nature of contraception (the same view that *all* Christian groups had before 1930). A Baptist minister who lived in my neighborhood told me about how he and his wife had used contraception until he was reading the Bible one night and, looking up at her, said, "Honey, I think we're sinning."

More than just a "contraceptive"

Among the many things that Christy and I learned about the chemical she was injecting into her body was that it was doing more than just preventing conception. Most chemical forms of contraception, including the pill, are also abortifacients. What this means is that, if an egg is released while a woman is on the pill (known as "break-through ovulation) and conception takes place, the womb becomes a hostile place for the newly conceived child. In many cases, the uterine walls dry up, preventing the egg from implanting there. This effectively aborts the child.

Many couples do not realize that contraception often works this way. We certainly didn't. Now, though we have four fantastic kids, the thought sometimes nags at me as to whether they might have brothers and sisters in Heaven whom my wife and I never had a chance to meet because we used chemicals to circumvent God's design.

Contraception vs. natural family planning

Individuals far removed from religion are also recognizing that contraception is harmful to their bodies, their relationships, and to the environment. The Catholic Church does not teach that a couple must have as many kids as possible, or that every act of intercourse must be with the intention to conceive. There are valid reasons why a couple may limit family size, such as financial situations or the health of the mother.

However, just as losing excessive weight is a virtuous goal, there are healthy and unhealthy ways to that end. Responsible diet and exercise – good. Binging and purging – bad. There is much spiritual harm that is created by a contraception mentality, but the reasons to reject birth control are obvious even outside of doctrine.

Effectiveness – when many hear of natural family planning (NFP), their minds automatically turn to the questionably reliable "rhythm method" from decades back. However, modern methods of natural family planning, such as the *Creighton Model*, are scientifically verified to be at 99% or higher effectiveness, more effective than most forms of artificial contraception.[36]

Personal health – The God who designed the vast and complex universe, as well as the microscopic beauty of an atom, is the very same God who designed our human body. There is a certain arrogance in telling that supreme designer that, *in this case – with my body – you might have gotten it wrong, sir. I'm going to shut down this part of me.* It shouldn't be surprising that artificial contraception has introduced so many health problems.

It is hard to watch a commercial for birth control without noticing the list of side-effects that could result from use, including tumors, birth defects, weight gain, reduced sex drive, depression,

---

[36] Aldred, David. "The Effectiveness of Natural Family Planning." *The Natural Family Planning Information Site.* Accessed 3/28/12.

strokes, and heart problems. If the commercials aren't alarming enough, the existence of class-action lawsuits against previously-assumed safe contraceptives should be. Natural family planning, on the other hand, does not introduce unnatural elements into the body and results in no side-effects. Instead, because the women is more in tune with her own body, she can often identify potential health problems early enough to seek early treatment. Considering that NFP's effectiveness is as high as most other forms of contraception, couples should ask why they would use an artificial contraceptive that would increase depression and reduce sex drive. Even more important is the question of why couples would introduce potential harm into their systems when a perfectly natural alternative exists. The question I eventually asked myself: *What kind of a man am I to allow my wife to put this poison into her body?*

Lower divorce rate – With a marriage-failure rate in our culture of over 50%, couples should desire to divorce-proof their relationships. Studies of couples who use natural family planning provide the answer; couples using NFP have a divorce rate of 1 to 3%.[37] There are many reasons for this, including the idea that NFP involves better communication and collaboration. In addition, the hormonal adjustment that comes with chemical contraceptives can often alter one's ability to identify a suitable mate. Studies show that, while on the pill, women are attracted to men who are not complimentary to them chemically.[38] As a result, when those women go off the pill, relationship breakdowns can occur as the body detects incompatibility. Children of couples, who do not have complimentary genes, may not be as fit.

In marriage we are to model the love that Christ had for each

---

[37] Wilson, Mercedes Arzu. "Divorce Rate Comparisons Between Couples Using Natural Family Planning and Artificial Birth Control." *Physiciansforlife.org*. 1-4 Mach 2001.
[38] Bryner, Jeanna. "The Pill Makes Women Pick Bad Mates." *Live Science*. 12 August, 2008.

of us. Christ loved us fully, giving his life up on our behalf. Husbands and wives are called to give themselves completely to one another. Through contraception, however, spouses are saying to one another, "You can have all of me, but not that part. I will put a piece of latex between us when we are together." Or, "I will shut down part of my body when I am with you." A marriage which is premised upon withholding part of one's gift to a spouse is a relationship that is more vulnerable to further division.

Building up temperance – The earlier analogy of an individual losing weight by binging and purging makes a good metaphor for one of the dangers of contraception. Eating disorders are often emotionally addictive, and individuals can end up dangerously emaciated, but with a compulsion to keep losing even more weight. Likewise, contraception removes the need for couples to practice occasional temperance in their relationships. This feeds into the earlier point regarding the divorce rate, as some of the symptoms of destroyed temperance in relationships are addictions to masturbation, pornography, and eventually adultery. Couples must train themselves to be in control of their desires, rather than let their desires be in control of them.

The spiritual harm of contraception

It was eye-opening to read the list of side-effects for the contraception my wife was using, but even that paled in comparison to what I discovered when I gave the Church the benefit of the doubt and actually read *why* contraception is taught to be a sin. This, too, is something that Christy and I should have done early on, rather than base our morality on the value system of the same culture that renewed *Jersey Shore* for several seasons.

Many Catholic couples, often advised by their Catholic parents to use contraception, do not realize that this act is a *mortal sin* if committed with full knowledge and intent. Scripture is clear on the immorality of contraception. In many Protestant communities, preachers actually make a point of advising couples to start considering their contraception options. Scripture gives no support for contraception. To the contrary, Genesis commands us to be fruitful and to multiply (1:27-28) and the Psalmist writes that children are a gift from God, that a man is blessed if he has a full quiver (127:3-5).

Onan, who takes his dead brother's wife in fulfillment of Levitical law, is struck dead for withdrawing during intercourse with her, spilling his seed (Gen 38:9-10). Some try to dismiss this, claiming he was punished for disobeying Levite law, but according to Deuteronomy, the harshest punishment for that is public humiliation (25:5-10).

Various forms of contraception are condemned in Scripture (insofar as they *could* contracept in those days), such as crushed testicles (Lev 21:17-20) and castration (Deut 23:1 & 25:11-12). Jesus curses the fruitless fig tree (Matt 21:19; Mark 11:14), yet many men intentionally become fruitless through surgery.

And while contraception is condemned, the practice of Natural Family Planning is upheld in Paul's first letter to the Corinthians, when he writes that married couples should not refuse each other, except by agreement for a season, when they come together through prayer instead (7:5).

In 1968, Pope Paul VI released a document called "On Human Life" (*Humanae Vitae*). This document, widely criticized by our sexually "enlightened" society, predicted several things for our culture if contraception were allowed to take root in marriages. Women would become sex objects, the morals of society would drop, there would be a break-down of the family, and the body would be viewed in a strictly utilitarian way. Each of these predictions has come to pass.

And of all of the evils that our society now faces, one of the worst is the abortion epidemic. Through contraception we treat pregnancy as if it is something to be avoided. As if conception is some unfortunate thing that happens when couples aren't careful. No wonder so many young women end up at the abortion clinic when our society has convinced them that it isn't a baby in the mother's womb, but a tumor. If Catholics and other Christians are truly going to be pro-life, the abortion mentality has to be absolutely rejected from our relationships.

Summary:

- Natural family planning is as effective as most forms of contraception;
- Contraception often introduces many dangerous side effects into one's body, whereas natural family planning has no such dangers;
- The divorce rate among couples who contracept is astonishingly high, compared to a very low divorce rate among couples who use natural family planning;
- Contraception is contrary to God's will and is, therefore, destructive to our spiritual health;
- In fulfillment of the predictions in *Humanae Vitae*, contraception has perpetuated many great evils in our society.

46

NO EASY WAY TO TALK ABOUT IT:
IN-VITRO FERTILIZATION

"You cannot be against embryonic stem cell research and be intellectually and therefore morally consistent, if you're not also against in vitro fertilization."
-Ronald "Ron" Reagan

Christy and I have always struggled to come up with names for our boys, but from very early in our marriage we both knew that our first daughter would be named Paige. As a teacher, I had a long list of names I would never give my child – some just sound more ornery to me now than they otherwise would – but girls named Paige had always turned out okay.

In a later chapter I write about how we had trouble conceiving for a very short period, and while that struggle did not last long, it gave me a glimpse into the very strong heartbreak that couples face when trying to conceive and experiencing ongoing disappointment.

The subtitle of this book promises to help answer even the *toughest* questions about the Catholic faith, and this chapter deals with one of the toughest. It's one thing to tell someone he needs to go to confession once in a while or to explain to a Southern Baptist why he is in error by using the Bible alone as his authority. But tell someone that her child was conceived in a sinful way? An issue like this strikes at our emotional core.

Couples who use in-vitro fertilization are seeking to do a *good* thing. In a society where kids are often viewed as a nuisance, these men and women put considerable emotional energy and finances into an attempt to bring children into the world, assuming for themselves the amazing responsibility of being a parent. And when a child results from this process, he is nothing short of a gift from God, who brings good from all things.

Many good, faithful Catholics have used this technique without even realizing *why* the Church teaches against it or even that it *does* teach against it.[39] Society has done a much better job of promoting the capability of science than the Church has sometimes done of promoting the moral considerations Christians must make in using the new promises of science.

It would be hypocritical for me to condemn a couple for the use of in-vitro since, as I explain in the chapter on contraception, Christy and I used contraception and very possibly contributed to the destruction of newly conceived children through an abortifacient "birth control."

I've been in conversations before when a sensitive issue of in-vitro has come up, and another individual issues the challenge that I would feel differently if I were in another man's shoes.

And this is absolutely correct. If I had an actively homosexual child, I would feel tempted to accept his lifestyle. If my wife were faced with possible death due to a delivery, I may very well be

---

[39] *Catechism of the Catholic Church*, No. 2377

tempted to end the pregnancy in order to save her. And if we found ourselves unable to conceive, I would almost certainly struggle with the Church's teaching on in-vitro fertilization.

Likewise, if we were unable to conceive, it would be very hard to accept that our parenting instincts could only be satisfied through adoption, babysitting or volunteering with youth.

Had we the funds, in-vitro would seem like an answer to our dreams, but this wouldn't be God's desire. Our emotions are fallible and often lead us astray. This is why God gave us revelation and an infallible Church, so that in those moments of emotional vulnerability, we have a pillar and foundation of truth.

Bringing children into the world is a good thing. But a *good* goal does not make every means of achieving that goal good also. A father, for example, may desire to put food on his family's table. There is a moral means of doing this (working an extra job and cutting back on expenses) and an immoral means (robbing a bank). The end does not justify the means (Rom 3:8)

There are some who are aware of a church teaching, but chose not to follow it anyway. "It's just a man-made rule," after all. We know, of course, that Scripture is very clear in stating that the leaders of the church have been entrusted to shepherd the flock (John 12), that these leaders had the power to bind and loose (Matt 6), and that the Holy Spirit would guide them to all truth in executing this power (John 6). When the church speaks on a given issue, we are called to trust in the guidance of God – that he would not have established a Church that would lead us astray morally.

Before examining in-vitro fertilization, it should be pointed out that there are many morally acceptable means of assisting couples that are having difficult conceiving. Natural Procreative Technology (NaPro) has been very effecting in helping struggling couples to identify physical obstacles to conception – obstacles that can then be treated medically. By extension, then, medical steps, such as fertilization drugs and egg-stimulation are fine as long as they do not propose a danger to the mother and child that is disproportionate to the benefit of the treatment. The Church isn't opposed to assisting the body to perform as it should, but in vitro does not do this. The procedure has a fairly low success rate, under 35% in the ideal age group and lower from there.[40] But even if the success rate were high, the following factors with this method testify to its intrinsic immorality:

IVF bypasses the marital act – The church opposes contraception, of course, because the primary ends of intercourse are procreation and unity. Contraception destroys both of these (which is why the birth rate is so low and the divorce rate is so high among couples who contracept). Neither the possibility of life nor a complete self-giving can be removed from the marital act without consequently removing its inherent sanctity. Likewise, once couples understand that children are a physical sign of their parents' love, it becomes clear that we must not have conception without the sexual act – the act of unity. Secular society has done a good job of convincing us that we are *owed* children. Sometimes couples are unable to conceive, even with the assistance of modern medicine. This is a truly sad fact of life. However, the act of baby-making is intrinsically tied to the marital act. Just as the Father and the Son love each other so completely that a third eternal person, the Holy Spirit, *spirates*[41] forth, a husband and wife are called to love each other so completely that a third human person is conceived.

IVF violates the exclusivity of the marital covenant – Marriage is a covenant between husband and wife. As explained in the last paragraph, children are a sacramental expression of that mutual and complete love. When a third party, such as a fertility

---

[40] http://www.americanpregnancy.org/infertility/ivf.html
[41] From the chapter on the Trinity, the theological term that describes the Spirit proceeding from the Father and Son.

doctor, enters into the act of conception (and actually completes the act of conception apart from the couple in a laboratory setting), the exclusivity of the marital covenant is violated. It is one thing, a perfectly acceptable thing, for a doctor to assist through medicine or surgery – the couple must still complete the marital act independently of his assistance. In-vitro fertilization makes the husband and wife secondary and passive participators.

IVF manufactures life – As explained above, children are meant to be a sacramental sign of his parent's love. IVF takes place through laboratory manipulation, rather than through the marital act shared between a husband and wife in the intimacy of their bedroom. When children are "manufactured" in this way, it adds fuel to the desensitizing of our society toward life. Christians must not allow any slack in the fight to hold onto the sanctity of life. If children can be manufactured simply because they are desired (as opposed to being a sign of the unbreakable bond between husband and wife), can they not be disposed of when they are not desired, such as in abortion?

IVF creates frozen embryos – Anytime something is "manufactured," there are discarded or defective products. In the process of in-vitro fertilization, not just one – but *numerous* embryos are created. Actual human children are created, but not implanted in the mother. Some of them are destroyed. Some of them are perpetually frozen. One of the more confusing problems in the area of bio-ethics today is the question of what, exactly, to do with all of the frozen embryos.

For every child who is conceived through in-vitro fertilization, there are a number who have been discarded or stored away. If for no other reason, in-vitro fertilization should be opposed because of the casual way in which newly conceived human life is abandoned in the laboratory.

IVF results in a higher number of birth defects - Father Tadeusz Pacholczyk, director of education at the National Catholic Bioethics Center in Philadelphia, writes, "Studies have shown a six-fold elevated risk for in-vitro fertilization for children contracting an eye disease called retinal blastoma versus normally conceived babies. In-vitro fertilization is very unnatural. You're extracting ova from the woman, culturing them and inspecting the developing embryo in a laboratory setting. They are in a completely unnatural environment for a very long time before they are put back into the womb."[42]

Understanding the moral threat caused by IVF should help couples understand the difference between the biblical command to welcome children and the modern sentiment that couples are owed a child, by any means necessary.

Summary:

- **In-vitro fertilization is a very sensitive subject and one that should only be addressed with great compassion and understanding;**
- **IVF bypasses the marital act and the exclusivity of the spousal relationship;**
- **IVF uses an immoral means of creating life;**
- **IVF results in frozen or destructed embryos;**
- **IVF results in a higher number of birth defects.**

---

[42] Tim Drake. "What's Wrong with In-Vitro Fertilization." www.staycatholic.com.

47

DOES GOD HATE SHRIMP?
HOMOSEXUALITY

"He who is guilty of unseemliness with males will be under discipline for the same time as adulterers."
-Basil the Great, Letters *217:62 (AD 367)*

If there was ever a hot-button issue in politics and religion today, it is concerning the level of acceptance that a society or church should give to people who engage in homosexual behavior. The earlier chapter on marriage gave the fundamental reasons why homosexual acts are immoral. Catholics reject homosexual acts, not as a judgment on those who struggle with their sexuality, but because God had specifically designed marriage to be between one man and one woman. A monogamous heterosexual marriage serves a sacramental and practical purpose, so any other type of sexual relationship is contrary to God's will.

However, not only are many Catholics unaware of the rationality the Church gives, but advocates for homosexual relationships are increasingly vocal in expressing their views politically and socially, and this chapter addresses many of these.

It is important to note that having a disordered attraction to something is not a sin unless one acts upon it. Many of us have loved ones who struggle with homosexuality, which makes this a sensitive issue, but objective truth must be defended, especially against our emotional struggles. However, our sympathy with friends and family who struggle with same-sex attractions serve as a reminder that, even as we present the truth to others, it must be done with "respect, compassion, and sensitivity. Every sign of unjust discrimination in their regard should be avoided."[43]

Homosexuals are born that way: There appears to be research, some good and some bad, on both sides of this issue. For those who are interested in trying to sort through it all, there are plenty of good resources. However, regardless of how the research shakes out, *it simply doesn't matter.* Let's say that, hypothetically, people *are* genetically predisposed to same-sex attraction, does this make it okay? Does this justify homosexual acts as being in accord with natural law? There is compelling evidence that people inherit alcoholism, but this does not excuse the father who drinks away his paycheck? Some court defenses have been built on the premise that a defendant was inherently psychotic, so do we excuse, as "perfectly normal," his habit of chopping people up and putting them in a freezer? None of this is to compare homosexuality with extreme violence, but rather to make the point that being "born with" some inclination does not qualify it as part of God's plan.

Homosexuality occurs in nature: State your objection to homosexual behavior, and someone will inevitably mention a study that was done somewhere that found that 10% of sheep engage in same-sex behavior. Yet, imagine what our society would be like if we used the animal kingdom as our measure of morality. Eating one's young is very common among our underwater friends, but God help the man found sprinkling salt on his newborn daughter.

---

[43] *Catechism of the Catholic Church*, No. 2358.

God doesn't make mistakes: No, he does not, but Adam and Eve did, and for that reason, original sin corrupted his otherwise beautiful creation. Many are born with physical disorders (a missing leg or blindness) and mental disorders (Down Syndrome). It was not God's doing or his intent that individuals would be born with handicaps or disabilities. God is order, so the original rejection of him moved humanity away from him and toward the state of chaos from which he formed the earth. And if this deterioration of our being can affect an individual physically and mentally, why should one suppose it wouldn't also be sexual?

Jesus never condemns homosexual behavior: First off, how do we know this? Doesn't John tell us at the end of his gospel that Jesus did many other things which are not recorded in Scripture. And even if Jesus didn't specifically mention homosexual behavior, he did institute marriage as a sacrament between a man and woman, and whenever he refers to marriage, he refers to a union of man and wife. And *even then*, let's say Jesus had been silent, Scripture condemns homosexual behavior (and extramarital sex, which include homosexual acts) all over the place (such as Rom 1, 1 Cor 6, and 1 Tim 1). And Scripture is inspired by God. And Jesus is God, so his views are one and the same with Scripture.

The Church should stay out of the bedroom - God invented the sexual act to allow us to participate in his miraculous act of creation. Since he invented it, he gets to make the rules. And the Church is the instrument through which he makes those rules known (1 Tim 3:15). So the Church sets the rules for morality, whether outside the bedroom or in.

The "shrimp" argument: Leviticus condemns both shellfish and homosexual actions as "abominations" (18:22; 20-13), which has given fuel to those who want to portray Christians as hypocritical bigots. If the Christian argument against homosexual behavior were predicated on Leviticus, there might be a point to be made. Rather, Leviticus is a listing of laws that were binding upon the Israelites. Some of these laws were ceremonial, some moral, and some civil laws that guided God's people to a well-ordered society and life. While shrimp was forbidden as a non-kosher food for the Jews, homosexual acts are condemned throughout the Bible, including the New Testament, where the Jewish ceremonial law is no longer binding. In addition, homosexual acts have been consistently condemned by the Holy Spirit-guided teaching authority of the Church. The Christian teaching on homosexuality comes, not from inclusion in an Old Testament list of laws, but from the realization that God established marriage between man and woman, and any distortion of that is a rejection of his plan.

There are straight marriages in worse shape: This argument is like saying that tax evasion shouldn't be illegal because rapists are rarely tax evaders. There are plenty of marriages in awful shape because they are embracing all the *other* threats to a healthy relationship, such as selfishness, drunkenness, adultery, and abandonment. However, homosexuals can fall victim to these same evils, and adding disorder on top of disorder does not suddenly create morality.

Homosexuals should have equal rights: Homosexuals actually already *do* have the same rights as straight individuals. If one is speaking of strictly civil marriage, then marriage is not a *right* at all, but a privilege from the state.

That privilege has been granted, traditionally, because society saw some benefit in marriage as an institution that would bring new producers and consumers and tax-payers into the world, and the benefits that same from legal recognition were designed to encourage this. Many of these benefits are available to same-sex couples through legal documents, such as power-of-attorney agreements and contracts. However, many advocates of same-sex recognition argue that all of these arrangements are inferior to the actual declaration of "marriage" for homosexual couples.

While several states have now legalized "gay marriage," even in those states that have not, heterosexuals do not have an unconditional "right" to marriage just because of love. Two people, to be married, must be of legal age and not otherwise prohibited from marriage, such as if one of them is already wed to another person. A man is also not allowed to marry his sister or someone who does not *agree* to marry him.

In all of the debate over gay marriage, those who wish to change the traditional definition of marriage do not, at the same time, typically come to the defense of polygamists. After all, if one can say that marriage between one man and one woman is subject to change, wouldn't more than just the gender be up for negotiation? Why not redefine marriage to include a relationship between three men and one woman?

People who oppose gay "rights" are homophobes: "Phobia" means fear, and Christians who object to homosexual actions do not do so out of fear. Such name-calling is a tactic used by people who have run out of logical arguments.

Nor would it be true to say that people who oppose homosexual relationships hate gay people. Rather, as Christians we are called to love one another, but also to correct others when they are engaged in behaviors that are dangerous to them, physically or spiritually. Love of one's neighbor means a desire to see that individual live in accord with God's will so that we might spend eternity together in Heaven. The real injustice within a Christian community are those who say, "live as you will, your eternal salvation is of less importance to me than whether or not you feel *accepted* in your personal choices."

My son (or daughter/friend/brother/uncle ...) is gay: Then he needs your support more than ever. It's hard for an individual to look at objective truth when it hits so close to home. Even somebody who is in favor of the death penalty might have second thoughts if it was his child in the electric chair, which is why the objective truth of God, not our own emotions, must be our guide in morality. If someone close to us struggles with same-sex attraction, this is certainly a difficult cross to bear. We each have our own crosses. However, 1 Corinthians 10:13 states that God will give each person sufficient graces to overcome any temptation. Of course we shouldn't reject a person because of his struggles, but the last thing our loved one needs is for us to make it easier for him to reject God by our accepting a sinful lifestyle.

We are all sinners: Before a Christian attempts to speak to anyone about his sinful actions, he should make sure there is not a log in his own eye (Matt 7:3). The chapter on objective truth explores this more, including the charge that pointing out sinful behavior is "judgmental." However, there is a difference between persistent sin and the individual who repents and attempts to rid his life of sin. A man who has a one night stand, realizes the sinfulness of his actions, and confesses has made use of the mercy and grace offered by Christ. Those who live in sin and have no intent to repent or ask forgiveness are in a state of persistent sin.

How could *loving someone* be sin? Many make the mistake of assuming that sin is only that action which directly hurts another. Rather, the definition of sin is an offense against God or a violation of his law, whether it directly hurts another person or not. However, it is also true that any sin, no matter how private, tears at the body of Christ, which includes all of humanity.

Summary:
- **Homosexual activity is contrary to the divine and natural law written on each human heart;**
- **Scripture defines marriage as a sacrament between a man and a woman, and any sexual conduct outside the confines of the marital union is sinful;**
- **Christians who speak out against homosexuality**

do so out of love and a desire to help others avoid harmful choices;

- We are all sinners and should make sure we are not engaging in behaviors that make us hypocrites when trying to guide others in Christian behavior.

48

RESPECTING GOD'S TIMELINE: END-OF-LIFE DECISIONS

"Grave men, near death, who see with blinding sight
Blind eyes could blaze like meteors and be gay,
Rage, rage against the dying of the light.
And you, my father, there on the sad height,
Curse, bless, me now with your fierce tears, I pray.
Do not go gentle into that good night.
Rage, rage against the dying of the light."
  -Dylan Thomas, from "Do Not Go Gentle Into That Dark
  Night"

"I wouldn't want to live like that," she said. "When God's calling me home, then just let me go."

The "she" in this case could be any number of relatives or acquaintances I've heard over the last few years, expressing their desire that they not be kept alive by artificial means. This type of conversation has been especially relevant since the 2005 Terri Shiavo case, when the husband and parents of a 41-year-old woman got into an argument over whether or not to remove her feeding tubes. The Shiavo case reverberated through the nation, as it received attention from the Florida Supreme Court and resulted in federal legislation signed by President George W. Bush.

But whatever the legal circumstances regarding one's decision to remove life-support, it is vital to know the moral implications. At the time this chapter was written, I have been a part of that discussion three times, twice regarding my mother, who is still alive, and once regarding my mother-in-law, who is not. In the latter case my wife's family was very insistent on following the teachings of the Church. However, on the flip side of the coin, I have even heard a Catholic doctor in a Catholic hospital stating his presumption that God would not want someone to live *this way*.

Natural law

Natural law, as well as the commandment that one shall not kill, holds that we must not only not end life, but we must preserve it within reason. The basic necessities of life – food, water, and medicine – are generally considered *ordinary* means. However, there are also *extraordinary* means of keeping one alive. These may provide an unusual burden of some sort. The Catechism explains that "discontinuing medical procedures that are burdensome, dangerous, extraordinary, or disproportionate to the expected outcome can be legitimate; it is the refusal of "over-zealous" treatment. Here one does not will to cause death; one's inability to impede it is merely accepted. The decisions should be made by the patient if he is competent and able or, if not, by those legally entitled to act for the patient, whose reasonable will and legitimate interests must always be respected."[44]

Families should then weigh whether ceasing a certain treatment simply lets nature take its course or in some way causes death? Is death the intent? This is key, especially when people say

---

[44] *Catechism of the Catholic Church*, No. 2278.

that, when God is calling them home, we should let them go. If God intends to call us home, he'll do it with certainty, stopping the heart or allowing some other devastating event to happen within the body. In the case of Shiavo, however, this was not happening. Despite the condition of her mind, her body was operating fine. She was not dying. The doctors withheld her food and water and *starved* her to death. Pope John Paul II addressed this very type of decision in an address to physicians in 2004, clarifying that removal of ordinary means was immoral.[45]

There may be legitimate reasons to remove a feeding tube, such as in the case of a cancer patient who will die anyway within the next few hours, and whose body no longer processes food. But in many cases of tube removal, the body is *not* dying. God is not yet calling the individual home.

Who would want to live that way?

We live in a very utilitarian society – one that often measures the worth of an individual by his ability to contribute to the whole or by the burden he places upon others. One justification for abortion is that the unborn child is an imposition upon the mother. A similar rationale threatens the elderly in our health care system. Many have, unfortunately, allowed this callous view of life to color their perception of their own self-worth or the quality of their lives based on their mobility and mental awareness. However, there are several reasons why the condition of one's life should not be the determining factor in whether that life is worth continuing:

It is God's decision, not ours – As mentioned above, our life is a gift from God, and it is he alone who should decide when it

---

[45] Pope John Paul II, *To the Congress on Life-Sustaining Treatments and Vegetative State*, 20 March 2004. In 2007, the Congregation for the Doctrine of the Faith, with approval from Pope Benedict XVI, reaffirmed this message, clarifying the obligation to provide food and water.

ends (Job 1:21). If the body is still able to process food and use it to create energy and new tissue, then removing these tubes is to treat a human being with less dignity than a plant upon our shelf. That an individual may not be conscious enough to chew or swallow is not the same as saying that he is dying.

God may have a purpose for us, even as we lay unconscious – While God does not actively will that bad things happen, he does allow them to happen when he foresees that good can come of them (Rom 8:28). While a woman with severe brain damage in a hospital bed may seem like a relatively useless individual, it may very well be through her that God's grace is bringing individuals to prayer who otherwise have let their spiritual lives go flat. He might be using her state to encourage her children to reconsider their lives and the opportunities they have let pass.

God might be allowing us to remain alive, even in an unconscious state, in order for us to repent – Stories of near-death experiences suggest that there is a level of consciousness that cannot be measured by brainwave machines. Our minds are not our souls. Our souls interact with the world through our minds and bodies, but the soul is the spiritual component of an individual and is not affected by disease or mental deterioration. While the woman in the bed may appear "brain dead" to those who visit, she may be very alert on a level we cannot perceive. God may be permitting a sinner time to reflect on her life and repent before dying, and removing a feeding tube robs her of that opportunity.

God might be allowing redemptive suffering - He may also be allowing a member of his flock to detach from those earthly things which have tempted her from a love of God, reducing the experience of Purgatory she might otherwise have encountered. As the final chapter explores, suffering atones for sin and purifies the soul (Prov 20:30; 2 Pet 4:1). Or, in her suffering, a patient might be uniting herself with that of Christ, possibly offering her experience to God on behalf of a loved one. Even if medication removes any physical suffering, she may experience an emotional pain through a spiritual knowledge of those who are hurting over their loss of her.

There are a number of stories of supposedly brain-dead individuals who have regained consciousness, sometimes just hours before the removal of a feeding tube. However, the immorality of removing ordinary means applies even to the patient who does not show signs of recovery.

The type of decisions discussed in this chapter are very complicated and emotionally painful, especially when a family is facing financial hardship or a possibly prolonged experience. It is a decision no family should make alone, nor is it a decision that can be made morally without having all of the medical facts, so consultation with a doctor and a priest are both necessary steps for individuals attempting to sort out end-of-life decisions. For difficult decisions, an excellent resource is the National Catholic Bioethics Center, which can be found at www.ncbcenter.org or, in emergencies, by telephone at (215) 877-2660.

Summary:

- For end-of-life decisions, one should distinguish between ordinary and extraordinary care;
- Consideration should be given to whether a patient is actually dying, or just unable to nourish and hydrate himself;
- God may have a purpose for keeping a non-responsive patient alive, such as to allow him to repent or to experience redemptive suffering;
- Decisions should be made with an understanding of the medical factors hand-in-hand with the teachings of the Church.

49

SEPARATION OF CHURCH AND VOTE?

"The way of light, then, is as follows. if anyone desires to travel to the appointed place, he must be zealous in his works. the knowledge, therefore, which is given to us for the purpose of walking in this way, is the following. . . . thou shalt not slay the child by procuring abortion; nor, again, shalt thou destroy it after it is born."
-Letter of Barnabas 19 (AD 74)

Abortion came up while I was discussing politics with a friend of mine. The two of us disagree sharply on most political issues, but we still manage to discuss them without slipping into insults or vilification.

I told him that, since life begins at conception, abortion is murder and should be outlawed.

"I don't think you can say for sure that life begins at conception," he said. "So you can't start making laws that only support your beliefs."

I disagreed, but his statement was worth pursuing to its logical conclusion. "You don't think there is scientific consensus that life begins at conception?" I asked. "Do you think there is scientific consensus that life *doesn't* begin at conception?"

"No, that's just it. We don't know, so we can't make laws criminalizing abortion without evidence."

"Fair enough," I said. "What about this – suppose you are a contractor and you have been hired to tear down a condemned building. You ask the owner of that building if it is vacant. You had heard that there might be some homeless people living in some of the old apartments. If he said there were absolutely no people in that building, you'd feel comfortable tearing it down, right?"

"Sure."

"And if he told you that, yes, there were people living in the building, would you tear it down?"

"Of course not."

"So what if he told you that he just wasn't sure if there were people there are not. What about then?"

"I'd have him make sure it was empty before I tore it down."

"Me too," I told him. "So if we aren't sure whether or not that is real life in a woman's womb, why are you okay with giving the destroy orders?"

As Christians, we are the Church Militant. We are God's army against the principalities and powers, and the world rulers of this present darkness. But when it comes to the voting booth, Christians have been more like the Church Impotent, letting the winds of secular values erode the foundations of our society. As a Catholic school principal, I've had individuals criticize our decision to put a pro-life message on the school's marquee as well as our practice of instructing our students to bring their Catholic values into the voting booth as adults.

As absurd as it seems that a Christ-centered school can be criticized for promoting life, the same absurdity pops up in conversations with Catholics near election time.

Should Catholics impose their views on others?

A conversation with a relative once turned to the issue of abortion. She assured me that, while she was pro-life, she didn't see how it was ethical to impose those views on others. Catholic politicians often justify pro-choice legislation in a similar way.

But as the chapter on objective truth made clear, there are some things which are true and some which are false. It would be one thing for a politician to say that his favorite color is blue, but that he doesn't want to impose his decorating preference on others. That is an opinion. The statement that life begins at conception is a factual assertion. It is either true or it is not.

If it is true and can be shown to be true that life begins at conception, then it doesn't matter at all whether or not someone else has a different religion (or no religion at all). Before the Civil War, there were individuals who believed black people were beasts of burden. Individuals at that time had a different belief system, and it was wrong. Was it unethical for society to outlaw slavery and to impose that view on those who disagreed?

One's view of slavery is not a matter of a value system. Either black people are human and deserving of equal rights, or they are not. Abortion is not a matter of values either. If it is a human life inside the mother's womb, then pro-choice voters are imposing *their views* on the child.

Despite what my liberal friend believes, science does show that life begins at conception. A newly-conceived child is highly organized, has the ability to acquire materials and energy, to respond to her environment, to reproduce cells, and to adapt, demonstrating the criteria for life.[46] At that point, the zygote has the 46 chromosomes that give it a human identity, and since species reproduce after their own kind, we know that the life within a mother's womb is human.

Dr. Jerome Lejeune, of the University of Descarte, Paris, is known as the Father of Modern Genetics. His conclusion: "To accept the fact that after fertilization has taken place a new human has come into being is no longer a matter of taste or opinion ... it is plain experimental evidence."[47]

Dr. Hymie Gordon, the former Chairman of the Mayo Clinic genetics department, wrote: "By all the criteria of modern molecular biology, life is present from the moment of conception."[48]

By this reasoning even abortion in the case of incest and rape is immoral. Suppose a woman conceived following a rape and carried the child to term, but started to have regrets when the infant was five months old and just starting to crawl. Just as it would be wrong to end the child's life at that point, it is wrong to end it while still within the womb. The child should not be punished for the sin of another, and by aborting the child of a rape, the violence of the rapist is allowed to take yet another victim.

Even those with Libertarian leanings have to admit some inconsistencies in the pro-choice views of so many in the group. Our rights end at the point that they threaten the life or liberty of another. A woman's right to choose ends at the point a child's life is at stake.

---

[46] "When Does Human Life Begin?" www.prolifephysicians.org
[47] Ibid.
[48] Ibid.

Notice that the issue of religion did not even come into this at all, but it certainly can. As voters in this great Republic, we are called to bring our individual values to the voting booth and to let the man who disagrees with us cast his own vote. The Constitution does not create a wall between the Church and state. The first amendment only forbids that Congress not make laws respecting the *establishment* of a religion. A law requiring everyone to worship in a Catholic Church would be a violation of this amendment. A law against the intentional death of another human being is not.

One-issue voters?

When Christians claim to vote pro-life, a common attack is to label them as closed-minded "one-issue voters." This isn't so.

After all, every voter becomes a one-issue voter if the right issue comes along. If a politician were to advocate for euthanizing all AIDS patients, it really wouldn't matter how great his tax plan is or what his thoughts are on health care reform, the vast majority of the country would reject him.

Even so, Catholics are not one-issue voters. There are a number of issues that a Catholic voter cares about, but some are more pressing than others. Some issues are matters of personal discretion, and others leave no room for flexibility. It will always be evil to intentionally take the life of an innocent human being, but matters of social policy leave room for personal interpretation.

As Christians, we are called to carry out the corporal works of mercy, such as feeding the poor and clothing the naked. The plight of the immigrant and the health of our neighbor are non-negotiable parts of our identity as disciples. However, two Christians can disagree, in good conscience, as to *how* one best helps the less fortunate. Many pieces of legislation sound compassionate, but really do not accomplish the good that they claim.

Take, for example, rent control. As compassionate as it sounds to put a cap on rental rates, homelessness actually *increases* in cities which have enacted this measure.[49] Similarly, social welfare programs that claim to help the poor might actually cause more harm than good. More than a compassionate heart, an understanding of how the economy works is necessary to be an effective voter.

One of the key components of Catholic social teaching is the idea of subsidiarity, which is the idea that our social concerns should be addressed on the most local level first, moving up to broader areas of political oversight as local levels fail.

All of this is to say that Catholics can disagree about the best way to help the poor, but not over whether or not human life should be protected. There are other areas that are beyond compromise for Catholics. The Catholic Answers Voting Guide identifies those issues as homosexual marriage, human cloning, embryonic stem cell research, and euthanasia.[50]

The teachings on abortion, homosexual marriage, cloning and other issues have a direct effect on the well-being of our country. Legislation is not designed to affirm lifestyle choices, but to promote those things which build up society. Marriage is the institution that brings new life into the world, and societies have afforded certain benefits to married individuals in order to bring stability and encouragement to this life-creating union.

With all of this presented, it is important to point out that, as the Catechism states, we are guided by the "certain judgment" of our consciences.[51] Some use the authority of the conscience as an

---

[49] "America's Homeless: Victims of Rent Control." www.heritage.org.

[50] http://www.catholic.com/sites/default/files/voters_guide_for_serious_catholics.pdf

[51] *Catechism of the Catholic Church. No. 1790.*

excuse to ignore Church teachings with which they disagree. However, as the Catechism explains, our conscience can remain unformed and ignorant, so for any Catholic voter, his conscience must first be formed by a clear and responsible understanding of the teachings of Christ and his Church.

Summary:

- Science tells us that a human life begins at conception;
- That life must be protected is not a matter of imposing religious views, but standing up for the those who cannot protect themselves;
- Some issues are up for discussion, such as how to best help the poor, while others are beyond negotiation, such as rejection of abortion.

50

BEARING OUR CROSS:
SUFFERING AND REDEMPTION

"I write to the Churches, and impress on them all, that I shall willingly die for God, unless you hinder me. I beseech of you not to show an unseasonable good-will towards me. Allow me to become food for the wild beasts, through whose instrumentality it will be granted me to attain to God. I am the wheat of God, and let me be ground by the teeth of the wild beasts, that I may be found the pure bread of Christ. Rather entice the wild beasts, that they may become my tomb, and may leave nothing of my body; so that when I have fallen asleep [in death], I may be no trouble to anyone. Then shall I truly be a disciple of Christ, when the world shall not see so much as my body. Entreat Christ for me, that by these instruments I may be found a sacrifice [to God]."
-Ignatius of Antioch, Epistle to the Romans

My dad was a kind man. He was the model of Christ in how he would sacrifice and serve others. It was that selflessness that was breaking him physically and emotionally and eventually wore down his body at an early age. Much of his last years can be summed up with one word: *suffering.*

It seemed a bit odd to me, at first, to put suffering as the last chapter in this book, but the mere fact that our physical and emotional pain is so uncomfortable to face head-on is an unfortunate thing, as suffering is a powerful topic in discussing the faith, and one that so few religious groups know how to address. The Hindus see it as karma and the Buddhists see it as the natural result of desire. Some groups link suffering to personal sin.

Jehovah's Witnesses will often start their evangelization by pointing out all of the suffering in the world, appealing to a sense of anxiety in the potential convert. The missionaries will then discuss God's promise of a new Heaven and a new Earth (Rev 21:1), concluding that this means a literal new Earth, upon which there is no pain, no broken hearts, and no stubbed toes.

Even some groups that do not promise health and wealth try to hook new members through an emotional fix to their everyday woes, evangelization through powerful music, exciting youth programs, and warm fellowship. There is nothing inherently wrong with any of these things, but truth must stand for itself, even if the casserole tastes bad and the music is torture. Christian joy must come through a realization that we are adopted children of God.

The meaning of suffering

God does not promise an end to suffering for those who believe in him. To the contrary, Christians are told to take up the cross in their lives (Matt 10:38-39) and suffer along with Christ (Rom 8:17-18; Phil 1:29). We will suffer various trials in our life so that our faith might be tested by fire (1 Pet 1:6-9).

This last verse is key. Having our faith *tested* by fire does not mean an assessment to see whether or not faith exists. Rather, metal was *tested*, or heated, in fire to strengthen it, much like the saying that "what does not kill me makes me stronger." The metaphor is used here to explain that our suffering, as long as we accept it and unite it with Christ, is a gift to strengthen our faith.

The apostle Paul was afflicted with some form of suffering, though he was always vague about its nature:

And to keep me from being too elated by the abundance of revelations, a thorn was given me in the flesh, a messenger of Satan, to harass me, to keep me from being too elated. Three times I besought the Lord about this, that it should leave me; but he said to me, "My grace is sufficient for you, for my power is made perfect in weakness." I will all the more gladly boast of my weaknesses, that the power of Christ may rest upon me. For the sake of Christ, then, I am content with weaknesses, insults, hardships, persecutions, and calamities; for when I am weak, then I am strong (2 Cor 12:7-10).

The power of the Lord was made perfect in Paul's weakness. He boasts of a "thorn" and finds the strength to be content in it. Even more than this, he accepts his persecution and writes: "Now I rejoice in my sufferings for your sake, and in my flesh I complete what is lacking in Christ's afflictions for the sake of his body, that is, the church" (Col 1:24).

Offering it up

We have become a culture so adverse to pain that the old Catholic advice to "offer it up" is rarely heard anymore. However, as this platitude expresses, we can take *ownership* of our suffering and unite it with Christ in a way that benefits his mystical body, especially if done as an offering of ourselves during the Mass.

Christians are members of a kingly priesthood (1 Pet 2:9-10), and are called to offer their bodies to God as living sacrifices (Rom 12:1). In our bodies, we bear the mortification of Jesus (2 Cor 4:8-12) and know the fellowship of his sufferings (Phil 3:8-11).

Christ suffered for us, and we are to follow his model (1 Pet 2:19-22). We can suffer on behalf of one another, just as Moses suffered for forty days and nights for the Israelites (Deut 9:15-20).

For if one member suffers, all members suffer with it (1 Cor 12:26). As Paul wrote earlier, it is not that the afflictions of Christ are not enough, but that his plan for salvation was that we build each other up through our prayers and through our sufferings. This includes voluntary suffering, such as fasting, which Scripture tells us is one of the most powerful forms of prayer (Matt 6:16-18; Mark 17:21), but how often do parents think to fast on behalf of their children?

My dad's legs were shot from years of standing on concrete to cut meat, and his body had deteriorated from the poverty of making sure everyone else was taken care of before he sought comfort for himself. As an adult and father myself now, I can only imagine his loneliness of living alone as his health and financial security failed. But if his life is any indication, he embraced even his suffering for me, my brother, and the eventual grandchildren he never got to meet. Whatever I know of Christ and his gift to humanity, I leaned first from the example of my father.

Not in this life, but in the next

The Jehovah's Witnesses are wrong. God does not promise that only a select few will get to Heaven. For all who accept Christ into our hearts, our reward for suffering with him is that we will be glorified *with* him, joint heirs in his eternal life (Rom 8:16-18).

Health and wealth Gospel preachers promise that, for the true believer in Christ, if you *name it*, you can *claim it!* If you *believe it*, you can *achieve it!* They use verses such as Matthew 6:26-30 to bolster their promise of earthly prosperity:

Look at the birds of the air: they neither sow nor reap nor gather into barns, and yet your heavenly Father feeds them. Are you not of more value than they? And which of you by being anxious can add one cubit to his span of life? And why are you anxious about clothing? Consider the lilies of the field, how they grow; they neither toil nor spin; yet I tell you, even

Solomon in all his glory was not arrayed like one of these. But if God so clothes the grass of the field, which today is alive and tomorrow is thrown into the oven, will he not much more clothe you, O men of little faith?

But it is not in this life that Christ was promising riches greater than Solomon, but in the next. Paul chastised his body and brought it into subjection so that he might win a "incorruptible crown" (1 Cor 9:25-27).

Christ did not promise health and wealth. His promise was not to those who sought to live like princes, but those who sought to live as Christ and the apostles, who had not a place to lie their head, no silver and gold, and sometimes no food or clothing (Matt 8:20; Acts 3:6; 1 Cor 4:11; 1 Tim 6:8).

His promise was not the gospel of luxury and comfort, but the Beatitudes from upon the Mount:

Blessed are the poor in spirit: for theirs is the kingdom of heaven.
Blessed are the meek: for they shall possess the land.
Blessed are they who mourn: for they shall be comforted.
Blessed are they that hunger and thirst after justice: for they shall have their fill.
Blessed are the merciful: for they shall obtain mercy.
Blessed are the clean of heart: for they shall see God.
Blessed are the peacemakers: for they shall be called the children of God.
Blessed are they that suffer persecution for justice' sake, for theirs is the kingdom of heaven (Matthew 5:3-12).

Summary:

- "Truth" is not determined by our emotions;
- Christ did not come to end suffering in this life;
- God allows suffering, but does not cause it;
- A Christian should learn to embrace suffering for its redemptive value, for himself and others;
- The end to earthly suffering comes in the next life, when we enter eternity with Christ.

CONCLUSION

When I started in apologetics, I was a lukewarm Catholic who didn't know much about his faith. But I was stubborn, so when I was challenged, I was determined to find an answer. One day it might have been a friend asking me why Catholics baptize babies. On another occasion, it was a co-worker explaining why he felt Purgatory is contrary to Scripture.

So, I went home, dug around through the internet and found an answer. And usually I found a question or two of my own.

Learning about the faith is addictive. There is a beauty in the complexity. Learning about the Eucharist leads into learning about confession, which leads into learning about Purgatory ...

But as much as I learned about the faith, I hadn't necessarily learned the best way to share that Good News with others. I was ready to give an explanation for the hope that exists within me, as Peter encourages, but not always with gentleness and respect.

I can recall awkward conversations where I triumphantly challenged the views of another, or debates in which I was more interested in scoring victories than in planting seeds.

Hopefully, the essays in this book are helpful. The analogies from my own life, together with Scripture and logic, provide the best explanations I know for Christianity.

But my knowledge of the faith, whatever it is worth, comes from a few years of study, and so does my understanding of how to share it.

The successful evangelist listens as much as he explains.

He recognizes the image of God in even the most hostile challenger.

He understands that study comes to nothing if the interior life is not nurtured by prayer and the sacraments.

He acknowledges his limitations and knows where to find the answers that weren't there before.

He is humble, yet confident in the truth that God exists and does not lie. And that our Lord's one, holy, Catholic and apostolic Church exists to guide each of us into truth, grace, and eternity with our Lord and Savior Jesus Christ.

INDEX

ABOUT THE AUTHOR

Spencer Allen is a writer and speaker on Catholic apologetics. His column has appeared in the *Catholic Missourian*, he appeared regularly as the apologist on the television show *Our Catholic Life* and he served for two years as President of *Apologetics from Scratch, Inc.*, a non-profit dedicated to bringing quality conferences to the Missouri area. He has publicly debated issues related to Catholic teaching. Currently, Spencer is principal of St. Joseph Cathedral School. He lives with his wife, Christy, and his four children in the Jefferson City Diocese.

For questions or to inquire about inviting Spencer to speak in your area, e-mail him at spencer@mackerelsnappers.org.

Made in the USA
San Bernardino, CA
05 May 2014